T0322281

A Modern
Way to Live

For Faye, Indigo, Wren and Etta
A house isn't a home without all of you in it

A Modern
Way to Live

5 Design Principles
from The Modern House

Matt Gibberd

PENGUIN LIFE
AN IMPRINT OF
PENGUIN BOOKS

1

Space

Prospect and refuge
Spaces for being together
Turning up the volume
Spaces for hibernating
The broken plan
The illusion of space
Using space to add drama
A space of one's own

023

2

Light

Light and emotion
Light and transparency
Light and layout
Reach for the sky
Playing with light
Don't be afraid of the dark
Light at night

077

3

Materials

Shaking hands with
  our homes
Truth to materials
The perfect imperfection
  of materials
Preserving original
  materials
Materials and health
Materials and the
  environment
Playing with materials

125

4 Nature

Putting nature first
Urban nature
Bringing nature in
My heart's in the savannah
    (ooh na-na)
A civilized wilderness
Kind of blue
The Ritalin of nature

183

5 Decoration

Adding colour
The importance of pattern
    and texture
The new Minimalism
The new Maximalism
Surround yourself with
    meaningful things
Wearing it well
How to arrange
How to collect

239

Introduction	02
Epilogue	300
Acknowledgements	304
Bookshelf	305

Introduction

When I was a child, weekends were often spent skimming planks of stale supermarket bread across the pond on Hampstead Heath, where they were hoovered with relish by expectant mallards. If I managed to achieve the right trajectory, the bread might even land in the garden of the house on the opposite side of the water. Sometimes I imagined the owner clearing crusts off his lawn with a shovel, muttering 'those pesky kids' under his breath. The place always fascinated me. With its exaggerated roof overhang and glass bricks stacked up in grids, it looked like the sort of fantastical folly I might build out of Lego on my bedroom floor.

Thirty years later, I am now standing inside the entrance hall of the house, where it is apparent that the glass bricks serve a practical purpose, editing out the view of the neighbouring houses and shattering the shafts of sunlight into coruscating pieces. A cast-concrete staircase zigzags through the space with the geometric drama of an M.C. Escher lithograph. Running my hand across the smooth pink-marble balustrade, I descend to the lower floor, where cooking, dining and relaxing all take place in a single open-plan room. I notice a network of tracks on the ceiling, and begin to pull primary-coloured curtains across the space to subdivide it, completely changing the atmosphere. The mosaic floor tiles shift from blue to white as they drop into the sunken dining area, which is presented as a celebration of the eating ritual. A set of Eames wire chairs surrounds a slate-topped table, its circular shape echoed by the mandala cast into the concrete ceiling above. As I move through to the back of the space, a built-in bench topped with a velvet-covered pad encourages me to sit down and admire the majesty of the trees outside.

Later, I ascend to the bedroom on the first floor, where the view of the heath is tantalizingly concealed behind a full wall of opaque glass bricks. But then I notice a band of clear glazing at thigh level, and, taking a seat on the bed, realize that my interaction with the landscape is being deliberately orchestrated. In one corner of the room is an open-plan shower and basin, with a loo tucked away behind a little blue door. The copper pipework is celebrated rather than concealed, and dramatically juts out across the room to act as an unconventional divider. This is, I conclude, the most thoughtful and intensely personal house I have ever visited, and exploring its interior takes me back to the childlike sense of wonder I experienced when I first encountered it all those years ago.

It spilt from the fertile mind of a little-known architect called Brian Housden, who took inspiration from the Maison de Verre in Paris and the Rietveld Schröder House in Utrecht to create a radical beacon of European Modernism in the genteel streets of North London. It was his life's work. Housden, his wife and their three young daughters moved into the house in 1964, but nothing was finished. There was a standpipe in the kitchen and a temporary lavatory. The structure was finally completed a couple of years later, but the interior evolved over the ensuing decades as funds allowed. One of their daughters, Tess Housden, explains:

> Slowly, doors, shelving and cabinets were added over a period of years. Dad did a City & Guilds course in woodworking and bought a machine in order to make the furniture himself. It took a long time, and it was definitely a labour of love. When we first moved here, when I was a baby, we slept in camp beds under the stairs. All the kids on the street would come over. We used to run through the house and then jump from the terrace on to the sand that was being used for the build. It was like a giant playground.

Brian Housden was always encouraged by his contemporaries to get the house listed. He approached English Heritage in 2002, but Brutalism was still regarded with suspicion, and nothing came of it. It wasn't until 2014 that its importance as a national monument was finally recognized, and the house was granted a Grade II listing. Housden died two days later.

His daughters sought a new custodian for it and appointed The Modern House, the estate agency that I co-founded with my friend Albert Hill, to handle the sale. For many people in the local community, it was regarded as a concrete carbuncle, but the family we sold it to were completely persuaded by the tactility of the materials, the life-enhancing natural light, the quality of the spaces and the connection to the landscape. For them, the Housden House promised a new way of living – a *better* way that places the human experience at the centre of everything.

The five elements for living well

The Modern House has been selling design-led homes since 2005. Back then, I was writing features and editing copy at *The World of Interiors*, and my old school friend Albert was the design editor at *Wallpaper*. Albert had come across a realtor in America who specialized in the sale of mid-century Modern houses, and our instincts told us that a curated approach would translate well to the UK.

Without a business plan, or any plan at all, in fact, we cold-called the owner of a Grade II-listed 1930s house, Six Pillars, that was currently for sale. Having been invited in for a meeting, we promptly rustled up some new headed paper and a set of business cards with a highfalutin strapline: 'Specialists in the sale of twentieth- and twenty-first-century homes of architectural distinction.' Catchy.

When the day of reckoning arrived, we dusted off our finest collarless shirts (channelling architect Richard Rogers but with none of the gravitas) and hopped on the train to Sydenham Hill. The client was as open-minded as we could have possibly hoped for. Glossing over the fact that we had zero experience of selling houses, he could see that we were educated and motivated, with a decent knowledge of design and architecture. My overriding memory involves the three of us standing in the double-height hallway, caressing the curves of his Marcel Breuer plywood lounge chair.

So we had a house to sell. What next? The phenomenon of online property sales hadn't got up to full speed yet. Rightmove was in its infancy and had a bit of a low-rent image, and Zoopla was still three years away from launching. Our 'office' was Albert's bedroom, which overlooked a cornfield in rural Hampshire, so we couldn't exactly stick one of those glossy photo cards in the window and rely on passing trade.

Therefore, we did the only thing we knew how to do, which was to take an editorial approach. We commissioned the accomplished interiors photographer Beth Evans to shoot the house. She used natural light rather than flash, and focused on the quality of the materials and architectural detailing. We went to the library and photocopied some excerpts about Valentine Harding, the architect of Six Pillars, and Jack Leakey, the former headmaster of Dulwich College prep school, who commissioned it in the 1930s. These formed the basis for a snazzy sales brochure, which highlighted the historical significance of the house and gave it a provenance. Kate Sclater and Tim Balaam from the graphic design agency Hyperkit put together a handsome website for us, using the offbeat colour chart developed by the Swiss-French Modernist Le Corbusier in the 1930s. Annabel Freyberg profiled us in the *Telegraph*, and a piece in *Wallpaper* followed. We were up and running.

The first few years weren't easy. We set up camp in a converted fire station in Godalming, Surrey, which subsidized local artists and start-ups. The rent was £55 a month (good), but the building didn't have any heating (bad), and the phone didn't ring much (very bad). Sometimes we felt like children playing 'shop'.

Looking back on it now, we were probably a bit early for online estate agency. The subsequent rise of web-based behemoths like Purplebricks has helped us, because, although they operate in an entirely different market, they have shifted public perception. Who shops for a new house on the high street these days? Where we really got it right, however, was that we identified a groundswell of interest in the idea of living well. From the outset, we considered each house not simply as a 'property' with a price tag attached to it but as a 'home' with the ability to transform someone's life.

Rather than focusing on a particular geographical area, The Modern House has always considered the quality of the building itself to be the starting point. We turn away some 50 per cent of the work that is offered to us, which might sound like commercial suicide, but this filter has served us well in an overcrowded marketplace. We represent flats and houses that excite us, and that we would want to live in ourselves. It could be a repurposed chapel with soaring ceilings; a loft apartment with raw concrete columns; a flat in a listed Brutalist block; or a dusty relic of the Modernist era that's waiting to be brought back to life. Above all, we always ask ourselves this: is it a home that lifts the spirits?

We have always remained alive to aesthetic shifts, evolving gradually from muscular Modernists to something a bit gentler and more accessible. In 2021 we launched a sister brand, Inigo. Named after the self-taught architect Inigo Jones, who imported Classical architecture to England in the early seventeenth century, it sells and celebrates refined rectories, Victorian villas and humble workers' cottages.

Much of this has been informed by my early experiences at *The World of Interiors*. I didn't fully comprehend it at the time, but the magazine provided an incomparable aesthetic training. We were encouraged to treat a mud hut in Mali with the same reverence as a Swedish palace. This democratic approach is something that Albert and I have tried to carry through to our own business, believing that a studio flat and a manor house are worthy of equal celebration – each, in its own way, can show us how to better utilize space or capture natural light.

I have been granted unique access through hundreds of firmly locked gates and sequestered doors, sometimes offering marketing advice to the homeowner, and at other times interviewing them for The Modern House's online magazine. I have also continued to write house features for *The World of Interiors*. The people I have met represent a great diversity of tribes and typologies, from renters to freeholders, empty nesters to families, commune-dwellers to single occupiers. While some live in compact urban apartments, others have big houses in the countryside or boltholes by the sea. And yet I have been fascinated to discover that all of these people live by the same set of unwritten design principles.

The purpose of this book is to show you what these are, and how you might implement them in your own home. I have grouped them together under deliberately broad headings: Space; Light; Materials; Nature; Decoration. Paying close attention to these five elements will, I believe, allow you to live a better and more fulfilled life.

So that you don't have to take my word for it, I have included a wide spectrum of real-life examples in these pages. Whenever someone is interviewed for The Modern House website, podcast or YouTube channel, the same question is posed to them: 'What does modern living mean to you?' Time and again, their responses equate thoughtful design with enhanced wellbeing. Take my friends Dominic and Rebecca Gaunt, for example. A few years ago they bought a nondescript bungalow beneath a railway embankment, which they replaced with an elegant modern house with full-height glazing and surprisingly generous proportions. Rebecca says:

The space, the light, the aesthetics in this house – they definitely have a feel-good effect on me. When we've been away, I'll walk back into our living space and it always hits me: the sense of space and light, and the calmness that it creates.

Design's timeless principles

The idea that the built environment is capable of having a positive effect on human happiness can be traced all the way back to Ancient Greece. The city-state of Epidaurus is considered to be the birthplace of modern medicine, and had more than two hundred healing centres set in beautiful natural landscapes with clear running waters and a favourable climate. Its Classical theatre, which dates from the fourth century BC, was a place where tunic-clad visitors could escape the burden of everyday ailments by watching plays and listening to music in stirring surroundings.

The influential Roman architect and civil engineer Vitruvius certainly saw a link between good design and the human experience. In his treatise *De architectura*, believed to have been written between 30 and 15 BC, he wrote:

Well building hath three conditions. Strength, utility and beauty.

Considered to be the first book on architectural theory, it touches on everything from mathematics to meteorology and medicine, encapsulating the Roman vision that architecture should improve the spiritual and intellectual life of man.

The Florentine scholar Poggio Bracciolini 'rediscovered' Vitruvius's manuscript in the early fifteenth century, and it became the definitive touchpoint for architects throughout the Renaissance, Baroque and Neoclassical periods, who subscribed to the Roman vision of clarity, order and symmetry. In fifteenth-century Italy, 'Renaissance men' such as Leon Battista Alberti trained as humanists and turned their well-manicured hands to everything from architecture to poetry, philosophy and art. They sought to create living environments that would appeal to both emotion and reason. Renaissance villas were built for wealthy families as a refuge from the noise and unsanitary conditions of the city, surrounded by formal gardens and dedicated to the pursuit of wellness.

Modernism fundamentally changed the language of design, but its chief protagonists continued to employ many of the doctrines set down by the Ancients. In 1927 Walter Gropius, founder of the Bauhaus School in Weimar, made a proclamation that bears a remarkable similarity to what Vitruvius wrote some two thousand years earlier: 'A house ... must fulfil its function usefully, be durable, economical and beautiful.' The revered German industrial designer Dieter Rams abided by his own set of perpetual rules. In the 1970s he came up with *Ten Principles for Good Design*, highlighting the honesty, beauty and longevity that characterize his products. It is remarkable how often I visit a modern house to find one of his masterful '606 Universal' shelving units on the wall. His legacy endures, in precisely the same way as that of Vitruvius and of Gropius, because the fundamental characteristics of successful design have always been the same, transcending any shifts in aesthetic preference. As Terence Conran wrote in *The Essential House Book*:

> *Fashions in decorating fluctuate like hemlines, whereas notions of comfort and intimacy date back hundreds of years. This is not to say that style isn't fun or even useful. But it is ultimately more important to find out what you really like, the unique combination of space, light, colour and materials which will continue to refresh your spirits long after the latest 'look' has had its day.*

Nourishing the senses

Human beings at every socio-economic level should have access to a home that gives them not only physical support but psychological support as well. Goldsmith Street in Norwich, designed by Mikhail Riches and Cathy Hawley, is rare example of an enlightened social-housing scheme. The houses are impeccably detailed, with angled roofs that maximize daylight and raise the spirits. The back gardens share a secure 'ginnel' where children can play together, and a verdant walkway runs right through the middle of the estate, promoting strong community engagement and social cohesion. Contrast this with the student digs that were thrown up in haste by the University of the West of England, to meet the increased demand for accommodation on campus. The 2.4 metre × 3 metre 'studio pods' were installed in a car park, loomed over by an existing hall of residence. Each unit had a minuscule window overlooking a communal walkway, with surface-mounted electrical conduit and faux-brick cladding. The students rightly complained about them being 'not fit for humans' and 'not mentally viable', and quickly abandoned them.

What the students were experiencing was design (if we can call it that) that failed to consider how it would make them *feel*. It didn't address the full range of human senses. There was no tactility or solidity in the materials, which were man-made laminates and plastics instead of those found in nature; wafer-thin walls and a lack of sound insulation led to a breakdown in the basic right to privacy; insufficient ventilation caused a build-up of smells; and so on.

There are commonly thought to be five distinct senses – sight, hearing, smell, touch and taste – but modern cognitive neuroscience suggests that there are as many as thirty-three. For example, 'touch' can mean many different things, depending on pressure or temperature. In his wonderful book *The Eyes of the Skin*, the Finnish architect Juhani Pallasmaa argues that vision has become overly dominant in design, to the neglect of the other senses. Indeed, if we think about the most inhumane of buildings, it is those corporate towers in built-up city centres that are designed to appeal purely to the eye. Occupying these structures, and interacting with them, is a strangely impersonal experience. Most have been conceived on a computer screen, with full consideration for how they look and very little for how they feel. The rise of social media hasn't helped, with architects falling over one another to conceive the most outlandish silhouette.

In response to this disheartening trend, the International WELL Building Institute has devised a commendable rating system that assesses architecture's effect on wellbeing within the workplace. Newly built commercial buildings are given scores in seven different areas – air, water, nourishment, light, fitness, comfort and mind – in an attempt to get designers and developers to think more holistically.

Within the residential realm, a handful of forward-thinking housebuilders are showing the way ahead. Walmer Yard in West London, designed by Peter Salter, is an extraordinary manifesto of multi-sensory design. The property developer Crispin Kelly studied under Salter at the Architectural Association, and in later life the pair came together to execute a poetic project that took ten years to realize. It consists of four interlocking houses in a courtyard setting. Walking around, you become acutely aware of the changes in sound, as if the Wizard of Oz is playing with a synthesizer behind a curtain: the reverberations of a metal staircase underfoot; the meditative twang of a copper hopper in the rain; the dampened intimacy of a dining room with walls of clay and straw. The interiors incorporate an array of tactile textures, including shiny lacquered wardrobes, cast-concrete walls, leather handrails and steel bathroom units with exposed spot welds. There are underground rooms clad from floor to ceiling in woven willow reeds, which give off the smell of country air and make you feel like you're in an outsized bird's nest.

The importance of home

It is worth pointing out that I am not a professional property developer, nor am I a trained designer, space planner, architectural historian, environmental psychologist or expert in biophilia. As the son of an architect, I spent a large part of my childhood on building sites, yet I can barely hang a picture on a wall without causing myself personal injury. This book is intended to be free of self-righteousness, and, in writing it, I am talking to myself as much as to you.

However, I have always understood that design is important. When I was a boy, I often accompanied my mum to the supermarket to help with the weekly shop (my primary role was to decant choc ices and processed cheese into the trolley while she wasn't looking). On one occasion, I needed a new toothbrush, and the two of us spent an inordinate amount of time in the toiletries aisle assessing the colour, material and ergonomics of each model before making our selection. This really stuck with me. My parents could never understand why someone would buy a product that didn't look good and function well, and they reinforced this constantly.

William Morris famously said: 'If you want a golden rule that will fit everything, this is it: have nothing in your houses that you do not know to be useful or believe to be beautiful.' This is certainly a mantra that I have lived by, whether consciously or not. A preoccupation with design seems to be one of those things that runs in families. My paternal grandfather, Sir Frederick Gibberd, was one of the leading figures in twentieth-century British architecture. He was principal of the Architectural Association during the Second World War, a Royal Academician, and a member of the Modern Architectural Research Society (MARS) alongside esteemed contemporaries such as Serge Chermayeff, Wells Coates and Berthold Lubetkin.

I was only six years old when my grandfather died, but his influence on my life has been considerable, mainly because he demonstrated that anything was possible. As a boy, of course, I saw him simply as an important member of the family. We called him Grandpa Whiskers because of his elaborate moustache. That he should also be deemed an important member of society only dawned on me when, as a teenager, I visited his most famous building: the Metropolitan Cathedral of Christ the King in Liverpool. A Catholic counterpoint to Giles

Gilbert Scott's Anglican cathedral nearby, it has been affectionately dubbed 'Paddy's Wigwam', because of its distinctive crown-of-thorns silhouette. Whereas Scott's building dazzles the visitor with its gargantuan scale, the Gibberd cathedral achieves the same effect using economy of form and fine detailing. My father took me up from London to see it, one of the most affecting experiences of my young life.

Whether by accident or design, I have also married someone for whom aesthetics define her very being. Faye Toogood is a self-confessed 'tinker' whose eponymous design studio operates across fashion, furniture, interiors and sculpture. Together, we have renovated many living spaces over the years, starting with a basement flat beside a railway line in Camden and culminating in a manor house in the South Downs National Park, making lots of mistakes and learning how to do things along the way.

Each of these homes has a deep emotional meaning. Shortly after Faye and I moved to our terraced house in Islington in 2009, I found out that my oldest friend Jedd was born there. By an amazing twist of fate, our first daughter, Indigo, was born in the house on the same day as he was, some thirty-five years later. We were in the middle of a major refurbishment at the time, and I remember asking the builder if he would be so kind as to stop drilling so that we could concentrate on the contractions.

During the coronavirus lockdown in spring 2020, we were living in a flat in Winchester. By this time, we had added two more girls to the family: our identical-twin daughters, Wren and Etta. With a pair of toddlers to look after, a seven-year-old who needed home-schooling and two businesses to run, our home quickly descended into chaos. Great tendrils of spaghetti spewed forth from cooking pots, and rivulets of wee-wee trickled under potties. Some people talked about using the self-isolation period to read *War and Peace*, but I was going through my own war to keep the peace, and there was certainly no time for reading.

For many of us, the lockdown served to amplify the inadequacies of our living environments (for me, the lack of a proper garden was the killer), and it was no surprise that the property market went into meltdown once the restrictions were eased. Others discovered new-found respect for their home, including my business partner, Albert, who wrote:

> *Now that we have the time and energy to revel in more meaningful relationships with our home, what emerges are not its deficiencies but its quotidian delights. The*

light that filters through the trees, casting evening shadows on the wall, for instance, or the snugness of the armchair that you have never before spent so much time in. As the outside world melts away, so does much of the noise, the one-upmanship, the aspiring to something other, and you are left living with what you have. And, as you look around your raft, the lifeboat on this turbulent sea, you see that it's actually rather pleasant and perhaps, even, previously a little underappreciated. Those Monstera deliciosa, *majestic plants that are native to the tropical forests of Mexico but have been cramped in the corner of the living room, are finally getting repotted into something more befitting of their majesty. Those windows, smeared with the thin grime of the city, have had their faces wiped. Those cupboards, guiltily harbouring out-of-date paperwork and unworn clothes, have been released of their heavy burden (or at least had their pain recognized). Those pictures on the wall that you've never really got on with have finally been stood down from duty.*

The Covid-19 pandemic has affected all of us in different ways, but what is clear is that it has caused a fundamental shift in working patterns. Nearly all of us spend more time at home than we did previously, and the demands we place on it are higher than ever. The American futurist Alvin Toffler anticipated this as long ago as 1980, when he declared:

> *I believe the home will assume a startling new importance in civilization. The rise of the prosumer, the spread of the electronic cottage, the invention of new organizational structures in business, the automation and de-massification of production, all point to the home's re-emergence as a central unit in the society of tomorrow – a unit with enhanced rather than diminished economic, medical, educational, and social functions.*

A home acts as a sanctuary and sometimes even a sanatorium during uncertain times. It is a place where we can truly be ourselves. Beyond our relationships with family and friends,

I would argue that it is the most important thing we have. The environmental psychologist Lily Bernheimer asserts that:

Our emotional attachment to our homes can be almost as strong as our emotional attachment to other people. Home environments are key in defining who we are, so much so that we almost feel they are part of us.

As a magazine journalist and entrepreneur, my life over the past twenty years has been about getting behind the scenes of people's homes, pulling back their curtains and rummaging through their pantries. Seeing how they choose to live, the objects they surround themselves with, the narratives they tell and the things that spark joy. It has been the greatest privilege imaginable, and I have learnt a lot. Every home has a story, and I want to help you write your own.

Space

'I like ruins, because what remains is not the
total design, but the clarity of thought, the
naked structure, the spirit of the thing.'
Tadao Ando

Prospect and refuge

If we imagine *Homo sapiens* casting around the African savannah throwing stones at hyenas, they would have depended upon the natural topography for survival. A lofty vantage point on top of a hill allowed them to assess threats and opportunities from a distance, while a cave or a clump of trees provided a welcome place to hide. In 1975 the British geographer Jay Appleton proffered the view that we are hard-wired to seek out similar environments in our everyday lives, because they once promoted our evolution. The spaces that we feel most comfortable in provide us with the ability to observe (prospect) without being seen (refuge), and our homes must be equipped with a combination of the two if they are to adequately support us.

The Finnish architect Alvar Aalto understood this concept more than most. His buildings contain a rich variety of different rooms at contrasting scales, and are full of dislocations and changes of level that challenge the user. Interestingly, they don't photograph particularly well, and the uninitiated may wonder what all the fuss is about. This is because they are designed to provide a multisensory experience rather than simply an appeal to the eye. An Aalto interior can be fully understood only when you walk around it, when you feel the shifts in atmosphere. In my view, a visit to Aalto's studio in Helsinki should be part of the curriculum for anyone thinking of designing a house. The main space has a curved ribbon of glazing overlooking a courtyard shaped like a Roman theatre, where the studio staff would watch slideshows and listen to lectures. Plants finger their way up the wall at the far end, beside a curious mezzanine hung with an assortment of Aalto's lighting prototypes. On the upper floor of the building is the drawing office, where the abruptly angled roof is supported on the slenderest of columns, and a high-level window gently washes the desks with ethereal light.

Scientific research suggests that a spatially uniform environment can cause us to feel unhappy. Prisons and hospitals, for example, feel inhumane because they are so cellular. 'A lack of complexity can have a negative effect on people's wellbeing,' Lily Bernheimer explains, 'because it mimics the sensation of a neurophysiological breakdown, of not having enough information about where you are in your environment and how to navigate it.' Even a large building like a church, which we think of as a single big space, is, in fact, a place of great

intricacy, with distinct 'rooms' such as the chancel, the nave and the transepts. For the Hunchback of Notre-Dame in Victor Hugo's novel, the cathedral was simultaneously his

> *egg, nest, house, country and universe . . . One might almost say that he had espoused its form the way a snail does the form of its shell. It was his home, his hole, his envelope . . . he adhered to it, as it were, like a turtle to its carapace.*

The more variation we experience within the built environment, the more pronounced our sense of stimulation and innervation. Sound performs differently in rooms of varying sizes. In a large space with high ceilings, voices and footsteps appear to be further away than they actually are, while the reverse is true in more modest rooms. If we want to throw a party for a hundred guests or whisper sweet nothings into the ear of our partner, we require very different environmental conditions. This is why the notion of the four-poster bed is such a romantic one, because its draped canopy provides us with acoustic intimacy. Smells, too, are more concentrated in confined spaces (which can be both a blessing and a curse). It makes sense that we should require differing ceiling heights if we are to experience the full range of sensory experiences available within the home.

In his book *The Poetics of Space*, the French philosopher Gaston Bachelard highlights the way in which a spatially complex home allows the mind to wander freely:

> *If the house is a bit elaborate, if it has a cellar and a garret, nooks and corridors, our memories have refuges that are all the more clearly delineated. All our lives we come back to them in our daydreams.*

Putting on my estate-agency hat for a moment, some of the homes that best represent the prospect–refuge theory have proven unusually popular with our buyers and significantly outperformed the market. A penthouse in London's Hoxton Square, for example, sold for more than 40 per cent above the local going rate, according to research by property-market analysts Dataloft. It is almost completely open-plan, with windows along the full length of the southern elevation, providing views over the trees of the garden square towards the twinkling City skyline. At one end of the space is a slatted-wood bed pod, measuring just 7-foot square: a little night-time nest where weary urban-dwellers can preen their feathers.

Another example is a house by Henning Stummel, built on the site of a furniture warehouse behind a Victorian terrace in Camden Town. Its centrepiece, a soaring social space with the proportions of a nineteenth-century factory, contains a kitchen, sitting room, dining area and architecture studio, all under one steel-framed roof. The sleeping accommodation is right at the back of the building, hidden within a stack of plywood boxes accessed via an invisible pivoting door.

Spaces for being together

Like the blood-red poppies of Flanders Fields, an optimistic flowering of architecture emerged from the devastation of the First World War. The bespectacled architect Le Corbusier, a rakish radical with a penchant for nudity, came up with a prototype for a new kind of modular housing that could be erected quickly and efficiently. It consisted of three open slabs of concrete, held up on slim columns and linked by staircases, without any supporting beams or load-bearing walls. 'Corb' called it the Maison Dom-Ino, a structure whose childlike simplicity defied its profound impact.

By exploiting the capabilities of concrete and steel, Le Corbusier and his fellow Modernists permanently altered the way in which buildings are inhabited. Households were less reliant on servants, and the result was a new world of non-hierarchical domesticity, of social and physical openness. Open-plan, lateral spaces are still the hallmark of modern residential interiors, fuelled by the mass repurposing of defunct factories, schools and barns with inherently generous footprints. People are naturally sociable creatures, and we enjoy having a space where everyone can be together.

It doesn't matter how large or small, how lateral or vertical, every home needs a room for congregating. Invariably this is a convivial, noisy, effervescent space. It should have high ceilings and an open plan, and suck in daylight through considerable openings. Above all, it should have a generosity of spirit.

Combining the kitchen and living space is the simplest way to achieve this feeling of bounteousness. Many years ago, we sold a flat on the sixth floor of Ernő Goldfinger's Trellick Tower, a brooding, Brutalist apartment block in London. The new owners, Gerard McAtamney and Andres Pajon-Leite, wisely decided to live in it for a year before carrying out a refurbishment, to fully assess how they occupied the space before committing to a layout (this is something I recommend to all new homeowners if they can manage it). Their conclusion provides a familiar summary of modern living habits:

> *We discovered that we spent 80 per cent of our time in the kitchen and around the kitchen table, next to no time in the living room, and the study was purely aspirational! So we decided to open the kitchen and living room into one space.*

Indeed, for a new generation of city-dwellers, a single room performs all of the key functions required during daylight hours. Rapid advances in technology mean that the home has assumed far more importance as a multifunctional place of work, rest and play. The most successful apartments are arranged around a table at the core of the space. During the day it might be a perch for a laptop, and by night a candlestick is placed ceremoniously at its centre, as it becomes a more formal backdrop for banqueting. People don't tend to crave a separate dining space any more, instead choosing to gather their friends in an informal way, inviting them to be a part of the process and giving them some vegetables to peel.

The act of cooking is a key part of the ritual of entertaining. In some ways it's an interactive theatrical performance, and the show begins as soon as the host flings open the front door in a distressed-linen pinafore. For a generation of amateur cooks, especially men, it was the image of Jamie Oliver carving up lamb for his friends in the late nineties that made us comfortable with the concept of preparing food in public. If it involved setting fire to red peppers on an open flame and throwing Maldon sea salt around the place, so much the better. The Naked Chef's city-centre apartment, with its open kitchen, generous dining table and spiral staircase, was the smoke-filled symbol of this sociable existence.

In our increasingly fractured society, sharing a meal with others is a way to build lasting relationships. For Sam and Sam Clark, founders of the much loved Moro Restaurant in London, their kitchen at home is very much the epicentre of daily activity, a place in which to bring friends together in the name of culinary adventure. They explain:

> Our fondest memories in the kitchen are when we've been able to show people what you can cook with a garden and allotment. We've got an almond tree that we planted in the garden, and a fig tree. We love to make a salsa with the early-summer green almonds, and a salad with the figs, or pick them when they're green and cook them like courgettes. We love wrapping fig or vine leaves around sardines and barbecuing them; using vine shoots in salads; making a dressing from green grape juice; or putting artichoke leaves into risottos and rice dishes. It's the greatest luxury to be able to pick and cook something unique, to give people taste experiences they've never had before.

At their home overlooking the sea in Devon, chef Gill Meller and his wife, Alice, host friends around a ten-person table. Gill says:

> *My father made us the table as a moving-in present, and everyone who eats at it signs underneath. Over the seven years we've been here, it's become a lovely thing, with lots of messages and notes of thanks, and jokes, and swearing. It's our visitors' book, so people eat and they sign it, and I really like that. It's a wonderful record of good times.*

For parents, the kitchen table often acts as a canvas for their kids' creativity. Families play games, make clay sculptures, do homework and eat around the table, sometimes all at the same time. My friends Tim and Emily Swift use brown paper as a makeshift tablecloth, rolling it out at the beginning of the week and letting their sons have creative free rein. Come Sunday, it is emblazoned with scrawls and doodles and splodges, as if Jackson Pollock has been let loose in a crayon factory.

It wasn't always thus. The rise of servants in middle-class households during the nineteenth century meant that the kitchen was deliberately placed away from the rest of the accommodation. Having a separate dining room was considered to be more genteel, as it separated the owners and their guests from the clang of pans and the pungent waft of snipe in savoury jelly being assembled by the cooks. As servants became less commonplace, this layout somehow persisted, and whoever drew the short straw of cooking the food needed to do so in solitary confinement.

Bringing the kitchen back to the forefront of everyday life has led to traditional layouts becoming unfit for purpose. As a result, it's amazing how many Victorian houses have been reconfigured to make them suitable for a modern way of living. If you ask me to pinpoint the most consistently popular genre of housing in London, it's the period terraced house with a modern extension on the back. We have sold hundreds of them over the years. They come in many different shapes, and are clad in everything from timber to slate. The rear extension is the simplest way to create a single space that's big enough for all of the conviviality that life can throw at it.

The most successful extensions are those that offer a point of difference to the other rooms in the house. The 'side return' is a redundant strip of land that runs alongside the ground floor of a building, which was originally used to store coal and provide access to the outside lavatory. By incorporating it into your extension, you can create a room that utilizes the full extent of the plot and is much wider than the rest of the accommodation. This usually fits a generous dining table, with perhaps enough space left over for a sofa to park your guests on while you prepare the lunch. A single-storey extension allows you to bring in light from various angles, including via the roof, and a seamless threshold on to the garden helps to blur the boundaries between inside and out. Sometimes a modestly scaled addition doesn't require planning permission, and can be built under permitted development.

Scientist Katy Davison worked with the architect Simon Astridge to extend her Victorian house in Islington, and it has transformed her experience of family living, as she explains:

> *The house had a typical side return, with a dead-space alley. We extended and opened everything up so that virtually every wall and door was moved. Only the staircase survived! Simon came up with the idea of a round window. The back of the house is quite overlooked, so we felt that having a big glass extension would be too much like a fishbowl. The circular window gives us a sense of privacy: we can look out, but people can't see in so much. I really love my house. When you come home and think, 'I love opening the door and coming inside,' it's the best feeling – it grounds you.*

When assessing the property market, keep an eye out for end-of-terrace houses, semis with unusually large spaces to the side, or those with attached garages that can be absorbed into the central living accommodation – anything that might give you a bit more width to create a proper congregation space. Perhaps the least successful rear extension I have seen was dedicated to a fully glazed laundry room. The owner suggested this was to afford her a view of the garden while she folded the kids' school uniforms, but to my mind it was a wasted opportunity to bring family and friends together in a single coherent space.

Turning up the volume

Valuing a house for selling purposes is a sophisticated art form, especially when you are assessing one that looks nothing like its neighbour. The starting point is always the gross internal floor area, which is why websites like Zoopla display a 'price per square foot' alongside each sales listing. That's the easy bit, of course. The true value of a home is bound up in all sorts of complexities: the quality of the light; the materials; the way the interior is presented – the kind of things that I described in my visit to the Housden House in the Introduction. Perhaps the least considered of all of these additional ingredients is volume.

High ceilings are an act of supreme generosity on behalf of the housebuilder. They require a greater quantity of building material, cost more to construct and steal valuable floor space from elsewhere, all the while contributing nothing to the sacred price per square foot. However, the truth is that people don't want to live in mean little boxes with no change of scale or sense of intrigue. The demands of the public have changed in recent times, and many property developers still haven't opened their eyes to the current landscape.

A few years ago we sold a flat belonging to my brother-in-law, Thomas. It measures less than 50 square metres (520 square feet) and has only one window. The bedroom, if you can call it that, is a mattress with a curtain around it on a mezzanine. And yet, because it has been converted from a school gymnasium, the living room is an exciting double-volume space with a parquet floor and full-height bookshelves. In spite of its humble footprint, the flat was snapped up for a significant premium.

Thankfully, there are certain enlightened developers who understand the value of volume. Roger Zogolovitch, for example, is a neckerchief-sporting visionary whose company, Solidspace, uses half levels to create dramatic open-plan spaces within terraced buildings of traditional proportion. Their 'split section' puts the key social spaces of the home – the areas for eating, living and working – on interlinked half levels, making them feel connected but private at the same time. This results in a decreased footprint, but the upshot is much greater ceiling height, more natural light and minimal wasted space such as hallways.

Neil Byrne, the founder of design agency Tomorrow PR, and his partner, fashion designer Eudon Choi, bought an apartment in a newly built Solidspace development in Shoreditch. Byrne says:

People expect a flat to have rooms off a central corridor and a kitchen at the end, but the layout of this is completely different. Amazingly for a flat, it's spread over five floors. Essentially, the rooms are stacked on top of each other and the stairways become the corridors. It means that it's filled with light even on dull days.

This idea has its roots in the Modern Movement and the work of the Austrian architect Adolf Loos, who developed the 'Raumplan'. Whereas Le Corbusier's Villa Savoye demonstrated the generosity of free-flowing lateral space, Loos's Villa Müller in Prague, built at around the same time, showed how to organize space vertically, with rooms positioned adjacent to each other at slightly different heights and linked by short staircases. He explained:

My architecture is in no sense conceived in plans, but instead in spaces (cubes). I do not design any floor plans, façades, cross-sections. I design spaces. For me, there is no ground floor, upper floor etc. . . . it is only about contiguous, continual spaces, rooms, halls, terraces.

Loos recognized that different rooms require different ceiling heights depending on their function. Contemporary research has shown that the volume of space can actually influence our mental capacity. Marketing scholars Joan Meyers-Levy and Rui Zhu took two groups of people and placed them in rooms that were identical in all respects except the ceiling height: one was 8-foot high and the other was 10-foot high. In a series of experiments designed to assess their psychological sense of freedom, the participants in the taller room demonstrated more pronounced creative and abstract thinking, while those in the lower room had a more confined mindset.

In another experiment, led by Dr Oshin Vartanian and published in the *Journal of Environmental Psychology*, volunteers were shown photographs of two hundred different rooms and asked to rate each one as 'beautiful' or 'not beautiful'. As you might expect, those with high ceilings came out more favourably in the judging process. Interestingly, however, the study went one stage further and monitored the volunteers' brain activity using an fMRI scanner. The images of rooms with high ceilings triggered heightened activity in two areas of the brain associated with visuospatial exploration, the left precuneus and left middle frontal gyrus. It would seem that a voluminous room engages our natural desire to observe our surroundings.

If you have a flat on the upper floor of a building, or a house with a pitched roof, it's often worth opening it up to the eaves, allowing the eye to travel all the way to the top. It sometimes works well to leave the original timber framework on display. Try to avoid false ceilings, which cramp a space unnecessarily; as we will discuss in the Light section, wall lights are always preferable to acne attacks of halogen spotlights. Steal volume wherever you can. An artist I know who owns a Victorian joiner's workshop removed half of the ceiling on the top floor to create a light-filled reception room, and left the other half *in situ* to form a sleeping platform, which is accessed via a set of space-saving paddle stairs.

I must admit that I have sometimes visited a newly built house and thought: this room is just *too* tall. A house should feel like a home rather than an aircraft hangar, with proportions that ground it in the domestic realm. American design duo Charles and Ray Eames just about got away with it when they built Case Study House No. 8 on a wooded bluff in Pacific Palisades, Los Angeles. Essentially a multicoloured shed in the trees, this influential edifice has cavernous double-height interiors that are never allowed to overwhelm. This is partly because the sitting room has two different ceiling heights, but it's also due to the interior arrangement: a pendant ceiling light on a long cord reaches right down through the space; mature pot plants fill the room with their bounteous foliage; and a ladder resting on top of the tall bookshelf extends all the way to top of the room, providing a physical connection between floor and ceiling.

Most of us have experienced the feeling of discombobulation induced by a huge space like a shopping centre. We grasp the handrail tightly as we ride the escalator, trying to anchor ourselves and overcome the feeling of vertigo. The shiny floors and hard surfaces serve only to increase our sense of detachment, as the sound bounces around like a grasshopper in a jam jar. Monolithic public architecture does little to consider the sensory needs of its occupants, and the same mistake must be avoided in the private realm. Early settlers got by with caves and huts, and Inuit made do with igloos – our current-day quest to build the most humongous house is surely flawed.

Spaces for hibernating

Not long ago, we were ambling along a country lane when Indigo spotted something out of the corner of her eye, dived into an unkempt hedgerow and emerged with an abandoned wren's nest in her palm. She was so enamoured with her discovery that, when we got home, she set about making her own nest using things from the garden. Gathering up handfuls of twigs and sponges of moss, she cajoled them into shape with great determination and dexterity. Both nests now have pride of place on our kitchen table, and the children fill them with treasures they have found, like petals and snail shells and pieces of discarded glitter.

A nest is a truly wondrous thing, because it is the physical manifestation of our primary instincts, a place that we would all like to crawl inside for a well-earned slumber. Vincent Van Gogh painted the birds' nests that he had found on his walks or acquired from local children. With their muted colours and strange protruding twigs, they have a haunting sense of melancholy, as if he had been trying to recapture the lost innocence of the infant's cradle. Of course, he famously painted his bedroom in Arles as well, a modest room with wooden furniture rendered, he said, in 'simple plain colours, like those in crêpes'.

Van Gogh intended his bedroom paintings to represent 'a certain rest or dream' and 'unswerving rest'. Indeed, only a small space such as this can conjure a primitive state of security and contentment, like a badger huddling in its sett or a vole taking refuge in its hole. Within the home, children create these nests for themselves instinctively, as the architectural historian John Summerson observed: 'There is a kind of play common to nearly every child; it is to get under a piece of furniture or some extemporized shelter of his own and to exclaim that he is in a "house".' When kids crawl underneath the dining table, they do so because it makes them feel more in control. It is the same for adults. Before a nerve-racking event like a public-speaking engagement, we are told to puff out our chests and extend our arms as far as they will go, to dominate the space around us and bring the walls closer.

We must all take inspiration from nature, and from children, by building in our own versions of the nurturing nest. In interior spaces with small proportions, the acoustics are reassuringly muffled, like a forest after a heavy burst of snow. They are perfectly suited to quiet activities such as meditation, contemplation and sleep. In deliberate contrast to the lofty

nature of congregation spaces, the ceilings should be lower and they should harness less natural light. They should be softly furnished and dimly lit, with effective sound insulation.

If we are to assume that the living space provides a place of prospect in the modern home, the most common place of refuge is the bedroom. This should be kept separate from the rest of the accommodation, if space allows. In newly built houses, bedrooms are often assigned to a separate 'wing' entirely, so that the occupant physically crosses a threshold and leaves the mental baggage of the day at the door. However, although a bedroom should unquestionably be a sanctuary, it must never be allowed to assume greater importance than the shared space.

In the first flat that Faye and I bought together, our bedroom was so small that there was barely any clearance around the bed (not helped by the builder's insistence on boxing in the services so that the skirting boards stuck out). I remember a friend of ours coming round for a cup of tea with her young son, who enquired innocently: 'Why do you sleep in a cupboard?' We had to keep our clothes somewhere, so we bought one of those lift-up storage beds. Unfortunately, as we hauled it into the bedroom on its side, it sprang open and got wedged in the doorway. Faye was stuck in the bedroom, on one side of it, while I was still out in the hallway muttering expletives. In the end, we had to remove the architrave to get it in. Despite these ignominious beginnings, it proved to be one of the best bedrooms we ever had, which held us in a tight embrace and encouraged us into the deepest of sleeps.

Morgwn Rimel, a creative director and former director of the School of Life, has created her own safe haven within a converted Methodist chapel in North London. The soaring proportions of the living space are counter-balanced by a cocoon-like bedroom, designed in conjunction with West Architecture. The walls, floors, doors and architraves are all made from birch- and spruce-faced plywood, while flush wardrobes and obscured glass further contribute to an atmosphere of complete serenity. She explains:

I'm American, and have lived all over the world, from Tokyo to Montreal. Before moving to London, I lived in a Modernist block in Sydney, which was poorly maintained. In Australia, you want to be outside at the beach, so it doesn't matter if your home is not a sanctuary. It's a different story in London. Life here can be wearing, and the weather is cold and dreary, so having a refuge to come back to is really important. I'm a total introvert, and being in the city, although I love it for the mental stimulation and the ideas that come from cross-disciplinary clashes, is something I find really exhausting. To be able to come back to a space that lets me recharge and literally find space to think is a real gift, and also quite necessary.

In the same way that a swaddle prevents a baby from flailing its limbs around, a small bedroom returns adults to the sanctuary of the womb. I have always found it strange that the price of a hotel room usually correlates to its size. If you want my opinion, go for the smallest one – it's not only the cheapest, but it gives you the most satisfactory sleeping experience. If it's positioned in the eaves at the top of the building, then so much the better: the ceiling height is usually lower, and you won't be woken in the early hours by the people in the room above doing squat thrusts.

The bathroom can also be considered a refuge space. En-suite bathrooms are always preferable because they promote seclusion. 'Man is the only animal that blushes,' pointed out Mark Twain, and a sense of shame and innate need for separation is a distinguishing element of our humanity. At home, I have my very own traditional water closet, a wardrobe-sized room containing a loo and a space-saving sink. It is hidden behind a jib door, and the walls are painted in gloss black to accentuate its diminutive proportions. I love that nobody knows it's there.

The late architect Richard Paxton and his wife, Heidi Locher, always incorporated his-and-hers bathrooms into every house they built. If space allows, this is a sensible way to keep the peace. Another couple I know each has their own bedroom, with separate access to a shared bathroom between the two, so that they can waft in and out without bumping into each other. Mornings are difficult enough without having to jostle for personal space. Tim Burton and Helena Bonham Carter famously took this sense of separation to extremes when they lived next door to each other in a pair of conjoined houses in Belsize Park.

I was once asked to value a Victorian terraced house that didn't have a door on the lavatory. The client had opened up the entire first floor to become one big room, including the master bedroom, the bathroom and a study. It was on the market with a local agent, and he couldn't work out why it wasn't selling. I had to gently explain that most people prefer a bit more privacy.

At the other end of the spectrum, we sold a house in East London where the singular sanitary space was its primary selling point. It had a walk-in shower, a bath with a horizontal slot window overlooking the garden, and a fully glazed roof. Dangling in one corner was a hammock, which could be hooked across the space to allow for daytime snoozes and night-time stargazing, while in another corner was a yoga mat, waiting to be unfurled across the pleasingly pockmarked floorboards.

The broken plan

If we are to assume that the ideal interior provides spaces for both stimulation and hibernation, how this can be achieved on a small footprint? The answer is by making it adaptable. Indeed, in recent years, designers have moved away from the open plan towards something more forgiving and adaptable: the broken plan.

Broken-plan living is about creating distinct areas within the home using partitions or changes of level. If we think about what we demand of our domestic environment, it serves as a place of entertainment, a retreat, a guest house, an office, a creative canvas and a place to decompress. It should also express our individuality. To achieve all of this, it needs to be malleable, to bend and twist in time with the rhythm of our daily existence.

The founding father of flexible living was the Dutch architect Gerrit Rietveld. His seminal Rietveld Schröder House in Utrecht was built in 1924 for Mrs Truus Schröder-Schräder, whose brief was to create a house 'without walls' for herself and her three children. Both architect and client sought to turn their backs on bourgeois notions of hierarchy and containment, instead embracing a spirit of emotional openness. The result is a dynamic, fluid interior that can be reconfigured using a system of sliding and revolving panels, providing an endless variety of spatial experiences. Rietveld was heavily influenced by the reductivist paintings of Piet Mondrian, a fellow member of the De Stijl art movement, which consist of pure planes in primary colours placed in asymmetrical patterns. Even the façade of the house is like a kinetic collage, with panels that seem ready to glide past one another.

Since the early days of the Modern Movement, flexible spaces have been utilized in small city flats as well. In 1936 my Grandpa Whiskers built an apartment block in Streatham called Pullman Court, a stuccoed ocean liner that helped to usher the spirit of European Modernism into the UK. The flats were given walnut sliding partitions, which could be pulled back to maximize the feeling of space during the day and closed off to create intimacy at night. Grandpa was only twenty-three years old when he designed it, a source of constant inadequacy for everyone else in the family. The commission came after he picked up a girl at a dance hall, who, as luck would have it, was the secretary of a property tycoon.

Such was the success of Pullman Court, he was asked to design a succession of London apartment blocks, including Park Court in Sydenham, Ellington Court in Southgate and the Somerford Estate in Hackney. He became known as the 'flat architect', and co-authored a book on the subject with his friend F. R. S. Yorke. *The Modern Flat* remains one of the defining publications of the age. They wrote: 'We believe that the problem of housing cannot be solved by the provision of millions of little cottages scattered over the face of the country.'

The Barbican Estate in the City of London, designed by Chamberlin, Powell & Bon and built between the 1960s and the 1980s, provided flexible living on a grander scale. It contains a variety of different flat layouts, each a blueprint for modern living. One of the most popular and prevalent is the 'Type 20', which has an L-shaped reception room with a sliding door that can be pulled across to create a study or a spare bedroom for itinerant friends.

When thinking about your own space, you might want to take inspiration from the Modernists and consider flexible partitions instead of walls. It's always useful to have a guest sleeping area or a workspace that can be sectioned off for privacy, but that can contribute to the sense of expansiveness in the living room when not in use. Pocket doors are particularly effective, as they slide out of sight, and I also like pivoting doors for their sense of drama. Full-height doors or those that seem unnecessarily tall can help to increase the perception of volume.

Almost as effective are static partitions that are partly glazed, thereby allowing the light to filter through from one space to another. This could be a Japanese-inspired screen – a simple timber grid with a strip of glazing at the top – or a more traditional-looking divider that mimics the elegant proportions and featherweight glazing bars of Georgian architecture, either in timber or steel. Rather than getting something made, it sometimes makes economic sense to source an old window: a Crittall unit from a redundant factory, perhaps, or a sash salvaged from a country house. Fluted glass is effective if you need visual separation between the two spaces. Free-standing bookcases can also be useful, especially those on castors that can be wheeled out of the way.

One of the most elegant flats we have sold measures just 45 square metres, and is contained within a converted printworks in London Fields. Its creators, designers Bentley Hagen Hall, have made expert use of the compact space, creating an L-shaped room that fulfils all of the requirements of living, dining and working. The little study area can be sectioned off with a curtain when required, with a step up that reinforces the sense of separation. A drop-leaf

dining table can be brought out when friends come round, or stashed neatly against the wall when not in use.

A converted warehouse in Islington by 6a Architects exemplifies flexible living on a grander scale. The first floor is 86 feet long, with a grid of steel beams and a profiled ceiling that create natural breaks in the space as you move through it: a kitchen at one end, a bed and free-standing bath at the other, and some seating and a dining table between the two that loosely define the various functions. The house was designed for an art collector, and it is the artworks themselves that help to subdivide the space. Along one side of the room is a row of glass vitrines set on floor runners, containing museum-quality ceramics and glassware. These can be repositioned to create different spatial arrangements and expose different artworks, like an ever evolving gallery. Similarly, books have been placed in archive storage units on runners, which can be pulled apart to reveal specific tomes or sandwiched together to save on space.

Michael Putman and Sara L'Espérance, founders of architectural studio Suprblk, took flexibility to its utmost extreme when converting a former biscuit factory in Bethnal Green. They deliberately set out to create a space that would work successfully for future occupants with circumstances different to their own, ensuring that the project has both longevity and commercial appeal. The couple have inserted a sequence of plywood joinery pieces into the building, including a sleeping platform accessed by a set of vertical steps, and a little desk perched on top of the kitchen units like an eagle's eyrie. Michael explains:

> When we started the design process, we were thinking, even though this place is for us, we should consider other people who might live here in years to come. We thought about three people. One was an individual who wanted to live and work here, so they could have the studio but all living spaces, too, which is how we use it. The second scenario was with two tenants. Because this is London, you need that flexibility in which two people could live, sharing the mortgage or rent, so a second bedroom could be created from where our dining room/meeting room currently is. The third one was a young, small family who could have a nursery or children's bedroom – that's when we started introducing playful elements like the ladder and the idea of a treehouse where the guest sleeping mezzanine is.

The illusion of space

Adjacent to a West London kebab shop, opposite a bookies, and a few doors down from a nail bar, you will find the discordantly discerning home of Duncan McLeod and Lyndsay Milne McLeod. If you plod along this prosaic high street at the right time of day, you might encounter Duncan riding a motorcycle through the door in his leathers like eighties TV cop Street Hawk. He explains:

> *I get around on a motorbike most of the time, and I didn't want it to get stolen or rusty. I asked Lyndsay if I could keep it indoors. Though resistant at first, she agreed as long as I could hide it somewhere.*

His ingenious solution was a retractable steel staircase, which winds across the entrance hall on runners. He has covered the treads with vivid green Astroturf, which he likens mischievously to a grocery-shop display:

> *It's a bit of fun. Lyndsay was pregnant with our son, Oban, and I've always dreamed of designing a house that a child would remember for ever. I stayed in a house in Hastings when I was five or six, and we played hide and seek; I went under the stairs, pushed a little door and suddenly found myself in a huge church. I couldn't believe it. Of course, the house was a vicarage, but I was still at the age when I believed in magic.*

If we are to magnify the visual impact of space, and capitalize on the feeling of contentment that it generates, it's essential to utilize every notable nook and credible cranny for squirrelling things away. Humans find untidiness inherently stressful, and storage makes us feel calmer and more organized.

Most buildings have natural niches and inlets where seamless cupboards can be introduced that don't compromise the bones of the thing. Is there scope for some built-in wardrobes in the bedroom? Can you create a spice rack in a recess in the kitchen? Might you be able to squeeze in some bookshelves above the door? Working with the natural contours of the building in this way will always be more efficient than plonking free-standing pieces of furniture around the place.

The architect Brian Heron demonstrated a particularly economical use of space when he converted the old water tank on top of Keeling House, a high-rise block of flats in East London designed by Denys Lasdun in the 1950s. The storage has been specifically configured for each piece of kitchenware, with dinner plates tucked into slots and rows of white mugs dangling from hooks like synchronized swimmers. In the bathroom, a free-standing Italian square bath doubles as a shower, with a vertically sliding tap. The family sleeps together in a single space with a bespoke two-tiered bed made from inexpensive OSB, with the parents on top and the kids underneath.

Despite my chequered history with storage beds, they are incredibly useful, and we have always had at least one in every place where we have lived. There is an amazing amount of redundant space beneath a double bed, which can be utilized for anything that you don't use daily, such as luggage or spare bedlinen. If you have a lot of clothes, consider splitting them into a summer and winter wardrobe, and keeping half beneath the bed when not in use.

Maximizing the space in a kitchen is a complex process. Faye and I worked with the specialist company Plain English on the design of our own kitchen, and, even then, the layout was altered many times during the process as we changed our minds about how we might use it. Unless you are very tight on space, I recommend avoiding wall cupboards wherever possible. They make the room seem much narrower, and the upper shelves become dumping grounds for redundant instruction manuals and 'Dad of the Year' mugs. Using open shelves instead allows the space to breathe; you just have to be disciplined about what you put on display.

Similarly, an island unit is a great way to buy yourself some more storage, but it can look overly bulky; treating it instead like a workbench – raised up on legs with space underneath – will lighten the visual load. Approaching the room as a collection of pieces of furniture is a great way to give it personality. Instead of fitted units, you could use, say, an antique dresser, a butcher's block and some free-standing stainless-steel appliances. This works especially well in old houses with walls that bow and bend.

The chef Mark Hix installed an 'unfitted' kitchen at his live/work apartment in Bermondsey, with a worktop supported on cast-concrete columns salvaged from a mid-century office block, and a refurbished nineteenth-century refrigerator that he bought in an antiques shop in Paris. He explains:

The fridge was made in the 1800s – originally they would have put a block of ice in the middle compartment to keep the whole thing cold. The refrigeration guy that I use for my restaurants converted it. It's got different sections: dairy; wine; glasses; negroni cabinet!

If you don't have space for a free-standing fridge–freezer in your own kitchen, you might consider a pair of under-counter refrigerators side by side. We have done this at many of the homes we have lived in over the years, usually adding a freezer in the basement if there is enough room.

Don't forget to think about the waste solutions in advance. A free-standing dustbin hangs around the kitchen like a foul-smelling Dalek, tripping people up and overflowing with the remains of yesterday's dinner. Storage for recycling should also be considered as part of the design process. The space beneath the sink is always a useful spot for food waste, for example.

It's best to keep the washing facilities out of the kitchen if space allows. There is something deeply unsatisfactory about the way in which fresh laundry is unloaded on to a crumb-filled floor, and the noise and heat generated by washing machines and tumble dryers contribute to an oppressive atmosphere within the most important room in the home. Ideally the washing should be carried out in a separate, well-ventilated space.

The modern bathroom tends to be a rather formal affair, with fitted baths, loos and sinks that all match perfectly, but I prefer to channel the spirit of Terence Conran by treating it in a more unstructured way. Much like an unfitted kitchen, a bathroom with a free-standing tub, a rug on the floor and an old cabinet nailed to the wall looks much more generous. Faye has a weakness for a traditional high-level toilet cistern with a long chain, although the power and noise of the flush tends to freak the children out.

There are many ways to trick the eye into thinking that a space is larger than it really is. Wall-hung mirrors are particularly effective, especially when placed close to windows, because they help to reflect the natural light and increase the size of the vista. Using the same material both inside and out also makes the brain feel that the room is physically expanding beyond its walls. One of the most effective examples of this is the architect John Pawson's house in London, which has a glass wall through which the concrete kitchen worktop appears to pass uninterrupted into the garden.

Another way is to shun traditional skirting boards in favour of shadow gaps: perfectly plastered little spaces where the wall meets the floor. These create a seamless visual effect and help the wall to feel like a larger expanse, which in turn generates an illusion of height. Walls used to be wet-plastered, and skirting was devised to hide injudicious junctions, as well as to provide a visual barrier for rising damp. Now that we have sheets of machine-cut plasterboard, metal-edge beads and damp-proof courses, skirting boards are more of a decorative conceit. In a similar vein, cupboards, wardrobes and cabinets should ideally be 'floating' on the wall rather than free-standing, so as to amplify the floor space and make the room feel bigger.

Minimizing areas of circulation such as lobbies, corridors, staircases and landings is another way to enhance the sense of space. Our old house in Highgate was designed in 1963 by the bustling, cigar-toting architect Walter Segal, who was a master at manipulating a floor plan to make the most of every square inch. Despite measuring no more than 140 square metres, the house feels far larger, because he carefully reduced the circulation so that it constitutes just 12 per cent of the overall area. It originally contained six bedrooms, a remarkable number for a building of modest size.

While the house was being built, Segal and his family lived in a wooden cabin at the bottom of the garden, a sort of Modern Movement static caravan. It cost £800 and took two weeks to build. Known as the Little House, this influential structure lasted over fifty years, before finally falling off its wooden stilts and being repurposed as a den for foxes. Segal was surprised by how much attention it attracted, and many architects made the pilgrimage to see it. The design – a wooden frame, insulation and weatherproof shell – was the prototype for what became known as the 'Segal Method', which he pursued for the rest of his career. This was a form of building that eliminated wet trades such as bricklaying and cement-pouring, in favour of a modular timber system reminiscent of traditional Japanese architecture. A number of enthusiastic self-builders adopted this approach, and there are little estates of 'Segal Method' houses in South-East London. Despite their humble proportions, they conjure a magical atmosphere that is both cosseting and uplifting. Segal was much influenced by the egalitarian principles of William Morris, as well as the early Modernists. He wrote:

The buildings of the International Style were by definition unassuming . . . They were meant to promote wellbeing.

At around the same time that Walter Segal was building his place in Highgate, David Levitt set to work on a new house with the eccentric name of Ansty Plum, nestled in the countryside on the Dorset/Wiltshire border. It sits on the side of a verdant valley, and has a pitched roof with the dramatic steepness of a perilous ski jump. We sold the house to its current owner, architect Sandra Coppin, who has breathed new life into the building and greatly appreciates its spatial parsimony:

> *The proportions of the house are dictated by the size of a brick and an uncut piece of Douglas Fir-veneered ply – there was no waste. It's that economy of means that, as an architect, I find compelling. We live in a time when everything is bigger and brighter, more open and supersized, and it's all about how much we can consume. This house is quite the opposite. It's about the least we can have, and the least we can use. There's a rawness and a lack of pretension, an honesty which makes it easy to grasp.*

One of the most important elements of space planning is the effective positioning of doors and windows, as it allows for satisfactory furniture placement. In a bedroom, for example, there should be a specific area of clear wall for the bed to shuffle into. A divan shoved up against a window spoils your visual connection to the outside world and is liable to give you a frosty head on a winter morning. If there is not enough wall allocation for storage, then invariably a free-standing wardrobe has to be shoehorned into a tight space close to the doorway, spoiling the entrance to the room and making it feel narrower than it is. If you have inherited an existing set-up that makes this scenario unavoidable, consider whether the door can be hung the other way around so that it opens against the wall rather than into the room.

Similarly, radiators should be placed beneath windows, so that wall space is kept clear for furniture. This is also preferable for energy-efficiency: induction causes the cold air coming in through the window to push the warmer air from the radiator into the room. Conversely, butting a sofa up against a radiator is liable to restrict the flow of heat.

Ironically, Baroque palaces can teach us a thing or two about how to save space. An 'enfilade' is a suite of rooms connected together along a single axis, with doorways that line up and provide a vista from one end to the other. In the seventeenth century, the first room was a public room, then there was a series of state rooms, culminating in the boudoir at the

furthest point – a guest was allowed to progress as far along the enfilade as their rank would allow. Putting the pomp and ceremony to one side, this arrangement maximizes space, because it dispenses with corridors, and there is a satisfying sense of flow as you move through the rooms.

The architect Laura Dewe Mathews has adopted this idea for her Gingerbread House in Hackney, East London, which is constructed from prefabricated cross-laminated timber panels and clad in cedar shingles. It measures just 80 square metres, but it's incredibly efficient, because the circulation is almost entirely dispensed with. In the Baroque tradition, the rooms on the ground floor run one into the other: the kitchen feeds the sitting room, which in turn opens on to the workspace.

An enfilade can transform even the most confined living environments. Alistair Langhorne and Claire Bunten of Lab Architects made the brave decision to uproot their two teenage children from a conventional family house in Fulham and plonk them on a working barge on the Thames. Aside from the ever present rocking, like the vague vertigo you get after a long-haul flight, it is surprisingly domesticated, with comfortable sofas and wood-panelled walls. It feels a bit like wearing your favourite fur-lined slippers, with skateboard wheels attached to the soles. The space below deck has been configured in three parts, with a bedroom and en-suite bathroom for the grown-ups at one end, kids' quarters at the other, and social spaces in the middle where the family comes together. Each part has its own staircase. You can see all the way down the full length of the boat when the doors are open, with shafts of daylight emitted by brass portholes. Every tiny bit of space has been utilized: cleverly sequestered in the bow is a glitzy little telly room, which is accessed by flinging open the original saloon doors and pulling off a balletic leap over a banquette.

The home should have a natural gradient of privacy, which enables guests to feel comfortable and saves them from embarrassment. If someone asks to use the bathroom, ideally they won't stumble into your bedroom by accident and see yesterday's Argyle socks on the carpet. In Peru the idea of having rooms with a range of different guest permissions is a common one, as outlined in the wonderfully opinionated 1970s architecture book *A Pattern Language*:

> *Casual neighbourhood friends will probably never enter the house at all. Formal friends, such as the priest, the daughter's boyfriend, and friends from work may be*

invited in, but tend to be limited to a well-furnished and maintained part of the house, the sala. *This room is sheltered from the clutter and more obvious informality of the rest of the house. Relatives and intimate friends may be made to feel at home in the family room (*comedor-estar*), where the family is likely to spend much of its time. A few relatives and friends, particularly women, will be allowed into the kitchen, other workspaces, and, perhaps, the bedrooms of the house. In this way, the family maintains both privacy and pride.*

Using space to add drama

The modern home should be full of spatial surprises, with rooms of varying sizes and shapes, and ceilings at different heights, some flat and others pitched. Even the smallest living spaces can be bounteous and big-hearted in their intent. As we have already seen, monotonous layouts and rooms that lack volume can adversely affect our feeling of happiness, which is why effective space planning should promote intrigue. What you're searching for is an ordered complexity, and anything that generates a feeling of contrast is to be encouraged.

This journey starts as soon as you step through the front door. The entrance hall is one of the most important rooms in a house: although it is rarely a place where we spend much time or carry out everyday activities, it sets expectations and generates a sense of arrival. It marks the transition point between the street and the home, between the public and the private domain, a place where we can cast off our metaphorical smog-soaked suits and don some freshly laundered pyjamas.

There is a pleasing decadence about a dramatically tall, brightly lit entrance hall. This, the visitor assumes, is a place with a welcoming atmosphere and a generosity of spirit. If you're fortunate enough to have sufficient space, think about dressing the hall as a supplementary room, with a chair to perch on and a table topped with flowers.

One of the most successful newly built houses I have visited in recent years is Nithurst Farm in West Sussex, designed by Adam Richards. Here, the entrance hall is the tallest space in the building, but also one of the most constricted. Adam explains:

> *When you come in, it's suddenly very dark, so your sense of sight is turned right down. But it's also where we store the logs, and it smells very strongly of wood. Because it's a tall concrete space, it echoes when you close the door, so your sense of hearing is also tuned up. So your senses get slightly rejigged, and then you pop through into the big main space, which provides a contrast of scale.*

A few years ago we sold a Georgian rectory in a country village, and the buyer explained with great enthusiasm how she had dreamt about the tinselled Christmas tree that she was planning to erect in the hall. Scottish textile designer Donna Wilson found a similarly romantic attachment to her house in Walthamstow, East London:

As soon as I walked through the door, I fell in love with it. And that was that! I think the hallway might still be my favourite part of the house. It feels like such a luxury to have that space. It's turned into a bit of a full-time job to keep it clear of jackets and shoes, but it's the one space that I like to keep really empty.

In *A Pattern Language*, the authors cite a study from 1962 that examined visitor habits at pavilions, fairs and trade shows:

[Robert Stuart Weiss and Serge Boutourline Jr] noticed that many exhibits failed to 'hold' people; people drifted in and then drifted out again within a very short time. However, in one exhibit people had to cross a huge, deep-pile, bright orange carpet on the way in. In this case, though the exhibit was no better than other exhibits, people stayed. The authors concluded that people were, in general, under the influence of their own 'street and crowd behaviour', and that while under this influence could not relax enough to make contact with the exhibits. But the bright carpet presented them with such a strong contrast as they walked in, that it broke the effect of their outside behaviour, in effect 'wiped them clean', with the result that they could then get absorbed in the exhibit.

Before you rush out and buy a luridly coloured shagpile, consider that this effect can be achieved using something as simple as a fitted doormat. At our office in London, which is converted from a 1930s ecclesiastical hall, we inherited a dingy and nondescript entrance hall, but by installing a huge lacquered front door and covering the floor entirely with coir matting, we conjured up a sense of occasion that was previously lacking. Even in a small space with no entrance hall to speak of, a change in material or a threshold of some kind will generate a sense of arrival. Of course, an entrance hall is also an 'exit hall' when it comes to saying your goodbyes. It needs to function effectively as a place of finality, with enough space that there's no awkwardness as you and your guests dance around each other trying to dish out hugs and kisses.

In smaller dwellings, providing a long view through the space and out into the garden immediately elevates the experience of arrival. As we shall analyse later in the book, any

opportunity to provide a connection to nature should be grasped. In larger houses, consider the journey towards the main entertaining space as an opportunity to build anticipation. Perhaps the visitor can be constricted through a narrow corridor: imagine a sailing boat tacking its way along a narrow tributary, before being unleashed into open waters.

Or else conceal the living space behind a door, which acts like a stage curtain to reveal the drama as it is pulled back. Consider making the door outsized and thick, so that it can be opened only with a run-up, or hide it seamlessly in the wall like something from a *Scooby-Doo* cartoon. Or perhaps make a diminutive opening, like the portal into the mind of John Malkovich, causing you to bend at the hip as you enter.

My architect friend Sally Mackereth played with scale in this way at her family home in King's Cross, which has been fashioned from a Victorian stable block. She explains:

> *It was built in 1878, which is shortly after Lewis Carroll wrote* Through the Looking-Glass. *It wasn't necessarily a conscious thing, but there is an* Alice in Wonderland *reference here – the feeling that all the doors are oversized, and the small, narrow staircases. I thought carefully about the way you might move through the house: the different thresholds, the element of surprise as you pass from one space to another, or perhaps the way you don't even understand that leaning against a wall might cause it to open. A lot of the doors into new spaces are concealed, either in the grain of the timber or the panelling.*

My own house was built by a Victorian landowner using an early method of *in situ* concrete. Nobody understands exactly how it has been put together, which is why, when we asked the builders to create a new doorway between the bathroom and the dressing room, they discovered a solid concrete ring beam rising out of the floor as they were drilling. Rather than block it back up again, we decided to keep the opening and accept that we would need to step over a threshold. We have made a virtue of it by giving it a curved cupboard frontage, so that there is a Narnia-like experience when you enter it. It's funny how happy accidents like this sometimes end up being the most engaging areas of the home.

Children are endlessly fascinated by these eccentricities and changes of scale. As we have discussed, they also appreciate places to hide, finding natural niches in the architecture and dens beneath the stairs to scurry into. Our twins, Wren and Etta, have built-in elevated beds with voids underneath that they crawl into when they are playing hide-and-seek.

Another way to create nuanced space is by varying the floor levels. The act of stepping up or down into a room is inevitably a more thought-provoking experience. Split-level spaces are a hallmark of Modernist living, because they allow for a sense of separation between rooms – usually the kitchen and the living room – while enabling the natural light to flow uninterrupted from one end of the building to the other. In my opinion, sunken sitting areas are one of the great legacies of the 1970s. In some cases, the entire sitting room is lowered, with free-standing or built-in sofas, while in others a simple square or rectangle filled with cushions makes a soft-centred conversation pit for friends and family.

Jonathan Tuckey is a designer who always considers the human experience as the starting point for any building, a by-product of his academic background in anthropology rather than architecture. His family home in Queen's Park, which he converted from a former steel factory more than twenty-five years ago, is one of the most richly textured and experiential spaces I have ever visited, and owes much of its success to the careful orchestration of space. He says:

> *There are changes of level between the rooms, which are purely psychological devices. You step up when you arrive in the house so that you leave the street behind, and then, equally, step down from the living room into the kitchen. It is only one step, but when the children were younger, it stopped the tide of toys drifting uninterrupted from one space to another. And then stepping up to the bedrooms provides a psychological separation between activities of the day and activities of the night.*

A staircase takes up a lot of room, but its impact should not be underestimated. At its best, a sweeping staircase or cunningly cantilevered set of steps can provide a moment of showmanship, reinforcing the aesthetic impact of the entrance hall. It can be used as a stage during a party, from which the host can raise a toast, or it might be the backdrop to a dramatic arrival by the hostess, as she sashays down to greet her guests in a phantasmagorical frock.

If it's designed in the right way, a staircase can be subsumed into the activities of everyday life. It should be open-hearted and embracing rather than tucked away apologetically. A stair that opens into the living space becomes a perch to sit on, especially if it splays out towards the bottom. It is also something that you use every day. Ascending (or descending) usually marks the physical transition between day and night, between the living spaces and the sleeping spaces, and the staircase should enable rather than constrict that progression. Personally, I am not a fan of spiral staircases, unless there really is no other option. Although they take up a smaller footprint, they require greater mental effort to use – inevitably they are tight on width and reverberate as you step. They also fail to contribute to the adaptability and durability of the home, as they are often unsuitable for young children, the elderly and pets.

The architect Alex Michaelis recognized the emotive power of a staircase when he was building a house for himself and his family in West London. He placed it right at the centre of the plan, so that it forms a natural division for the various functions of the home, with a kitchen and dining space on one side, and a sitting room on the other. The staircase is lit from above by a massive rooflight, reinforcing its importance. Best of all are the stairs themselves: thick, open treads with a reassuring solidity, and an adjacent slide that enables the kids to propel themselves down on their bottoms at high speed.

A few years ago I visited the celebrated architect Richard Rogers and his equally legendary wife Ruth Rogers, owner of the River Café restaurant, at their extraordinary house in Chelsea. I will never forget the sight of Richard coming down the stairs dressed in a shocking-pink shirt and orange braces. The couple have removed one of the floors and inserted a perforated-steel staircase that descends through two storeys; it acts as both a form of sculpture and a dramatic means of arrival.

Inspired by his father, perhaps, designer Ab Rogers has indulged in some staircase sorcery of his own at the aptly named Rainbow House, a whimsical world of vivid colour behind an unassuming façade. Here, the fibreglass-and-steel spiral stair reveals itself like the unfurling of a colour fan, moving through the entire spectrum of the rainbow, tread by tread. As if that weren't fanciful enough, a hatch in the floor of the master bedroom provides access to a steel chute that cascades down into the kitchen, which comes in handy if you need a midnight feast (make mine a slider).

A space of one's own

The demands we place on personal space tend to change as we get older. Our three children will happily pile into the same tiny room with their friends, splayed out contentedly on bunks and truckles. When we were travelling through Cornwall as teenagers, my friend Jedd and I would often sleep in the front seats of his elderly Triumph Herald; if we were feeling particularly decadent, we might share a one-man tent, along with a pair of rucksacks and the remains of yesterday's pasties. As an adult, I find myself being infinitely less tolerant of the presence of others. I never used to understand why my grandparents slept in separate single beds, but now it makes complete sense to me. Much as I love my daughters, there are times when I long for a sound-proofed Nissen hut that their howling cannot penetrate.

Most of us cohabit with others, whether they be friends, lodgers, flatmates or family members. Sometimes we don't know these people very well, or we have little in common with them. Their presence in our inhabited space is, in many ways, a barrier to our own creativity, to our daydreaming. As human beings, we talk about being *alone* with our thoughts, and *at one* with nature. Yi-Fu Tuan writes:

> *Solitude is a condition for acquiring a sense of immensity. Alone, one's thoughts wander freely over space. In the presence of others they are pulled back by an awareness of other personalities who project their own worlds into the same area . . . people crowd us; people rather than things are likely to restrict our freedom and deprive us of space.*

The same is true of pets. My mum, who lives on her own, depends on the company of her devoted Yorkie-Poo, but there is a point at which being shadowed everywhere by a dog becomes tiresome (or even downright dangerous, if you are trying to get down the stairs). Regardless of our personal circumstances, we all need a place in the home that is distinctly our own.

While the home as a whole provides us with a buffer against the outside world, so an individual room gives us autonomy and privacy from those we live with. Its physical boundaries – the walls and the door – allow us to withdraw from social interaction when we need to.

This private sanctuary is often a study or work room, which doesn't have to be big, but it does have to be self-contained. Children and pets will accept separation from their carers only if they can't see or hear them. Amateur artists and dilettante designers will feel the mental benefit of a separate studio: somewhere they can coil clay or weave wool while listening to their favourite vinyl records. Others may prefer to tend to their saplings in the potting shed, with the *Shipping Forecast* as a soundtrack. A supplementary space like this can be fashioned from a redundant outbuilding, converted from a garage, tacked on to the house as a lean-to or newly built in the garden. Whatever form it takes, it should be simple, humble and honest. Cobwebs are welcomed; paint-spattered floors are positively encouraged. If a space is to be your own, you must allow the sediment of life to settle over it.

This is the space where your own self is allowed to be truly articulated. If you want to nail a rusty horseshoe above the door or paint the whole thing gloss red, that's your prerogative. Making your own space expresses your ego and gives you a personal identity.

Kids, too, will benefit from their own domain. If you have enough space for a games room or a play area, try to parcel it off from the primary living accommodation, so that the carnage is self-contained. Toddlers should be able to build teetering timber towers without causing anxiety in their parents. Teenagers will appreciate a space where the outside world won't interfere with what they are doing. Let your children have a say in how it's decorated. The increasing prevalence of helicopter parenting has allowed children very little room for creative manoeuvre.

When you have guests to stay, consider that they will also crave their own defensible space. One of the most satisfactory modern-house layouts I have come across is a single-storey arrangement where the kitchen and sitting room are in the middle of the plan, the principal sleeping accommodation is placed at one end of it and the guest accommodation is at the other. This provides the utmost physical and acoustic separation for all of its occupants, who can come together in the middle of the house when they want to socialize and retreat to their private quarters when they need some respite. At the very least, try to ensure that the guest bedroom is not placed directly next to the master bedroom, so that visitors can feel a sense of segregation from their hosts.

If you can put the guest quarters in a stand-alone studio or garden room, expect to be flooded with visitations from long-lost relatives and estranged friends. Achieving complete separation is one of the greatest gifts you can impart to house guests. A spill-over space like this can serve a variety of different functions: when people are not in residence, the ping-pong table can be wheeled out or the climbing wall can be put to use. It can become a child's place of refuge as they grow into a teenager, or accommodate an elderly family member as they become increasingly reliant on others. It can even be an infirmary for someone recovering from illness or injury. Human beings are unique among primates in using their home in this way – an ailing ape, for example, risks death if it cannot keep up with the other members of the troop as they strike out in search of sustenance and shelter.

For flatmates and sharers, finding your own space within the household can be a challenge, but even the most communal of dwellings requires some level of separation. There might be a place for your most treasured books, or a chair that fits you particularly well. Can you negotiate your own shelf in the fridge or the food cupboard? Is there a window seat available to be commandeered, where you could place a cushion and bask in the sunshine like a house cat? The most valuable spaces of all are those that allow us to find a rare moment of respite and allow our daydreams to take hold. In the inimitable words of Gaston Bachelard:

> *In our houses we have nooks and corners in which we like to curl up comfortably. To curl up belongs to the phenomenology of the verb 'to inhabit', and only those who have learned to do so can inhabit with intensity.*

Light

'The sun never knew how
wonderful it was until it fell
on the wall of a building.'
Louis Kahn

Light and emotion

Built in the mid-1950s by Le Corbusier, the Chapel of Notre-Dame du Haut in Ronchamp sprouts from a Gallic hillock like a plump autumnal toadstool. With its swelled masonry walls and upturned roof, it looks like the sort of fairy-tale folly you might find in a toddler's playroom.

One afternoon, Faye and I shoehorned some baguettes into a knapsack and hiked up the hill for a look. Catching our breath, we stumbled through the chapel's pivoting portal. The overwhelming quietude told us that there was no one else around – which was just as well, really, because we promptly burst into tears.

You don't have to be deeply religious to have a spiritual experience inside a building. As Le Corbusier himself said, 'I have not experienced the miracle of faith, but I have often known the miracle of inexpressible space.'

At Ronchamp, the building's ability to stir the emotions is all to do with its masterful manipulation of natural light. A celestial glow washes down the mortared walls of the apse, where a single candle flickers with painful poignancy. Powerful shafts of sunlight penetrate the hulking south wall through asymmetric windows set at alternating depths. The spaces left between the walls and the ceiling are filled with clerestory glazing, eroding the darkness progressively and revealing the board marks in the concrete. Little bursts of stained glass sparkle like rubies and emeralds.

We sat in silence, on our own, for what must have been an hour. By the time we emerged from the chapel, the evening was descending and the site had become enveloped in mist. The building now looked muted, more like a musty milkcap in a damp forest.

Just as the light gives a religious building its atmosphere, so it brings character, emotion and comfort into our homes. It creates warmth underfoot as we move through the interior; it projects animations of rustling leaves on to the walls; it brings interior objects into relief and gives them their depth; it creates kaleidoscopes of colour as it reflects and refracts around the building. As a client of ours with a Modernist house poetically described it: 'When the sun comes out, everything starts to dance.'

We spend so much time in our home environment that we need to feel an emotional connection to it; this is largely informed by the quality of the light. When looking for a place to buy or rent, people tend to be swayed by the weather conditions on the day of their viewing. We would all find it hard to fall in love with a single-glazed relic of early Modernism on a drizzly morning in February, for example, but on a balmy August afternoon . . . well, that's a different matter.

When Marie Laurent and Édouard de Pomyers bought a Postmodern house in Clerkenwell designed by Piers Gough, the light was the most important factor in their decision-making, as Marie explains:

> *We just had a total crush. It was a beautiful sunny day. I remember the light, and I remember the big tree in the small square, almost entering the house, almost part of the house. We had a cup of tea on the rooftop terrace with the owners. Édouard and I looked at each other and said, 'Okay, this is clearly our place, this is our house.' The light was the most impressive thing. It's so luminous, even in a country where the sun isn't that reliable.*

Sunlight stimulates our imaginations. It is easy to understand why St Ives, which resides like a bunion on the big toe of England's outstretched foot, became a haven of creative endeavour in the inter-war period. The quality of the Cornish light, cascading in from the North Atlantic, proved inspirational for a generation of artists: the inscrutable Barbara Hepworth feverishly chiselled away at great lumps of stone in her garden in the middle of town; Patrick Heron abstracted the drystone walls and vivid foliage in Zennor; and the untrained seafarer Alfred Wallis painted the glinting crests of the waves on to bits of old board.

Natural light is also integral to human health. Vitamin D, the 'sunshine vitamin', has been shown to reduce the risk of heart disease, weight gain and certain forms of cancer, and promote strong bone development. Most importantly of all, it makes us feel good. There is a simple reason why, every summer, seaside resorts swell with holidaymakers, jostling for space around swimming pools. Sunshine triggers the release of serotonin, the 'happy chemical'. When used in combination with Continental lager, the effect can be positively euphoric.

Light and transparency

The inebriating effects of alcohol and sunlight might go some way towards explaining Paul Scheerbart's obsession with glazing. Scheerbart was a heavy-drinking German author who propped up the bar with Edvard Munch and August Strindberg. In 1914 he wrote a persuasive treatise entitled *Glasarchitektur*, proposing a brand of architecture that 'lets the sunlight and the light of the moon and stars into our rooms not merely through a few windows, but simultaneously through the greatest possible number of walls that are made entirely of glass'.

Scheerbart believed that transparency would make the built environment 'paradise on earth'. His ideas proved influential, and thereafter the Modernists went berserk with picture windows and curtain walling, garnishing their buildings with whitewashed roof terraces like the dazzling sun decks of ocean-faring liners. Two of the most iconic buildings conceived in the 1940s, Mies van der Rohe's Farnsworth House in Illinois and Philip Johnson's Glass House in Connecticut, were entirely see-through, to the extent that the landscape itself became the primary form of interior decoration. 'I have expensive wallpaper,' quipped Johnson. Although these audacious dwellings were undoubtedly extreme, they acknowledged the importance of natural light and its ability to positively affect the human psyche.

The first fully glazed building designed for human use was actually built almost a century earlier, by the English gardener-turned-architect Joseph Paxton. Having landed the job of head gardener of Chatsworth House in Derbyshire at the age of twenty-six, Paxton developed increasingly elaborate glasshouses to help him cultivate rare lilies, prize pineapples and the Cavendish banana, which went on to become the most-consumed banana in the Western world. His experiments with iron and prefabricated glass culminated in his great masterpiece of 1851, the Crystal Palace, a gargantuan greenhouse masquerading as an exhibition venue. Paxton intended it to provide an optimistic haven for sooty city-dwellers. Despite its life-affirming beauty, however, it suffered from severe overheating. Paxton's design incorporated natural ventilation, with hundreds of louvres in the walls, but this proved inadequate on a hot midsummer day, and the organizers were forced to remove parts of the glazing and replace them with canvas curtains to block out the sun.

The truth is, glass is a terrible thermal insulator. Most of us can recall an uncomfortably sweaty lunch in a conservatory on a summer day, when it feels like you might be cultivating

cress beneath your shirt collar. We need to modulate and regulate light in the right way, rather than allow it in thoughtlessly.

The late architect Walter Greaves certainly believed this. His family home in West Sussex, built in 1981, is one of the most memorable houses we have ever sold, and is cited by many of our staff at The Modern House as their all-time favourite. Greaves worked on the design of the Royal Festival Hall in London, with Peter Moro, before setting up his own practice to focus on smaller projects. His love of his craft and his retiring disposition were, perhaps, at the expense of gaining a bigger reputation, and he remains less known than contemporaries like James Stirling and the Smithsons. It took him more than five years to achieve permission for his house, a complex of gently curved forms wrapped in cedar. Nowadays, it is protected by a rare Grade II* listing, which serves to highlight the seemingly arbitrary nature of UK planning laws. Internally, the house has a hushed beauty that derives from its masterful modulation of natural light. Greaves's daughter Hannah explains:

> *My mother likes direct sunlight, but my father wasn't so keen. His office was north-facing but the house itself has lots of high-level windows to let the sun in – a compromise. And that worked. He made a house that was cool for him and light for my mother. Because that's what he believed a house should do: it should function . . . The setting of the house is so beautiful that you never quite get used to it. I am always surprised by it when I come back, even after just half an hour. There isn't one great big window from which you see the garden all the time so that it becomes commonplace. He once designed a house on the seafront and the clients said, 'You haven't put enough windows in – we want to be able to see the sea all of the time.' My father's response was, 'If you don't see the sea for a couple of minutes, you come back to it and see it all over again, time and time again.'*

In many ways, Walter Greaves was ahead of his time. These days we are acutely aware of the potentially harmful effects of the sun, and more conscious of environmental sustainability. We have an obligation to use openings more sparingly. A window is not there to replace a wall but to act as an intermediary between the public and private domains, between the harsh reality of the world outside and the reassuring embrace of the space within.

Windows are the weak point in the efficiency of a building. Effective ones should maximize the amount of solar gain, while preventing as much heat as possible from leaking out again. The rate at which heat escapes through glass is measured using a 'U-value', which is decidedly different depending on the window type: approximately 5 for single glazing, 3 for double and less than 1.6 for triple. To meet the requirements of Passivhaus, which is a standard for low-energy building, it must be no more than 0.8. Much in the way that shaving razors started out with a single blade and now have three or four, so it is with windowpanes: triple, and even quadruple, glazing has become customary.

Architects Anna and Russel Hayden bought a straightforward 1960s house in Stockport and brought it up to Passivhaus standard using extra insulation, a mechanical ventilation system and, crucially, efficient modern glazing. The effect on their lives has been considerable, as Anna explains:

> We've slept through thunderstorms and even a police car chase that ended in our next-door neighbour's front garden! The triple glazing cuts out almost all external noise. I had knee surgery last year and spent three months in the house, not really leaving. It made a big impact on my recovery because I was comfortable, so I really believe in the power of architecture to make people feel better.

Personally, I have a preference for fixed panels of glass rather than those that open and close. A picture window – free of obtrusive handles and mechanisms – does a better job of framing the views and looks far more beautiful. The structural supports can be hidden in the structure of the building, making it appear frameless. Adding a deep sill gives the room greater flexibility, acting as a light-flooded perch for a guest, a daybed for an afternoon nap or a plinth for a collection of ceramics.

Bifold doors balance the need for access and ventilation, but they break up the views unnecessarily when closed, and bunch together like an unappealing club sandwich when open. For a room that links to a garden or terrace, consider installing a glass pivot door instead: this provides the unsullied aesthetic benefits of frameless glazing, along with a seamless transition between inside and out.

It must be acknowledged that glazing can be extremely expensive, so you should be

looking to achieve the greatest amount of transparency with the budget you have available. In a kitchen extension, for example, there is nothing wrong with a fixed window alongside a good old-fashioned door. The most important thing is to ensure that the frame is as minimal as possible, and that the glazing bars, if there are any, are lightweight.

There is much to admire about Georgian architecture, but perhaps its greatest legacy is the exquisite purity of its windows. Alain de Botton, a philosopher who has written compellingly about architecture's ability to stir the emotions, sums it up well:

> *The Georgian houses of Bath charm us by the ethereal way in which the windows appear to hover over their façades. Recognizing, as their subsequent colleagues often have not, the intense beauty of the tenderly held pane, the city's eighteenth-century architects competed with each other to develop frames in which the slenderest fingers of wood could fasten around the greatest expanses of glass. Pushing at the technological boundaries, they [made] windows with some of the same impelling grace as a Degas ballerina, fluidly pirouetting her sylph-like body on an axis of a mere five toes.*

When replacing the windows on a pre-existing building, it is crucial to use a sympathetic product. One of the most popular housing types that we sell is the humble 'Span' house. Between 1948 and 1984, architect Eric Lyons and developer Geoffrey Townsend built thirty housing estates across the Home Counties that were intended to 'span the gap' between jerry-built suburbia and architect-designed city homes. Many of them work particularly well as starter homes for young families: there is usually a reception room and kitchen downstairs, with a fully glazed elevation on to a private garden, and three modest bedrooms and a bathroom upstairs. To the uninitiated, these look like any other mid-century terraced house, but closer inspection reveals solid-wood parquet floors, elegant door furniture and attractive signage with considered typography. One of the key features is the glazing, which is framed in timber or aluminium and set out in thoughtful configurations. Although many of these houses are now protected by listing status, unfortunately there are countless examples that have been ruined by uPVC glazing, the ultimate scourge of modern buildings. Having marketed many of them over the years, I can vouch for the fact that the presence of plastic windows limits the number of interested buyers and severely compromises saleability.

It is worth getting your windows cleaned regularly, and ensuring that they are kept clear of blockages, especially hulking items of furniture such as wardrobes and sofas. Think about what's happening outside as well. Is your wilful wisteria taking away all of that celestial sunlight?

As well as the glazing itself, it's important to consider the window treatments. Shutters block out the light effectively, prevent heat loss and tuck away neatly. In my kitchen at home, there is an arched Victorian sash window with original shutters that stash away in a lidded compartment set within the sill. In the rooms of the house where we need more cosiness, including the bedrooms and the dining room, we have heavy curtains because of their ability to block out the light while providing extra insulation.

I admit to being a bit obsessive about curtains. Every night, I check them to make sure that there are no gaps around the sides where a shaft of dawn sun might be able to penetrate – there's nothing worse than being awoken early by a light sabre in your cornea. In the morning, I do the reverse, wrestling them back to allow maximum light penetration. When we were refurbishing the house, I made sure that our curtain poles were extra wide, so that the full extent of the windows can be revealed during the day. In the children's bedrooms, we have hung blackout blinds behind the curtains as a secondary line of defence against early waking.

When I lived in London, it always surprised me how many homeowners failed to consider the lack of privacy after dark, especially in basement flats. Walking home after work, I could see right inside their illuminated interiors. Installing a window covering made from a gauzy material can provide a visual barrier while allowing the light to permeate. Net curtains have a sleazy reputation, but natural linen voiles are a far cry from the twitching, smoke-stained polyester of 1970s suburbia. In historic houses such as those owned by the National Trust, you will often find Holland blinds behind the curtains, which provided screening from the sunshine and prying eyes.

Many years ago we sold a Grade II-listed 1930s house in Hertfordshire to designers Steve Gibbons and Heidi Lightfoot, who were attracted by the inherent transparency of the building. Due to the sheer number of windows in the house, they have put up no fewer than thirty Venetian blinds, which help them to moderate both privacy and light levels. These have become an integral part of the experience of the interior, casting a kaleidoscope of stripes, chevrons and grids on to the walls and furniture. The downside of metal blinds, of course, is that they are liable to get bent out of shape and sometimes refuse to go up or down; we have all spent far too much of our lives wrestling with strong-willed Venetians.

Light and layout

Using natural light in the right way should inform almost every decision we make in relation to our homes. When searching through the property listings, make sure you consider the natural attributes of the building. Flats situated on the lower-ground floor are nearly always cheaper, but there are several reasons for this: they are less secure from intruders, closer to street-level pollution and, crucially, often suffer from a lack of light. I recommend going for something higher up, if you can.

Journalist Vishaka Robinson recognized this when she bought her flat in Bath, which is arranged across the upper floors of a house on a hilltop. The trade-off for a daily hike up the stairs is a life-affirming spillage of sunshine – the result of its lofty position and double aspect. She says:

> It feels like a house in the sky. One side gets all the morning light, and the other gets all the afternoon sun. So, during the day, even in the middle of winter, we rarely turn on the lights.

It is best to find a home with some semblance of separation from those around it. A Dickensian alleyway may hold a romantic appeal, but don't expect to have great expectations of daylight. The depth of a building can also have a significant effect. Deep floor plans inevitably create areas of deadness and darkness, and, in my view, any given part of a building should be within 15 feet or so of a window. If we imagine a room as a cuboid, it should have openings on at least two of its faces. This not only increases light penetration; it also enables us to read people's expressions more clearly and makes for a much more flattering room.

When architect Jason Syrett built a house in a woodland clearing for his family of four, he took the opportunity to incorporate natural light seemingly from every angle. The result, he believes, has a positive effect on their collective state of mind:

> The quality of light that comes through the surrounding canopy is amazing, and changes through the seasons. When it snowed a lot recently, my wife noticed that the light created a serene quality throughout the house as it reflected through the windows

and around the different elevations. Because the top floor of the house has four different aspects, we get views of the trees beyond the garden on one side and sunlight coming in from another. I think it contributes to a qualitative sense of wellbeing.

Take account of the orientation of the building when choosing how to configure the space. Design that acknowledges the movement of the sun reduces the need for auxiliary heating and cooling, resulting in lower energy bills, reduced greenhouse-gas emissions and a more comfortable living experience. In the Northern Hemisphere, a home should ideally be stretched out along an east–west axis, with the principal living spaces splashed liberally along the southern side to draw in the sunshine. The eastern side is ideal for bedrooms, so that the sun's salutation stimulates natural waking, much like a child's sleep-training clock. In the same vein, dining spaces work well on the western side, where they capture the radiant embers of the day. Utility rooms, garages, storage spaces and services can be squirrelled away at the northern end, or in areas of the home that are naturally darker. Artists and photographers benefit from the flat light of a north-facing window, so this is also a good place for a studio.

When considering how to furnish her family home, a listed fifteenth-century hall house in Kent, the artist Sarah Kaye Rodden was guided by the light conditions she inherited with the building:

> *The front room was always going to be my studio because it has a lot of natural light. But it's also the room that we spend all our time in as a family during the day. The back of the house gets less light but that works for us because it's a cosy space to spend our evenings. I make a point to light candles after the children have gone to bed, not because it's romantic but because it just seems like that's how the house wants to be.*

It is surprising how even the most exalted designers have sometimes neglected to consider the implications of orientation. Red House in Bexleyheath, which was built for William Morris by his friend Philip Webb in 1859, is one such example. It was conceived as a celebration of craftsmanship and the ideal of the medieval guild; Morris and his Pre-Raphaelite brethren made virtually everything by hand, from the wallpaper to the stained-glass windows and the built-in cabinets. Edward Burne-Jones called it 'the beautifullest place on earth', but it was also ruddy freezing, because the principal rooms faced north to address Watling Way, the ancient pilgrimage route to Canterbury. The chill aggravated Morris's medical conditions and, after just five years, he scarpered back to Bloomsbury clutching a hand-embroidered blanket.

If you work from home for any significant period of the week – as many of us do these days – try to position your designer desk or wobbly workbench as close as possible to a window. A shortage of natural light has been shown to disrupt the body's carefully regulated circadian rhythm. In a study published in the *Journal of Clinical Sleep Medicine* in 2014, one group of people were asked to carry out their work in windowless rooms, while another were placed in sun-filled spaces, and it was found that those who were starved of natural light suffered from markedly worse sleep quality.

We should also apply the same consideration to our children's workspaces. It can be tempting to bundle recalcitrant teenagers into the basement study and let them get on with it, but encouraging them to carry out their revision in a light-filled space can actually boost their exam grades. A report commissioned by the Pacific Gas & Electric Company in California concluded that a significant uplift in test results could be attributed directly to the amount of natural light in the room.

For little ones, try to reserve one of the brighter rooms in the house for use as a playroom, or, if you have less space, set them up with a table beneath a window in the kitchen. Don't park your baby on a play mat in a depressing corner: bring him out into the room so that he can experience the brilliance of the day. Natural light generates dopamine and is essential for the healthy development of eyesight.

If your home has more than one level, consider inverting the traditional layout for a more satisfactory result. Admittedly, you might never get used to the idea of declaring 'I'm going downstairs to bed', but in most other respects it makes a lot of sense, unlocking the light and views for the living spaces, and using the naturally darker areas lower down the building for sleeping. This works well in a range of different contexts, from urban penthouses poking above the rooftops like vigilant meerkats to country houses with views over rolling fields.

The key thing is to work with the natural attributes of the building, as Stuart Piercy and Duncan Jackson did when they converted an early-nineteenth-century Martello tower in Suffolk into an extraordinary modern dwelling. A cylindrical brick fortress with hardly any

windows was an inauspicious starting point, but the architects turned that to their advantage, creating intimate bedrooms with lightwells in the bowels, and an evening sitting room with a wood-burning stove set within a womb of brick. For the kitchen and dining space, they popped off the lid of the building to create a rooftop eyrie, with a wraparound band of glazing and polka dots cut into the roof that provides views of passing ships and scudding clouds.

When talking about natural attributes, I also mean ceiling heights. Inverting the layout works best when each storey is fairly uniform throughout the building. In a Classical house, the rules of Palladian proportion apply: the *piano nobile* (on the first floor), with its high ceilings, sizeable sashes and generous natural light, is optimized for entertaining, while the proportions are less grand and the windows are smaller on the higher floors, lending themselves better to sleeping spaces.

The problem with many period buildings, of course, is that they were built to accommodate servants, with the food prep taking place in the dingy depths. Even the most imposing and expensive Georgian houses in London still tend to have kitchens in the basement. Money might buy you period splendour, but it doesn't always get you light.

There are exceptions, though. Witness the Spitalfields area of London, which, to take an olfactory metaphor, is sandwiched improbably between the pungent whiff of cumin emanating from Banglatown to the east and the schlocky aftershave of the City execs in their Postmodern ziggurats to the west. Spitalfields was settled in the seventeenth century by Huguenot silk weavers, who installed light-filled lofts with tall ceilings to accommodate their looms – in recent times, many of these have been repurposed to become surprisingly modern kitchen spaces.

Natural light should also be used to guide visitors through the building, to give them a clear direction and a nuanced experience. Entrances, and places of particular architectural or decorative beauty, should be especially well lit. As the authors of *A Pattern Language* point out:

> *People are by nature phototropic – they move toward light, and, when stationary, they orient themselves toward the light. As a result, the much loved and much used places in buildings, where the most things happen, are places like window seats, verandas, fireside corners, trellised arbours; all of them defined by non-uniformities*

in light, and all of them allowing the people who are in them to orient themselves
toward the light.

As we saw in the Space section, we can use flexible layouts and a broken plan to encourage the light to permeate. Even the smallest spaces are granted a sense of importance by the presence of 'borrowed' light. Many homes built in the 1960s and 1970s have open shelving or a transparent partition between the kitchen and dining room, making even the most modest preparation space feel larger and brighter. In my house, we have a small laundry room that is sectioned off with a partially glazed screen, so that the light passes through but unsightly washing is hidden from view. Messy utility spaces like this tend to look respectable when you view them through glass – it has the ability to elevate everything.

To my mind, courtyard houses offer the optimal layout for absorbing the sunshine's restorative rays. With the accommodation arranged around an enclosed garden, all of the rooms have a connection to nature and are naturally shallow in plan. There are some wonderful historical examples in Britain, including a staggered terrace of twenty-eight modest single-storey dwellings in Hatfield, Hertfordshire, known as the Cockaigne Houses. These have flat roofs, blockwork party walls and frames made from black-stained timber. We have sold many of them over the years, and they are always highly prized. The architects, Phippen, Randall & Parkes, were likely influenced by the Russian-born émigré Serge Chermayeff's family home in New Haven, Connecticut, which was built as a prototype for a single-family urban housing development. It is composed of three connected single-storey pavilions enclosing open courtyards, with a deliberately nondescript frontage. Chermayeff not only sought to maximize the levels of natural light in his design; he also wanted to maintain privacy by turning his back on the streetscape – an idea that was engagingly outlined in his book *Community and Privacy*, co-authored with architect and theorist Christopher Alexander.

The courtyard layout continues to be favoured by current-day architects. Thomas Croft, for example, has completely transformed his modest mews house in West London. He explains:

> *The original layout was very cellular, with lots of small windows, and the result was*
> *that the space was very dark in all seasons and felt quite pokey. We demolished almost*

the whole house and rebuilt it in a much more open-plan way. The resulting house is 40 per cent bigger and also makes much more of the courtyard garden, which is now the focal point. Like lots of architects, I love Japanese courtyard houses, and the renovation has some of that spirit; it's almost as if the garden is a pristine object and we're forever walking around the outside, looking into it. The oak floorboards used inside and out are on the same plane, aligned in size and direction, and are made from identical oak, the intention being that the different environmental conditions would totally transform the exterior ones while leaving the interior ones unchanged – a sort of meditation on ageing.

Reach for the sky

Despite being built almost two thousand years ago, the Pantheon in Rome has the largest unreinforced-concrete dome in the world, with a hole punched unceremoniously through its centre like the valve on a football. On a fair-weather day, an intense circle of sunlight is projected on to the wall, while during a storm, raindrops fall though the opening and clatter against the marble floor, as lightning scissors through the ill-tempered clouds above. To Emperor Hadrian and the citizens of Rome, the Pantheon's oculus symbolized the eye of the gods looking down upon their city, and there was never any doubt as to what kind of mood they were in.

The oculus was to become a key feature of the architecture of the Roman Empire, allowing rainfall to provide natural cooling on a hot day, and architects from Byzantium to the Islamic East later adopted it for their own ecclesiastical masterworks.

A building that opens itself to the sky will always take on a celestial atmosphere. Santiago Calatrava's Oculus transportation hub, built on the site of the former World Trade Center in New York, was designed to resemble a dove taking flight. Running down the centre of its ribbed wings is a backbone of glass, which emits a ribbon of illumination that Calatrava calls the 'Way of Light'. Every year, in a poignant memorial to those who lost their lives in the 11 September attacks, this vast skylight peels back to embrace the air and the sky.

The extravagantly bearded artist James Turrell, a lifelong Quaker, has made a career out of the same concept. Turrell is a keen pilot, with a fascination for the relationship between the earth and the heavens. Each of his 'skyspaces' is designed to be a place of contemplative thought: an intimate room with an opening cut into the ceiling, which frames the sky and casts abstracted shapes of light that shift throughout the day. It's like sitting inside an eyeball looking up at the moon.

Beyond its metaphysical properties, a rooftop opening can also serve a practical purpose. Ernő Goldfinger's 1930s house at No. 2 Willow Road in Hampstead, for example, is topped by a glazed oculus that spills natural light on to the spiral staircase, illuminating the treads and drawing the visitor up through the building.

Top light can transform basements, turning them from seedy Underground carriages into genuinely useable, inspiriting spaces. It also opens up opportunities to convert lofts and attics. Rooflights emit more daylight than traditional windows, because they are angled towards the sky, so even a rudimentary one in the pitch can be hugely effective. They create the illusion of space, improve the internal air quality with effective ventilation and prevent overheating in the summer.

In tight-knit urban environments, where buildings bump heads like sheep in a pen, it is essential to harness the sun's rays wherever there is space to do so. Gianni Botsford's aptly named Light House is a beguiling manifesto of top-lit tomfoolery. It was built on a backland site in Notting Hill, surrounded on all sides by other buildings (the owners were required to obtain fourteen party-wall awards with neighbouring houses). Working with the environmental engineers Arup, Botsford produced a computerized plan of solar and daylight conditions throughout the year, taking into account weather patterns specific to London. This led to the development of a fully glazed 'sky façade' roof, which is the house's only outward-facing element. It has four different grades and patterns of glass, creating an ever changing showreel of light and shade throughout the day.

Apartments in converted warehouses often employ similar methods. Factories were built to provide sufficient light for industrial activity, with no need for outward-facing views. Now that factories have been repurposed as homes, young professionals are attracted to the honesty of the building fabric and the quality of light from the original single-glazed rooflights.

For photographer Sophie Harris-Taylor, who prefers to shoot without flash, the natural light was always going to be a deciding factor when choosing a first home for herself, her partner, Misha, their one-year-old son and an acquiescent greyhound. Having bought a typical one-bedroom flat on the ground floor of a Victorian house, they cleverly converted the adjoining garage into a modern living space, which is gently lit from above by a pair of rooflights. As Sophie explains:

> *You always feel under the sky in some way or another. And throughout the day, you get these amazing pools of light that move organically through the space and draw your eye to different spots. In fact, it's the light and openness that we value most about it – we've never felt enclosed at all. A friend of ours once described it as 'a bit of a sanctuary', and I feel the same. I think modern living today seems more humble than in the past. It's much more about the simpler pleasures that make living more comfortable and truer to yourself, and less about external appearances.*

Adding an extension to an existing building creates an elongated plan, resulting in a dark spot, usually at the point at which it meets the original structure. The solution is to add a rooflight, which supplements the sunlight coming from either end.

Most rooflights are manually operated, but you can also get electric ones that retract like the sunroof of an executive saloon, with rain sensors that close the roof automatically during a sudden downpour. In the most extreme examples, the whole roof of the house can lift off. The past masters of this were Richard Paxton and Heidi Locher, who built a series of experimental homes around London on unprepossessing strips of land. Their house just off Hampstead High Street is set around a 40-foot double-volume reception room with a pair of huge retractable glass rooflights. When open, these turn the sitting room into an outdoor piazza, with full-height trees planted in outsized terracotta pots. On a summer's day, you can pull up a deckchair and bask in the benefits of Vitamin D without leaving the house (there's no danger of getting rickets here). A glass-sided indoor swimming pool runs parallel to the sitting room and refracts the light like a mirror ball.

For those with more modest budgets and ambitions, high-level windows placed just below the roofline – clerestory glazing – can be just as effective, especially in rooms requiring privacy or security. Mid-century terraced houses, for example, often have a bathroom in the middle of the plan on the first floor, with a wash of natural light provided by a strip window beneath the mono-pitched roof.

Clerestory fenestration dates back to the temples of Ancient Egypt, but is most clearly associated with Gothic churches. By using flying buttresses as external supports, architects were able to incorporate windows of increased size into their designs, until the upper section of the church became almost entirely glazed – a 'clear story' of glass. Frank Lloyd Wright is credited with adapting this art form to small-scale residential architecture.

Clerestory windows emit a more ambient form of light than conventional openings, and, because they are placed high up the wall, they allow the light to penetrate further into the space. They help to free up space for showers, kitchen units, pieces of furniture or artworks, and can be used in place of conventional windows if you want to block out the view of your neighbour's underpants drying on the washing line.

Playing with light

As Le Corbusier proved with his chapel at Ronchamp, light has far more than a functional benefit: it is the material with which we can tell a story. The Japanese architect Tadao Ando was heavily influenced by Ronchamp when creating his own ecclesiastical masterpiece, the Church of the Light, in a town to the north of Osaka. Behind the altar, light passes through a cross-shaped opening that runs the full width and height of the concrete wall. The profound emptiness of the space, with rudimentary benches made from scaffolding planks, reinforces its sacred atmosphere. Ando believes that there should be no difference in approach between designing a religious building and a home. He explains:

We do not need to differentiate one from the other. Dwelling in a house is not only a functional issue, but also a spiritual one.

The aptly named Fog House in Clerkenwell, designed by the celebrated Ghanaian-British architect David Adjaye, has an entire wall of sand-blasted glass that cleverly diffuses the light like a passing cumulus cloud. It was commissioned by Janet Street-Porter, who acquired the artist Marc Quinn's studio and set about converting it for residential occupation. We sold it to the lawyer and investor Della Burnside, who finds it a truly life-enhancing place to be:

Everything is geared around brightness and light. Glass opens up the spaces on each floor, and on the top floor there is glazing on three sides and the best views of the park from the rooftop terrace. It's a complete contrast to my previous home, a late-Victorian house. I was looking for a house with more light, a modern layout and outdoor spaces that could accommodate my dogs. Coming here and having the large balconies and being near the park was mind-blowing – I didn't think I would be able to find something like this.

Using reflective materials in your home allows you to play with the light and increase its intensity. An artfully placed mirror not only enhances the sense of space, it boosts the light level as well. The nineteenth-century Neoclassicist Sir John Soane was a wizard with a mirror.

Plagued by cataracts and failing eyesight, he grasped every opportunity to experiment with light when creating his home in Lincoln's Inn Fields. In the red-painted library, he put mirrors in the fireplace, on the back of the window shutters and even above the bookcases, creating the sense that you were glimpsing the rooms next door. In the breakfast room, he fashioned a 'handkerchief dome' ceiling with a convex mirror in each of its corners, and further light-enhancing mirrors lining the insides of the arches.

In our old house in Islington, Faye and I propped up a salvaged refectory mirror against the wall of the master bedroom, so that it appeared to double the number of windows when you looked at it from an oblique angle. The bathroom was lacking in space and character, so we clad the walls in shimmering Zellige tiles, replaced the standard door with a partially glazed version with hand-blown glass, used an inky-blue gloss paint for the woodwork and hung a foxed antique mirror above the sink.

When thinking about your own interior, consider each material's ability to bounce the sunlight around. Polished concrete is a good choice for floors because it combines hardiness with reflectivity, and polished metals like brass create bursts of light. Glazed doors, glass partitions and open-tread stairs all allow the light to travel through the interior. One thing I don't necessarily endorse, however, is glass staircases, which seemed like a good idea in the 1990s but now bear the scratches and scuffs of a thousand careless footsteps.

The World of Interiors once commissioned me to interview the industrial designer Michael Anastassiades at his home-cum-studio in South London, and I was struck by his clever use of reflective surfaces. Rather than decorate the space with conventional artworks, he chose instead to showcase his own product designs, like a three-dimensional portfolio. In the workspace on the ground floor, his 'Waxing Gibbous' mirrors looked as if they were dripping from the ceilings and oozing across the floors. Upstairs in his apartment, faceted copper mirrors provided warped and whimsical plays of light, and a chandelier waltzed gently above the desk like an Alexander Calder mobile.

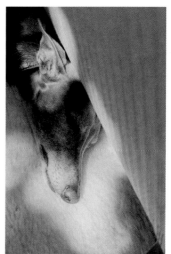

Don't be afraid of the dark

For natural light to be truly effective, it must be used in conjunction with its brooding antipode: darkness. Within the realm of fine art, the two have always been ascribed equal importance. Caravaggio's powerful paintings achieve their tension through the use of *chiaroscuro* (which translates as 'light-dark') and tenebrism (dramatic illumination). Brightly lit faces leap from the oil-black depths of the canvas, their mouths agape and foreheads etched with melancholy. The eighteenth-century English painter Joseph Wright of Derby broke with tradition by applying these techniques not to religious scenes but to the marvels of the technological age. *An Experiment on a Bird in the Air Pump*, which is on display in the National Gallery in London, fizzes with the excitement and tension of a scientific 'miracle'.

These extremes of glitter and gloom are as important in architecture as they are in art. Unlike painters, we don't need to conjure such effects from a brush when playing with *chiaroscuro* in our homes. We have the real thing. As the Victorian art critic John Ruskin pointed out, the light and shade found in the natural world 'is a very much finer thing than most artists can put together'.

Without areas of contrast, our homes would be one-dimensional and monotonous. As we saw in the Space section, playing with the scale of different rooms and areas of circulation provides us with the opportunity to build expectancy and vary the user experience. And so it is with light. There is nothing wrong with a dark and mysterious corridor, since this is not intended to be a space for pause or reflection. Once you arrive at its culmination point – a sunny sitting room or blazing courtyard – the brightness seems all the more exhilarating.

Architect Sean Ronnie Hill and fashion designer Mallika Chaudhuri employed this technique when renovating their ground-floor flat in Harlesden. Mallika explains:

> We were both in agreement that we wanted to keep the hallways dark, because hallways are dark spaces in general. We're both great lovers of the sea, so we thought, 'Let's make it like you're going into this deep blue sea.' Then when you come out into the lighter space, a sense of drama hits you. Sometimes people don't get it. They're like, 'Why is it so dark? Where are the lights?' But it's deliberate.

Squirrelled away in a wooded hamlet on the outskirts of Billericay, Essex, is the aptly named Dapple House, another home that utilizes darkness as a theatrical device. From the front, it presents itself as a blank black box, with bedrooms, bathrooms and a boot room all lit by minimal amounts of glazing. The brightness builds progressively through the building, culminating in a voluminous living space with full-height glazing that opens on to a terrace. Owner David Parsons explains:

> *The concept for the design became one of a clearing within a forest, with the idea of light and shade coming through the foliage of the tree canopy. You approach the house and see it surrounded by trees, and when you first enter, it's a bit darker. Then, as you move through the house the focus is on the terrace, it becomes lighter and lighter, rooflights and big sheets of glazing appear, and the light starts to play, as if you're reaching a glade within a forest.*

Bedrooms don't actually need huge amounts of light. They should cuddle us to sleep at night and prod us gently into action in the morning. Similarly, formal dining rooms are at their best when they conjure the decadent fug of a gentlemen's club. We should build in dark spaces for reading and thinking, acknowledging that the unfocused atmosphere of a dimly lit nook allows our daydreams to take hold.

Architect Peter Culley bought a run-down flat on the Whittington Estate, a 1970s social-housing scheme in North London, and carried out a renovation before selling it on. He decided to introduce darkness into the interior scheme, which traditionally might have been seen as commercial suicide (cue the image of a property developer with pointy shoes rollering the walls in magnolia). He explains:

> *One of the bedrooms is very dark, because it's the last space you come to – it's very retreated. I always like the richness of dark rooms, and I made my own blue paint for a project in Memphis – it's very ambiguous because it can feel black, it can feel purple, or at times indigo or regular blue. The colour schemes between the two bedrooms were a bit of an experiment, too, with one dark and one light. They're like doppelgängers, in that they're symmetrical and spatially the same but have been treated like a flip of*

each other. There's a balance in that contrast, though. I did this final renovation to sell, and people often advise that you should take the richness out of a home if you're doing that. This is the complete opposite approach, where we have been bold but also offered two opportunities for how the rooms can look. I like them as a pair, but looking at them individually allows you to see how you could approach them differently, with colour and furnishings.

In his fabulous essay *In Praise of Shadows*, the Japanese novelist Jun'ichirō Tanizaki argues that darkness is completely fundamental to Japanese culture, from the dark lips of a geisha to the mysterious depths of a bowl of miso soup. He draws attention to the deliberate variation of shadows found in traditional houses, with their extended eaves that diffuse the sunlight and deep alcoves that enhance the richness of lacquerware on a shelf:

A Japanese room might be likened to an inkwash painting, the paper-panelled shoji *being the expanse where the ink is thinnest, and the alcove where it is darkest. Whenever I see the alcove of a tastefully built Japanese room, I marvel at our comprehension of the secrets of shadows, our sensitive use of shadow and light. For the beauty of the alcove is not the work of some clever device. An empty space is marked off with plain wood and plain walls, so that the light drawn into it forms dim shadows within emptiness. There is nothing more. And, yet, when we gaze into the darkness that gathers behind the crossbeam, around the flower vase, behind the shelves, though we know perfectly well it is mere shadow, we are overcome with the feeling that in this small corner of the atmosphere there reigns complete and utter silence; that here in the darkness immutable tranquillity holds sway.*

David Adjaye's Lost House, which is shoehorned into a former goods yard in King's Cross, plays with darkness in a radical and thought-provoking way. With only one outward-facing window, it is illuminated instead by three lightwells that puncture the space. The walls, floor, ceiling and kitchen cabinets are all black, and there is a subterranean lap pool that seems more suited to caving than swimming. Amazingly, however, none of this feels overly oppressive, because the light bounces merrily off the fishpond and the mirrored surfaces and the lustrous poured-resin floor. The studio, which is set on a half level above the kitchen and separated by a wall of opaque glazing, is illuminated from behind and acts like a stage for shadow puppetry. Owner Jessica Robinson explains:

> *The architecture has definitely changed the way that I live. I grew up in a house laden with pictures and wall-to-wall carpets, and in New York I lived in a bohemian brownstone. This house is like an artwork in itself, so I live more simply here. Some people can see the space as intimidating, but I find it incredibly relaxing and quiet. It really does feel a little lost amid the bustle of the train station and the canal . . . it's like opening a door into a hidden world and you just wouldn't expect it to be here.*

Light at night

The image of modern Los Angeles was defined by a single photograph: Julius Shulman's iconic night-time shot of the Stahl House, designed by Pierre Koenig in 1959. Projecting from a Hollywood hillside is a rationalist glass box, in which two nattily dressed ladies engage in relaxed conversation, seeming to float above the city. This, we think, must be the place where dreams are made. On a visit to the house a few years back, Faye and I stood in Julius Shulman's distinguished footprints. As darkness descended, we observed that the spherical pendant lights in the sitting room lined up precisely with the boulevards of streetlights twinkling in the city below.

As Koenig demonstrated so skilfully, a modern home should consider the selection and placement of artificial lighting in a holistic way, as an essential part of the design process. Lights are not like baubles to be hung on a Christmas tree by the children.

The first thing to remember is that built-in lighting should be indirect rather than direct. My personal golden rule is this: if you can look straight into the bulb's blinding filament, then it's in the wrong place. The biggest scourge of modern interiors is the endless runways of ceiling spotlights that you find in kitchens, illuminating the island unit as if it were a Ming vase in a museum. You shouldn't have to wear a visor when you're chopping the onions.

As we have seen, every interior needs its shadowy depths, and ceiling lights succeed only in homogenizing and flattening everything. Jun'ichirō Tanizaki amusingly bemoans the overuse of artificial lighting in the lobby of the Miyako Hotel in Kyoto:

> Should a person on a summer's evening set out to refresh himself among purple hills and crystal streams, to take in the cool breeze that blows through the tower on the heights, he will only find himself beneath a white ceiling dotted with huge milk glass lights, each sending forth a blinding blaze. As in most recent Western-style buildings, the ceilings are so low that one feels as if balls of fire were blazing directly above one's head. 'Hot' is no word for the effect, and the closer to the ceiling the worse it is – your head and neck and spine feel as if they were being roasted. One of these balls of fire alone would suffice to light the place, yet three or four blaze down from the ceiling,

and there are smaller versions on the walls and pillars, serving no function but to eradicate every trace of shadow.

Public spaces such as shopping centres and airports are so intensely bright that we have become desensitized to excessive illumination. It must be acknowledged that artificial light is not good for us. It disrupts our sleep patterns, and adversely affects our immune systems. Nightshift workers have been proven to be at increased risk of a range of health problems, from stress and stomach ulcers to depression, heart disease and cancer. For the majority of us working more conventional hours, we still spend our afternoons in dazzlingly bright offices, while our children beaver away beneath flickering fluorescents. We owe it to our assaulted senses to turn things down a bit at home.

Artificial light is generally required towards the beginning and end of each day, when the sun is at its lowest point and our bodies are either waking gradually from a slumber or winding down after the stresses of the day. It makes sense, therefore, that it should promote a gentle atmosphere rather than the floodlit energy of a sports stadium. Subscribing to this notion will support your wellbeing, have a beneficial environmental impact and reduce your lighting bills.

Ceiling lights should either be recessed so that they are invisible, or surface-mounted and angled so that they provide a wash of light across the walls or the corners of the room. Personally, I much prefer wall sconces, and I always ensure that every light is placed on a dimmer, so that the atmosphere can be varied and the intensity can be managed.

When choosing where to position the lights, consider how flattering they are. Take a cue from fashion retailers, who have a vested interest in making you look like the best version of yourself, with fitting rooms equipped with seductive low-level lighting to complement the considerate pattern-cutting. In a bathroom or dressing room, the lights should ideally be positioned at head height – with bulbs that are covered, frosted or shaded. The light should arrive from multiple sources, much like on a theatre set, so that all sides of the face are considered. Overhead lights cast shadows beneath the eyes and accentuate our bumps, blemishes and wrinkles. Whatever you do, don't put a ceiling light above the mirror, unless you want the rumpled jowls of an English bulldog.

Think about how you use your living space in the evenings and go for subtle, isolated task lighting. Once dinner is on the table, turn the lights down and bring out some candles.

Candlelight is still the healthiest, most flattering, romantic and atmospheric form of illumination. Interior designer Hollie Bowden says:

> In the evenings, I like to turn all the main lights off and have more of a soft glow. I'll light some candles and curl up on the sofa with my books or magazines looking for inspiration. I think what needs to happen to cope with modern living in a city is to create a sanctuary. It's about finding a quiet place, or making a space where you can have peace, calm and tranquillity in order to balance and offset the noise and the stress of busy modern life.

The lighting at my house is so muted that, if you were to approach it after nightfall, you might well assume that no one was in. My dad invented a word for it, accusing me of what he called 'lightism'. We don't have any built-in ceiling lights at all, and instead have standing lamps and table lamps plugged into 5-amp sockets. We use candles in the dining room and a desk light in the study. Our bathroom has discreet low-level lights with sensors either side of the fireplace, so that we can use the loo at night without waking each other up. There are plug-in night lights in the corridors, which allow the children to navigate around without switching on the main lights.

A helpful way to think about lighting is to consider its colour: 'blue' for waking up and 'red' for winding down. Exposure to a cooler light temperature during the day helps to suppress melatonin secretion, keeping us alert and improving cognitive performance. Conversely, too much blue light in the evening interferes with the circadian rhythm, so problems arise when we watch television or use a mobile phone before bedtime. One of the reasons why we find the flickering of candles so intoxicating in the evening is that the warm light eases us into a slumber.

Once we recognize this, we can start to make the right choices at home. For example, the quality and temperature of ambient light are heavily affected by the type of bulb you use. Compact fluorescents are liable to give your home the clinical glare of an operating theatre, whereas traditional incandescent bulbs tend to give off a much warmer, more human-friendly light. There is a great variety of different LED bulbs available, and some people choose different colours for the different rooms in the home: a warm white in living spaces and bedrooms, a cool white in kitchens and bathrooms, and daylight in art studios.

When I needed to buy a digital clock for Indigo's bedroom, I spent a long time looking for one with red numbers, so that it doesn't keep her awake as it sits on her bedside table. In my opinion, a 40-watt, or 400-lumen, bulb is plenty for most light fittings, especially bedside lamps. If the design of a particular light fitting means that the bulb is left on show, consider using a crown silver bulb, which throws a towel around the naked filament and reflects the light back on to the wall.

Given that they are switched off for the vast majority of the day, lights need to be beautiful objects in their own right. The young designer Oscar Piccolo has recognized this with his 'Lampada Cappello' lamp, which is notable for its graceful silhouette: a pleated shade atop a lithe, squiggly iron base. He explains:

> *When I was designing the lamp, I wasn't thinking about how it could bring light. I was thinking of it as an object that might be switched off just as much, or more than, it's turned on.*

'Everything is sculpture,' said the Japanese-American designer Isamu Noguchi, who reimagined the traditional paper lantern into an electrically lit product with the refinement of an artwork. Noguchi turned his hand to everything from furniture to gardens, architecture and ceramics, but perhaps his most enduring legacy is the 'Akari' light, which is still hand-made in the original family-run workshop in Gifu, Japan. Hinting at the longevity of his design, he declared: 'All that you require to start a home are a room, a *tatami* and an Akari.'

Curator Oscar Humphries, who has amassed a collection of museum-quality pieces by Isamu Noguchi, lives with a contemporary version of the artist's 'Akari 10A' floor lamp. He says:

> *I'm a total snob about Noguchi design and I have some really important pieces but, with the lights, I just buy new ones. They're the perfect light: beautifully designed and not too expensive.*

To my mind, the timelessness of a vintage design will always trump the more clinical forms of contemporary 'architectural' lighting. My house is littered with obscure European examples from yesteryear. For interior designer Louisa Grey, Vico Magistretti's 'Atollo' lamp, designed in the 1970s, is her favourite possession. Its pleasingly rudimentary shape – a hemisphere balanced tantalizingly on a cylinder and a cone – gives it a sense of permanence that would work just as well in a newly built home as it does in Louisa's Victorian townhouse. At night, it glows gently like a magical mushroom. 'The light from it is just stunning,' she enthuses. 'It makes me really happy!' There can be no finer endorsement than that.

Materials

'A good building must be capable of absorbing the
traces of human life and taking on a specific richness . . .
I think of the patina of age on materials, of
innumerable small scratches on surfaces.'
Peter Zumthor

Shaking hands with our homes

Parents complain about the 'Terrible Twos', but, in my experience, they're nothing compared to the 'Sulky Sevens'. When she was seven, Indigo was so proficient in the art of psychological warfare that I sometimes imagined her sprawled across her bunkbed, glitter shimmering on her thunderous brow, poring over battle plans about how to engineer our downfall.

In our old flat in Winchester, she channelled much of her scorn at the door furniture. The kitchen door was garnished with a rusted metal knob so arthritic that it could be opened only by a grown-up with a strong wrist. This proved quite useful in high-pressure parenting scenarios, until the day that she decided to slam it repeatedly until the latch broke. After that, she came and went as she pleased, her chest puffed out like a vainglorious unicorn.

To be fair to her, a door handle has one basic function, which is to provide admission to a room. Every time I approached the kitchen door in our flat, I would have to inhale deeply, drop my shoulder and wrestle with the wretched thing until it opened. It was a small scar on the rockface of my day. In *The Eyes of the Skin*, Juhani Pallasmaa poetically describes the door handle as 'the handshake of the building'. He writes:

> *The surface of an old object, polished to perfection by the tool of the craftsman and the assiduous hands of its users, seduces the stroking of the hand. It is pleasurable to press a door handle shining from the thousands of hands that have entered the door before us; the clean shimmer of ageless wear has turned into an image of welcome and hospitality.*

Indeed, a handle should offer you an amicable greeting, not challenge you to a scuffle. Pallasmaa himself designed door furniture, and a number of other twentieth-century Nordic designers got their carefully sanitized mitts on it, notably Arne Jacobsen and Erik Gunnar Asplund.

Touch is the most underestimated of the human senses, certainly when it comes to our homes. Helen Keller, who could neither see not hear, poignantly described her reliance on haptic discovery in *The World I Live In*:

I have just touched my dog. He was rolling on the grass, with pleasure in every muscle and limb. I wanted to catch a picture of him in my fingers, and I touched him as lightly as I would cobwebs; but lo, his fat body revolved, stiffened and solidified into an upright position, and his tongue gave my hand a lick! He pressed close to me, as if he were fain to crowd himself into my hand. He loved it with his tail, with his paw, with his tongue. If he could speak, I believe he would say with me that paradise is attained by touch; for in touch is all love and intelligence.

Within the home environment, dogs naturally seek out the most comfortable places, stretching out in front of the fire or settling themselves on to the sofa with a satisfied sigh. Above all things, a home should be a place of great comfort, an infirmary for weary bodies at the end of a long day. It's all very well filling it with avant-garde furniture, but if you can't sit down for fear of ending up on the floor in a heap of broken wood, then it has failed in its purpose.

Over the years, I have been invited into hundreds of houses and been asked the same question: what should we spend our money on? The answer is simple: it's the things you come into physical contact with every day – the light switches, the cistern lever, the door furniture, the kitchen worktops, and so on. The choice we make of materials – the way they feel against our limbs – can have a significant effect on our experience. The designer Ilse Crawford writes:

When we touch, we feel. Our feet, for example, are one of the most sensitive parts of our bodies (they have as many nerve endings as our genitals); the pressure points on our feet also carry signals directly to the brain. A tactile, high-quality floor, therefore, should be a given in a building designed for human wellbeing. This sensibility should apply to anything we touch. The materials we use create atmosphere and carry hidden messages, which largely determine the mood of a space and our relationship to it.

You don't have to spend a huge amount of money to achieve a richer and more tactile interior. When Faye and I once rented a cottage for eighteen months between house moves, we purged the walls of their yellowness using a vat of white emulsion, switched out the chrome-effect plastic knobs on the cupboards for black metal ones, and hung some simple linen curtains.

The place became completely unrecognizable. When our tenancy came to an end, the cottage rented again straight away with no void period, so the landlord was happy, too.

Barny Read and Becky Nolan took a similar approach to their rented flat in Bow, as Becky explains:

> We ripped up the brown carpets everywhere to expose the concrete floors, which we lacquered for a nice quick Brutalist fix. We changed the kitchen worktops, all the door handles, all the fixtures and fittings for the lights and changed the curtains in every room. It was only cosmetic and not super-expensive, but it's changed the whole feel of the place.

Buy-to-let landlords tend to make decisions based on cost rather than quality, which is why rental properties often feel so inhuman, but we are all guilty of making the wrong material choices from time to time. My bedside table at home was salvaged from a dental practice: a wobbly wooden cabinet with a top made from pockmarked metal, bent out of shape from thousands of procedures. After I've taken a slurp of water, I have to place the glass down with great care to avoid waking Faye. I often misjudge it in the darkness, and the bedroom resounds with a sonorous clang. A night-time call of nature can be a similarly fractious experience. I sometimes forget that our loo seat doesn't have a soft-close mechanism, drop it from a height and shudder as it slams against the porcelain. We all experience moments like these in our homes every day, little sensory assaults and flashes of inconvenience that adversely affect our mood.

Fortunately, there are lots of other things in the house that have a positive influence on my day. When we bought it, we inherited some old brass light switches, with ergonomic dolly switches and pleasingly patinated wall plates. The floor in the entrance hall also makes me happy: old oak planks in varying widths, which are always warm and accommodating underfoot. But my favourite thing is the doorknob on my wardrobe. Designed by Faye, it's made of solid bronze, cast from a stone that she found on a mud-larking trip along the Thames. The imperfection of the shape, with its softly rounded edges forged by thousands of high tides, somehow works perfectly in the palm. Every morning I shake hands with it, and find a brief connection with nature.

Physically coming into contact with the natural world is an important thing, as we will analyse in depth later in the book. The curator and writer Glenn Adamson says:

> As a culture we are in danger of falling out of touch, not only with objects, but with the intelligence they embody: the empathy that is bound up in tangible things. I am speaking here of material intelligence: a deep understanding of the material world around us, an ability to read that material environment, and the know-how required to give it new form. This skill set was once nearly universal in the human population, but it has gradually shifted to specialists. Meanwhile, materials themselves have proliferated, becoming more numerous and complicated thanks to scientific research.

That's not to say that we should all be building our own houses from scratch. Many of us, myself included, would struggle to construct even the most basic shelter. But working with our hands, even if it's chopping logs for the winter, making a mug out of clay or building a treehouse for the kids, helps us to reconnect with the planet and make more informed choices about how we treat it.

Truth to materials

Back in 2001, some family friends of mine, Carol and Philip Thomas, built an audacious modern house on a patch of greenery just behind the high street in Highgate, which is one of those well-preserved Georgian villages that's been subsumed into the throbbing mass of London. Given the highly sensitive nature of the site, and the increasing prevalence of nimbyism, it's unsurprising that a few local residents got their knickers in a twist about it. One neighbour, when he saw the gleaming copper roof going on, complained to the planning department that they were building a mosque. We can only imagine what he thought when he pulled back the curtains one day to see the builders, standing on the roof with wide-legged sangfroid, urinating on the copper to make it go green.

Materials are at their best when they are left in their raw state and allowed to age gracefully. Copper was chosen for the roof not because of its religious connotations but because it develops a verdigris encrustation with the most beautiful layering of textures. Similarly, corten steel, which corrodes through exposure to the atmosphere, develops an oxidized layer that gives it a unique character. The artist Richard Serra, who worked in the steel mills of California as a teenager, has forged a career out of the material's painterly scuffs, scars and scrapes.

For a sculptor, the intrinsic quality of a given material is something to be celebrated, and ageing is an accepted part of the artistic process. Henry Moore said:

> . . . *sculpture in stone should look honestly like stone, [and] that to make it look like flesh and blood, hair and dimples, is coming down to the level of stage conjuror.*

Moore's majestic *Recumbent Figure* (1938), now in the collection of the Tate Gallery, is an unadorned mass of Jurassic Oxfordshire limestone, its fossilized surfaces and craggy contours making it seem as much an ancient geological fragment as a figurative artwork. It was commissioned by the Russian-born émigré architect Serge Chermayeff, who installed it on the terrace at Bentley Wood, his newly built estate in East Sussex. The undulating forms of the green Hornton stone acted as a visual bridge between the architecture and the landscape.

Much like Moore's sculpture, the house itself celebrates the character and natural beauty

of a single material: Chermayeff used timber both for the frame and the cladding. John Summerson enthused: '[Its] beautifully sited hollow rectangles suppressed every vanity of "style" and merely touched the environment into conscience of form.'

We sold the house in 2020, and, despite post-war extensions and alterations, the architect's original vision was still intact: a low-lying box with a ground level of floor-to-ceiling glass that spilt into the green waves of the countryside.

The intellectual notion of treating materials with 'honesty' was pioneered by the nineteenth-century Gothic Revival architect Augustus Pugin, who designed the interior of the Palace of Westminster, along with its Big Ben bell. He wrote:

> *The two great rules for design are these: 1st, that there should be no features about a building which are not necessary for convenience, construction, or propriety; 2nd, that all ornament should consist of enrichment of the essential construction of the building. The neglect of these two rules is the cause of all the bad architecture of the present time.*

Pugin's ideas were taken up by the dashing art critic John Ruskin. His *Seven Lamps of Architecture* was a Victorian manifesto on the principles of good design, one of which was 'Truth': the honest display of materials and construction.

Ruskin considered the mechanization of the Industrial Revolution to be the cause of great misery, generating soulless products and depriving workers of the personal satisfaction derived from making something by hand. He advocated a return to the medieval-guild model, in which artisans crafted each piece from beginning to end, and his ideas provided the spark for the Pre-Raphaelite Brotherhood and the Arts and Crafts Movement.

Ruskin's philosophical outpourings found physical manifestation at William Morris's Red House (1859). Morris wanted to create a home within striking distance of London that was constructed from natural materials, which he saw as healthier and better-looking than industrial products. Whereas most villas during this period were finished in wedding-cake stucco, the Red House flaunted its crimson brickwork like a sun-tanned visage. Internally, Webb left the timber framing and structural brick arches exposed, as an honest reminder of the house's construction methods and its external appearance. As we saw in the Light section,

Red House is far from a flawless building, but there is much we can learn from its straightforward approach to materiality.

The same could be said of Rudolf Schindler's house in Los Angeles, a highly experimental dwelling that provided the spark for Californian Modernism in the early 1920s. When I interviewed the artist Edmund de Waal, he spoke with great enthusiasm about its authenticity:

> *The beauty of the house is that all of the materials are unadorned. The concrete is barely polished; the wood is local Californian redwood that's not been hewn beyond the mildest of working; the glass – where there is glass, because often there are just spaces – is not grand or stained. It's a tactile house, one that unfolds through haptic discovery. You run your hands along the concrete walls and understand that material, you touch the beams or the inlay in the walls and understand the grain of the wood, so what you're doing at every point is being returned to lots of decisions about how you relate to the world.*

The perfect imperfection of materials

Having worked with clay since he was five years old, Edmund de Waal has spent a lifetime investigating how the smallest of interventions can reveal the innate character and texture of a material. He is best described as a perfectionist of imperfection, producing porcelain vessels with just the right amount of indentation and wobbliness. Much like his mentor, Bernard Leach, Edmund is heavily influenced by the aesthetics of Japan, where he studied at the age of seventeen. The Japanese have always embraced the notion of flawed beauty in a way that we in the West have never managed. *Wabi-sabi* teaches us to accept transience and asymmetry, and find joy in weathered surfaces, mismatched materials and natural ageing. This mindset is exemplified by the traditional tea ceremony, a spiritual experience that enables those taking part to escape everyday anxieties by preparing and sharing tea in humble surroundings.

Our seemingly relentless quest for perfection in life, from work to relationships and the way we live, is a cause of constant anguish. When creating a home, it is essential to let go of the idea that it will be immaculate or unblemished. This mindset doesn't always come naturally. In our garden at home, we have some fibre-cement planters designed by the Swiss Neofunctionalist Willy Guhl. Many years of exposure to the elements led them to develop a life of their own, with layers of beautiful lichen and moss. Unfortunately, our window cleaner came round one day and took it upon himself to do us a 'favour' by jet-washing them, and now they look like something from a mail-order catalogue.

For designers, imperfection is, in many ways, a much harder quality to work with than perfection. At the Neues Museum in Berlin, for example, British architect David Chipperfield chose to painstakingly patch up the original building, which meant that every decision he made about materials, finishes and detailing was an individual one. The notion of a young intern, or 'CAD monkey', sat in the corner of an architect's office, cutting and pasting exactly the same toilet block on to every drawing, is depressing because it is so prevalent. Deyan Sudjic, former director of the Design Museum in London, writes:

> *If you aspire to be perfect, as opposed to being imperfect, at least you have a template for what you want to get from an object. To be perfect is to know what to try for, when you design every joint, create every seam, and shape every surface. But to look*

for the positive qualities inherent in imperfection, you cannot simply put yourself in the hands of a process and expect the outcome you would like simply through the exercise of skill and persistence.

Children seem to have an innate understanding of transience. The emotional weight assigned to toys and teddies is often commensurate with the amount of wear and tear they have suffered. Indigo's most treasured possession is 'Rabbity', who has been by her side since she was born, a bedraggled bunny with frayed fur and a neck so deprived of stuffing that her head lolls helplessly to one side. Rabbity has endured some dark days, including the occasion when she was run over by the No. 19 bus. Such is her importance to our collective sanity, Faye and I decided to buy a back-up toy of identical type and proportion, in case she ever went missing or suffered a fatal traffic accident. This doe-eyed doppelgänger, who was appropriately christened 'New Rabbity', has been permanently discarded in a corner of the playroom since she arrived. Both of these toys came from the same factory, but each has a very different material character brought about by ageing. Rabbity has a colour, a texture and a smell that is uniquely her own; her lack of 'newness' is her greatest strength.

In the same way that a much loved toy bears the marks of a life well lived, so our homes tell stories about their past experiences. The materials we live with are in a state of constant flux, and we should celebrate their flaws and allow them to age gracefully. The food editor and writer Mina Holland embraced imperfection when renovating her flat in South London, a first-time purchase with her husband, Freddie. She says:

It was really important to us to work with the original features, like the fireplace, cornices and doors. But we've used them like a line drawing that we've coloured around – albeit in a neutral palette – with exposed plaster, plywood units, painted floorboards and encaustic tiles.

Even newly built houses, which haven't yet developed their own narratives, can borrow character from natural materials. Rather than plastering a brick wall, for example, there might be more beauty in leaving it exposed. Brick is one of man's oldest materials, and was used to build our earliest cities. It has a texture and porosity that makes it feel alive, even when

painted over. If you own an older house, try gently stripping back the internal walls to reveal the abstract beauty wrought by layer upon layer of historic paint.

Rupert Thomas, my erstwhile editor at *The World of Interiors*, lives on an early-Victorian crescent with his husband, the playwright Alan Bennett. Whereas the façades of the surrounding houses are all bedecked in pastel-perfect powder-blues and lemon-yellows, theirs has been dry-scraped, revealing the blemishes and crumples in the old stucco. It's like one of those anxiety dreams in which you turn up to a party with no clothes on. Rupert once told me that the neighbours think they are mad, but, to my mind, it's easily the most beautiful house on the street.

Mat Barnes, founder of architecture practice CAN, and his wife, Laura Dubeck, went to greater extremes when renovating and extending their dilapidated red-brick Edwardian house in Sydenham. The couple deliberately set out to preserve the spirit of the semi-derelict building they fell in love with, which meant leaving the original back wall between the kitchen and the extension in a partially demolished state. Mat says:

> *It was inspired by the stereotypical crumbling wall in a scene in* Trainspotting, *but its staggered shape also means it's very good for putting plants on. Our starting point for most rooms was to strip everything back and see if we could use the finish or material we'd exposed. In the kitchen area, we stripped back the wall to bricks, and then decided to leave it and just paint it to tie in with the crumbling end wall. We wanted to include some reference to the construction process, so had the structural steel columns in the extension painted red and white to mirror the ranging poles used in surveys.*

Most of the materials we produce nowadays are slick, standardized and lacking in personality. One example is laminate flooring, with its overly shiny, faux-wood boards that squeak as you walk across them. Even real timber floors are mercilessly sanded and buffed so that they look brand new. If your house has an original wooden floor – whether Georgian oak boards, Victorian pine planks or 1930s parquet – let its bruises, scars and freckles tell the story of its life. Try not to obliterate its character with a sander. If there are gaps between the boards, leave them rather than filling them in. Finish it with an oil or a wax that will lightly protect it without making it look like a glistening tenpin-bowling alley.

Have you ever sat in an old house, gazed out of the sash window, and noted the difference between the original windowpanes and those that have been replaced? As we discussed in the Light section, modern glazing has advantages for its transparency and energy-efficiency, but, in the right setting, there is no substitute for the refinement of historic, hand-made glass, the way it twists and swirls like an Edvard Munch painting.

Zellige tiles, which are hand-made in Morocco using traditional techniques and non-refined natural clay, have a similar appeal for their undulating surfaces. They can be trickier to fit than standard tiles, so your contractor might not thank you for specifying them, but their inconsistency in size and shape lends natural movement to a room.

Once we accept the idea that the house needn't be perfect, entertaining becomes a lot easier. *Wabi-sabi* is about making do with what you have, so a dinner party might involve a bandy-legged table garnished with a simple cloth, some cow parsley from a nearby hedgerow, mismatched plates and an assortment of drinking vessels. There's nothing wrong with cracked crockery. Indeed, the Japanese have made a virtue of such things – the centuries-old art of *Kintsugi* involves repairing broken pots using tree-sap lacquer dusted with powdered gold, giving them veins that glisten as they catch the light. And forget about burnishing the cutlery – it looks much nicer when it's a bit tarnished and neglected.

Jun'ichirō Tanizaki summarizes it perfectly:

> As a general matter we [in the East] find it hard to be really at home with things that shine and glitter. The Westerner uses silver and steel and nickel tableware, and polishes it to a fine brilliance, but we object to the practice. While we do sometimes indeed use silver for tea kettles, decanters or sake cups, we prefer not to polish it. On the contrary, we begin to enjoy it only when the lustre has worn off, when it has begun to take on a dark, smoky patina. I suppose I shall sound terribly defensive if I say that Westerners attempt to expose every speck of grime and eradicate it, while we Orientals carefully preserve and even idealize it. Yet for better or worse we do love things that bear the marks of grime, soot and weather, and we love the colours and sheen that call to mind the past that made them.

Preserving original materials

If *wabi-sabi* teaches us to be humble and accept things as they are, then it makes sense that we should do our best to preserve existing materials rather than replace them. This is an obvious statement when applied to, say, an eighteenth-century manor, with its elegant flagstones and intricate cornicing. Sure enough, Historic England exists to protect important building fabric, and most countries have a similar regulatory system. But what about more modern buildings, and those that are not protected by listing? In my view, even the most mundane houses have raw ingredients that we can work with. Creating a home is a bit like making soup. Original materials like fireplaces, door handles, panelling, windows and banisters are the decorative equivalent of garlic, herbs and heavily sweated shallots; without them, we're left with a tasteless broth devoid of any depth.

In any home from any era, we should acknowledge the original design intent and ask ourselves how the building wants to be. Utilizing pre-existing materials has clear environmental benefits, and reinstating natural materials that have been lost over the years gives the building back its character. When we buy or rent a place, the temptation is to purge it of its previous occupants. While it's certainly true that your home should reflect your own view of the world, think carefully before you make any major interventions. Live in it for a while, if you can. That wooden floor you thought was a bit beaten-up when you moved in might start to take on some significance – its warmth beneath bare feet, or its ability to absorb the comings and goings of daily life. Those old cast-iron radiators might rattle a bit and struggle to push out heat, but they tell the history of the place, and can be refurbished to improve their performance. The great thing about pre-existing materials is that they induce less anxiety, because we don't obsess over their upkeep; they are what they are.

They also tell stories. We once sold a characterful maisonette converted from a Victorian butcher's shop. The original retail space at the front had been repurposed as a kitchen, complete with marble counters, ominous-looking hooks, weighing scales and a glazed frieze of Art Nouveau tiles. At the back, the old wooden payment kiosk had become an unconventional study.

The penthouse apartment at the Isokon Building in Hampstead, which we sold to Tom Broughton, founder of spectacles company Cubitts, remains almost exactly as it was in the

1930s. Jack Pritchard, who was a salesman for Venesta, set out to demonstrate the aesthetic and structural potential of plywood, which the general public saw as an inferior substitute for solid wood. The panelled walls, the chequer-board floor and much of the original furniture are made from beautifully patinated ply, all protected by a rare Grade I listing. Tom says:

> *There are a few existing holes that I have to use when I'm hanging art, but I think that's beautiful – at some point in time, this hole was made, and on the pin that sat out of it there was probably a Ben Nicholson. You become extremely cognizant and aware of every little bit of the building, every design detail, every piece of material, and form an incredibly strong relationship with it. I was attracted to it because it felt so timeless, but also because of what it represented – in the late twenties and early thirties there was a positive outlook about doing things differently and challenging the status quo. Walter Gropius, Marcel Breuer and László Moholy-Nagy from the Bauhaus all lived here, along with Agatha Christie and a whole bunch of Soviet spies. Without trying to sound too grand, it's like living in an art piece. You feel less a resident, and more a custodian.*

One of the most astonishing homes I have visited in recent years belongs to the artist Sue Webster, who has used materiality as a narrative device. Webster stumbled across an abandoned double-fronted Victorian villa in De Beauvoir, surrounded by corrugated fencing. She discovered that its owner had been maniacally digging tunnels and caverns beneath it since the 1960s, to the extent that the road was folding in on itself. When the council finally evicted the 'Mole Man of Hackney', they removed 30 tonnes of debris from the site, including three cars and a boat, and filled up the holes with aerated concrete. He had dug down as far as the water table. Working with David Adjaye, Webster decided to treat the design process like an archaeological dig, revealing and preserving both the tunnels and the council's crude interventions, and adding her own layer of crisp modern concrete to an already textured site. The outside of the building looks like a beaten-up bunker, with scuffed render, reclaimed bricks and a knackered front gate. It is a house that suits the anarchic demeanour of its owner who, after all, has a son called Spider Webster.

The Spanish architect Ricardo Bofill adopted a similar approach when he converted an

abandoned cement factory near Barcelona into a family home and studio. While most people would have razed it to the ground and built something else, Bofill made it his life's mission to resuscitate this belching industrial relic of 31,000 square metres and repurpose it as a spellbinding modern living space.

Even without such grandiose intentions or ingredients, we can all learn from Sue Webster's and Ricardo Bofill's desire to conserve the built environment, to repurpose pre-existing materials rather than starting again. There is a certain humility in taking a house, a flat or an individual room on its merits, and accepting it for what it is rather than fighting against it.

Graphic designer Amy Yalland showed admirable modesty when she converted a manufacturing plant in Auckland into a surprisingly liveable home. Her starting point was a faceless box on an industrial estate, next door to a food-packaging company. However, she was attracted to the proportions: more than 2,000 square feet of floor space, and ceilings fit for a cherry-picker. Her light-touch refurbishment made a virtue of the building's industrial heritage, and she even retained the steel-roller shutter and disfigured concrete floor. The utilitarian aesthetic wouldn't be for everyone, but, within constrained cities with prohibitively high prices, people need to find space where they can. Amy explains:

> *The concrete floor in the main space had traces of the floor plans of each room, which I left to document the space's history. The mezzanine was a closed-in double-height set of rooms that I gutted to open everything up, clad with Monterey cypress from a local timber mill. It really needed some storage, so I designed a series of modular ply units, some built-in to house the pantry, laundry and kitchen, and some on wheels for studio materials, books and paper.*

When converting an industrial building, it is worth spending some time identifying how the space would have been used and which materials survive from the original build, to ensure that it feels authentic. Try to get hold of some archive photographs, search local planning records and speak to neighbours who have lived in the area for a long time. Floors and windows are particularly important. Carlo Viscione, who is a spatial designer, identified this when he refurbished a 1930s school block in Forest Gate, East London:

We kept the original concrete stairwell, the parquet floor and the tiling that goes all the way around the perimeter – I think it must have been used as a protective surface where the workbenches would have been. We put a lot of thought into the windows, because we wanted something that worked really well with the period of the property. They were all uPVC, but there was one original steel window on the ground floor by the door where the old school caretaker would have had access, so we used that as a reference and specified new ones. Some people will spend a lot on a kitchen, but I'd rather invest in windows and the fabric of the building to make the most of a space.

This conservationist approach to materials is just as valid for modern housing developments. Over the years, we have sold hundreds of flats on thoughtfully designed council estates, especially those in the London Borough of Camden. Under the stewardship of Sydney Cook in the 1960s and 1970s, architects including Benson & Forsyth, Neave Brown and Peter Tabori conjured up some of the world's most radical social housing in this area. Flats that have passed into private hands through 'right to buy' are now highly prized, and those with their original materials in place are the most sought after of all.

A fine example is Sam and Nelli Turner's home on the Alexandra & Ainsworth Estate, an avant-garde Modernist vision of concrete terraces and pedestrian walkways beside a railway line in well-to-do St John's Wood. The couple have painstakingly restored it to how it would have been. They explain:

We remade just about everything. The original banisters to the staircase were here, but we re-created the treads with reclaimed Iroko wood and made the same corner cut-outs that are in the steps that run up and down the ziggurats outside. The decision to paint the banisters black came about when we found some old photographs of it like this. The original floors were lino, so we've installed a contemporary version from Sinclair Till. The biggest things were the kitchen and the bathroom, as we wanted to re-create the tiling that was part of the original interiors. We eventually sourced some that are normally used in industrial spaces and swimming pools. The wardrobes in the bedrooms are exactly as they would have been, and still have the glass panel that can be pulled across to dampen any train noise.

Chris and Susannah Burke undertook a similarly respectful refurbishment of their Grade II-listed 1960s Modernist house in Suffolk, upholding the original vision of architect Birkin Haward while adapting it for modern use. The house was constructed without any of the green credentials expected today, with materials more suited to the commercial buildings that Haward worked on, so the couple sought to make it as eco-friendly as possible within the confines of the listed status. Chris explains:

> *It was cold! Most of the internal pine-boarded and plaster walls were without insulation, whilst the outer skin had the bare minimum – most of the windows were single-glazed, so the original oil boiler was basically just pumping heat into the atmosphere. We really had to take it back to a shell to make it liveable and sustainable. At first, we put a new highly insulated roof on and then we replaced 167 bespoke sealed window units – quite a challenge, as we were living here at the time with our school-aged children, and I remember it being a particularly wet autumn that year! The second phase required us to vacate for six months whilst the main structure was exposed to instal new electrics and plumbing plus an air-source heating system. From the outside, it looks very much the same, set in its secluded woodland plot, but we were able to add a large paved terrace at the back that really adds to the inside/outside living through large sliding doors.*

Materials and health

Humans have lived in agrarian settings for many thousands of years, so it is logical that we derive great comfort and solace from natural materials – an enveloping cuddle from a cashmere blanket, say, or the bolstering solidity of a wooden table. As Alvar Aalto put it: 'We should work for simple, good, undecorated things, but things which are in harmony with the human being and organically suited to the little man in the street.' Aalto was born among the forests and lakes of rural Finland, with an innate awareness of nature's curative powers. His Paimio tuberculosis sanatorium (1929–33) was conceived as an 'instrument of healing', with non-glare lighting, a natural gravity ventilation system, a soothing colour scheme and warm wooden furniture that hugged fragile physiques. Acknowledging the importance of effective hygiene, Aalto gave each patient their own wash basin, which he designed in a specific shape to emit almost no sound as the water hit it. The 'Paimio' armchair was designed with the backrest at a prescribed angle to open up the airways and help the patient's respiration.

In design, we talk about 'clean lines', referring to the aesthetic impact of rectilinear forms and clearly defined volumes, but the sanitary connotation of the term is worth dwelling on. Reductivist architectural elements like shadow gaps and flush cupboards collect less dust than heavily contoured skirtings, architraves and mouldings. The Victorians became interested in the health aspect of interior materials, developing wipe-clean wallpaper, for example, and Modernists like Alvar Aalto took it to a hospital level of cleanliness.

A century on from Aalto's pioneering sanatorium, and in the devastating wake of the Covid-19 pandemic, we are even more aware of the need for effective hygiene. We now place a higher demand on our interior materials, which must not only look good and provide comfort but also be uncontaminated and non-toxic. We have talked about the tactility of a well-designed door handle, but the germs transmitted by countless handshakes now make us wary. Designers are increasingly being asked to specify push catches and foot-operated doors, which are less likely to transmit germs from one person to another. And do we even need all of those doors anyway? Some might argue that open-plan living, with its absence of thresholds and ease of ventilation, also means cleaner living.

Kitchens and bathrooms are particularly sensitive areas of the home in which the choice of materials plays an essential role. Dirt tends to build up in gaps and junctions, so using a single material is more sanitary, and feels both generous and celebratory. Natural materials such as marble and glazed clay tiles have a gentle sheen and are easy to clean.

Copper, along with its corrosion-resistant alloys brass, bronze and cupronickel, has inherent antimicrobial characteristics, making it a wise choice for high-contact interior elements like bathroom and kitchen fixtures. Bacteria, viruses and fungi all struggle for traction in its lustrous presence. Copper is man's oldest metal. The Smith Papyrus, an Egyptian medical text, describes how it was used to sterilize drinking water and wounds, and the Romans, Greeks and Aztecs all adopted it for its hygienic attributes, treating everything from headaches to ear infections. Medical interest was heightened during the nineteenth century, when it was observed that copper-workers seemed to be immune to cholera. More pertinently for modern use, the coronavirus can survive for days on a stainless-steel or glass surface, yet dies within hours of landing on copper.

Twin basins or his-and-hers taps in a bathroom are a luxury, but they reduce the transmission of germs. Anyone who has put a hand down the back of the sofa to retrieve an errant coin will know that soft furnishings are a repository for biscuit crumbs and pet hair, therefore they should have washable covers and cushions that are detachable rather than built-in. Faye and I have a pair of off-white Gervasoni 'Ghost' sofas designed by Paola Navone – on the face of it, these are a brave choice with young children, but we bought two sets of loose covers so that they can be bundled into the wash every now and again.

Perhaps it's a generational thing, but my dad could never understand why he was asked to remove his shoes on arrival at our house. When you have twin girls breakdancing across the floor in nappies, as we did, you become acutely aware of tread-shaped mud deposits and tumbleweeds of lint. A simple shoe rack beside the front door is a worthwhile investment. If you get cold feet, physically as well as metaphorically, treat yourself to a fetching pair of gingham house slippers. Grander houses need a boot room at the most heavily utilized entrance point, where muddy shoes can be stored, soggy coats hung up and dogs towelled down, ideally with a basin so that everyone can wash their hands upon arrival.

We have become much more aware of outdoor air quality in recent years, and yet we still pay little heed to the build-up of harmful gases and particulate matter inside. Given that more than half of the air we breathe in a lifetime is within the walls of our homes, this is a significant oversight. Indoor pollution can be caused by everything from chemical cleaning products to

damp penetration, tobacco smoke and toxic building materials. This is particularly relevant for people with pre-existing health conditions like asthma and pulmonary disease, and for children, whose still-developing lungs are especially vulnerable. According to the World Health Organization, more than 50 per cent of pneumonia deaths among children under five are linked to household air pollution. For all of us, though, long-term exposure to pollutants increases the risk of death from respiratory disease, heart disease, cancer or stroke.

Glenn Adamson tells a remarkable story about an experiment undertaken by NASA, which set up a simulated life-support chamber completely cut off from the outside world. In a scene reminiscent of the film *The Martian*, in which a lugubrious Matt Damon uses his own excrement to grow potatoes, the six crew members had to survive without any air, water or external resources:

> *The experiment was going particularly well; the crew had been in the habitat for more than eighty days, breaking their existing record for consecutive time spent in total isolation. To celebrate, the support staff who had been monitoring them printed up T-shirts commemorating the milestone and put them into the enclosure via an airlock. What happened next surprised everyone involved: within twenty-four hours, all the plants that the team had been growing for food wilted and died. It took them a while to realize what had gone wrong. The iron-on transfers on the T-shirts had released minute amounts of formaldehyde into the air supply. It was just enough to knock the biosphere out of balance. End of experiment.*

The substances we live with release fumes into the air all the time without our knowing about it, like a flatulent uncle at Christmas. While much of this is fairly harmless, it's when we introduce new materials or start disturbing existing ones that they become much more dangerous. If you're carrying out any building works, my advice would be to move out if you can. If not, make sure that the interior is well ventilated, and choose products that emit low levels of formaldehyde and Volatile Organic Compounds (VOCs), especially if you're doing the work yourself.

When I was excitedly refurbishing my first flat in my twenties, my favourite afternoon activity was to wrap a bandana around my head, put the cricket on the radio and unleash a paint roller on to the walls. However, the post-decorative headache was less enjoyable. Our nostrils don't lie, and the powerful pong of a newly decorated room is a sign that chemicals are being released into the air. Paint can be full of harmful solvents, especially oil-based trim paints like gloss and eggshell, so do your research before falling in love with a particular shade on the colour chart. Farrow & Ball have transitioned to entirely water-based products, for example, and Edward Bulmer uses naturally occurring raw materials like linseed oil, chalk and earth. Manufacturer Airlite has developed an air-purifying paint that actually absorbs pollutants, and has been shown to kill certain strains of coronavirus in less than fifteen minutes.

Carpets are among the worst offenders. The latex backing and the adhesive used to stick them down, which are responsible for that familiar new-carpet smell, can continue to off-gas for years after installation. Try layering rugs on to the floor instead – they do the same job of insulating the space and providing comfort, and you can switch them around easily if you fancy a change.

Try to get into the habit of opening the windows and doors, and add extractor fans, trickle vents and ceiling fans to encourage the flow of air. You might consider using an indoor air purifier, and natural cleaning products. I also recommend ordering a radon testing kit. Radon is a naturally occurring radioactive gas caused by the decay of uranium in rocks and soil. Exposure to excessive levels has been proven to cause lung cancer, but remedial action can be taken to reduce its presence in the home.

Sheena Murphy, who runs the interiors practice Nune, is part of a new breed of designers who are passionate about creating healthy living spaces. She explains:

> We avoid bringing in things that are toxic and mass-produced, when we're not really sure what the materials are, and letting them off-gas in people's homes. But we also think about who's making those pieces, where they are coming from, what conditions they are being made in, the age of the people making them. It becomes an ethical question. We try really hard to shop small, to support people who care about the process and the material.

As a general rule, it is advisable to use natural building materials – without coatings, glues or processing chemicals – whenever possible. For example, untreated wood like cedar is non-toxic and naturally resistant to rot and pests, and can be used for anything from cladding to decking and interior joinery. Clay is a healthy and seldom-used alternative to conventional gypsum plaster. Not only does it absorb smells, it is also hygroscopic, helping to maintain an optimal humidity level and preventing the growth of mould and fungi. Architect Simon Astridge worked with the specialist company Clayworks to apply Cornish clay to the walls and ceilings of his flat in North London, using a Japanese technique called *arakabe*, which incorporates chopped straw. The result is a beautifully textured and atmospheric interior. He explains:

> *The lovely greenish-grey colour of the clay in the living space was designed to mirror the typical London sky. The walls and clouds merge into each other and draw your eye out to the view. The rest of the home was designed around the human body, so it's a very sensual space. We specified the materials in each area to support their different purposes and the experiences you would want to have within them. We used a jute tatami-style matting throughout the hallways and communal areas for a comforting warmth and softness beneath your feet. The walls and ceiling of the dressing space are clad in timber, and distinguish it from the grey-stone bathing area. You have to cross a threshold between the two, which enhances the specific use of the separate spaces and makes them more enjoyable as a result.*

Much like clay, *tadelakt* is a natural, non-toxic plaster that provides an animated, highly textured finish. It is made from lime plaster, which is rammed, polished and treated with olive-oil soap to waterproof it, making it a great choice for bathrooms. *Tadelakt* is traditional in Morocco, where it's usually pigmented in a deep red, but it can be specified in all manner of beautifully offbeat colours. Faye and I used it in the bathrooms of our house in Highgate, even covering the cupboard doors to provide a seamless finish. Regrettably, one of the cupboards chipped after heavy use and had to be patched up, and it never quite looked the same, so my advice is to use it on walls without junctions.

Materials and the environment

As a bleary-eyed commuter gazes out of the train carriage on their way to King's Cross station, past the Emirates football stadium and a scattering of misjudged housing developments, they might find their attention drawn to a monumental wall of sandbags abutting the railway line, with little windows cut out of it like modern-day arrow-slits. What looks like the fortress of a demented war veteran actually happens to be one of the most experimental private houses in London. It was built in 2001 by the architects Sarah Wigglesworth and Jeremy Till, the latter of whom is also the Head of Central Saint Martins art school. The sandbags, filled with cement, are an ingenious way of buffering the sound from the trains; over the years, they have burst forth like hundreds of beer bellies beneath ill-fitting T-shirts.

The visitor's first encounter with the house is the front gate, made from willow hurdles woven around a galvanized-steel frame, a prelude to the symphony of ancient and modern behind. Sarah's architecture studio looks like it has been wrapped in a blanket to keep it warm, in a deliberate challenge to the unyielding nature of the corporate edifices nearby. The 'blanket' is actually a silicone-faced fibreglass that has been quilted with an insulating layer. Moving through to the courtyard, which resounds with the busy clucking of chickens, you become aware of another unusual building material: straw bales. Used in construction for thousands of years, straw is cheap and easy to instal, and performs excellently as a thermal insulator. The half-metre-thick bales, sourced from a farmer, are illustrative of the ingenuity and resourcefulness Sarah and Jeremy applied to constructing their home, and also of the way they sought to draw from age-old wisdom, to relearn what has been forgotten.

Their eco-friendly approach may seem fairly customary more than twenty years on, but the couple were pioneers at a time when sustainable design was in its infancy and had yet to find a mass following. Through the project's far-reaching press coverage, and, crucially, their participation in the first season of the TV programme *Grand Designs*, the house shifted the public's perception of what a sustainable home could look like. Just as architecture was hitting the zeitgeist with a lifestyle-orientated rebrand, the Straw Bale House, with its urbane owners creating a bucolic eco-home in the middle of Islington, became a willing cover star. Sarah says:

One of the things that I think is really important about sustainability is that sense of wellbeing, ownership, enjoyment and care that you have over a building that you love. If you don't value your environment, you don't have those relationships with your surroundings. In the summer, when the leaves are dappling light into this place, it's absolutely gorgeous. And I think that's part of it. It's just a beautiful space to live in.

It has been a long time coming, but climate change is finally being taken seriously across all areas of society, and zero-carbon buildings are set to become the norm rather than the exception. We should all be conscious about using recycled and renewable materials, and about building at a modest scale that will meet our basic needs.

Aside from straw bales, the farmyard provides us with another excellent source of sustainable and effective insulation: sheep's wool. This naturally hygroscopic fibre absorbs moisture from the air and generates heat as it does so. When packed into a wall, ceiling or roof space, it helps to prevent the loss of energy, reduce carbon emissions and keep heating costs down. Your home feels the cold just like you do, so wrapping it in the equivalent of a thick jumper or bobble hat is a worthwhile investment.

Wool can be bought on the roll, and comes in all sheeps and sizes. It's much less flammable than synthetic materials, and can be returned to the soil at the end of its life, where it decomposes quickly and returns nutrients to the ground. Of course, sheep produce a new fleece every year, so wool is a renewable fibre source. And it even comes with a royal seal of approval, having been championed by the Prince of Wales via his commendable Campaign for Wool.

Another eco-friendly material that keeps popping up is cork. By its very nature, cork is regenerative, as it's the only tree that grows back its bark. It is waterproof, lightweight and an effective insulator, making it an ideal material for insulation and flooring. It also has a retro aesthetic that some find enticing (including me) and others find slightly horrifying. Bella Freud used cork tiles to cover the walls of the show flat she designed at the former BBC Television Centre in West London, imparting natural texture and inviting works of art to be hung on them.

One of the primary benefits of cork is its ability to deaden the acoustics, giving a room the

reassuring thud of a recording studio. It was famously used by Proust to line the bedroom walls of his boulevard Haussmann apartment. Indeed, the wonder of sustainable natural materials is their ability to appeal to all of our senses. In my bathroom at home, the floor is covered in rush matting, which gives off a lovely gentle aroma that nourishes neglected nostrils.

'Rush' is something of a misnomer, in fact, because this humble material is harvested in a slow and measured way that goes back many centuries. Felicity Irons is a highly skilled maker who, during the summer months, can be found in a 17-foot-long punt on the River Great Ouse, scything the bulrushes by hand with members of her extended family. The day's cut is transported back to the farm, and leant against a hedge to allow the sun and wind to dry it. Once it is ready, Felicity plaits the rush by hand into 3-foot lengths, which she then sews together with jute twine to make free-standing mats and specially commissioned full-sized carpets. She even replicates the historic practice of weaving in herbs like lavender, chamomile and southernwood, conjuring the mellow fragrance of a hazy summer day.

Looking to the future of what sustainable materials we might use for the structural elements of our homes, bamboo has greater tensile strength than steel and is stronger in compression than concrete. In Hong Kong they use it as scaffolding, which is far quicker to erect than steel because of its light weight. As anyone who has grown bamboo in their garden will also know, it shoots up at a prodigious rate (sometimes up to 3 feet a day) and is virtually indestructible because of its rampant roots and rhizomes. There are all sorts of other outlandish options available as well, including Ferrock, which is made from recycled steel dust and silica from ground-up glass, Timbercrete, essentially a mixture of sawdust and concrete, and Hempcrete, which is the inner fibres of hemp plants.

Good old-fashioned wood is a common and widely available resource that has many advantages over alternatives like concrete and steel. It is natural, renewable, recyclable and non-toxic, has strong thermal characteristics, and is the structural element with the lowest embodied energy. It has also been proven to have a calming effect on humans. In a study published in the *International Journal of Environmental Research and Public Health*, participants were asked to place the palm of a hand on a series of different materials, including marble, stainless steel and white oak. Touching wood was found to calm activity in the prefrontal cortex and induce parasympathetic nervous activity more than the other materials, bringing about a state of physiological relaxation.

Modern derivatives like Cross Laminated Timber (CLT) are significantly more fire-resistant than traditional timber. CLT is made from gluing together layers of solid-sawn lumber to form panels, which can then be erected quickly and efficiently on comparatively minimal foundations. Its environmental benefits are still being debated, but it has a much lower embodied carbon footprint than steel and concrete, and generates less waste on site. It can be left exposed internally, minimizing the need for finishing materials like plasterboard, suspended ceilings, cornicing and skirting.

Accoya is another form of modified timber, which is known for its durability and is sold with a warranty of up to fifty years. Anyone who played conkers as a child will remember that dipping them in vinegar made them almost indestructible. Accoya is produced using a similar process: by taking sustainably sourced softwood and treating it with acetic anhydride to make it as durable as any tropical hardwood.

There's nothing wrong with using brick either. Some of man's earliest cities are made of it, such as Uruk in Mesopotamia, which was founded some six thousand years ago. There is something irrefutable about a material that's made by combining three of the basic elements of the universe – earth, water and fire. As the Three Little Pigs demonstrated, brick is one of the most enduring materials we have, but, even if the Big Bad Wolf had managed to blow the house down, the good news is that it would have been fully recyclable. We see reclaimed bricks all the time, in everything from garden walls to newly built houses, and they have a craggy beauty that newer materials cannot replicate.

In his Introduction to the book *Brick* by William Hall, the architectural historian Dan Cruickshank writes:

> *Unlike many other hard building materials, bricks breathe, almost as living beings. Their open cell structure makes them wind-proof but breathable, which means they are the ideal materials for homes. They also offer superb insulation – helping interiors remain cool during a hot summer and warm in cold winters. Since they also function as heat reservoirs because of their high heat retention capacity, bricks can actively help warm a room.*

Louis Kahn was a magician with bricks, fashioning them into monumental structures with the gravitas and immortality of ruins. Kahn was a professor of architecture at Yale, and later at the University of Pennsylvania, always garnished with a dickie bow and with his hair combed over his scarred face. If his students were stuck for inspiration, he would counsel them to listen to their building materials, to take guidance from their natural attributes:

> You say to a brick, 'What do you want, brick?' And brick says to you, 'I like an arch.' And you say to brick, 'Look, I want one, too, but arches are expensive and I can use a concrete lintel.' And then you say: 'What do you think of that, brick?' Brick says: 'I like an arch.'

Alvar Aalto also had a great time playing with bricks, using more than fifty different types to build his Experimental House in Muuratsalo. This variegated summerhouse allowed him to create patterns and grids in the façade like a child using building blocks, and acted as a testbed to explore the efficacy of the material in an unforgiving climate.

Back in 2014, we sold a house made of brick in Deptford, South-East London, designed by the architects DSDHA. The client, Geoffrey Fisher, is an art historian with a healthy respect for both the environment and the historic fabric of the city. Every day on his way home from the library, he would walk down to the River Thames, pick up the best abandoned bricks he could find along the shoreline and cart them home in his backpack. He repeated this process for several decades, amassing a haul that eventually formed the basis for his wonderfully evocative new house. The buying public clearly recognize the poignancy of a building like this: we sold it for 58 per cent more than the average house of the same size in the area.

Much like Geoffrey Fisher's house, the Palais Idéal in Hauterives, France, is a monument to obsession, craftsmanship and love. It was built by the postman Ferdinand Cheval, who was doing his rounds one day when he tripped over a stone. Its strange shape sparked the memory of a dream he once had, in which he built himself a whimsical castle. Interpreting this incident as a sign from above, Cheval spent the next thirty-three years alone in his garden cobbling together an extraordinary pleasure palace, often working at night by the light of an oil lamp.

With no architectural training to speak of, he took inspiration from nature, postcards, early illustrated magazines and his own imagination.

Employing locally sourced materials should be the basis for any building, as it reduces the environmental cost implicit in transportation and ensures that there is an aesthetic context, especially if elements of the local vernacular are incorporated into the design. My own house, located in the South Downs National Park, was built in the nineteenth century using Hampshire stone and a smattering of fish bones from the river. Materials define a sense of place, from the sandstone terraces of Edinburgh to the brick-and-flint cottages of north Norfolk.

The work of the Japanese architect Shigeru Ban is defined by its materiality. When he was a child, his parents extended their house several times, and he would pick up the carpenter's offcuts and make model trains out of them. Later in life, he figured out how to use paper tubes as a structural material. After the Great Hanshin earthquake in Kobe, in 1995, left some three hundred thousand people homeless, Ban created the Paper Log House, with walls made from paper tubes and foundations consisting of donated beer crates weighed down with sandbags. This became the prototype for cheaply built, environmentally friendly disaster-relief buildings, and in the ensuing years Ban has used paper to build housing projects in places like Haiti and Rwanda.

Of course, what's right for a temporary building like this isn't necessarily appropriate for a private dwelling. Perhaps the most important lesson for us to absorb in a transient and throwaway society is that the material choices we make should be for the long term. When converting their Victorian flat in Bristol, Agatha and Robert Appleton-Sas shunned the idea of a modern fitted kitchen and instead combined pre-existing pieces of furniture. Robert explains:

> *A new kitchen is not necessarily sustainable, and what's amazing is that if someone doesn't like ours, they don't need to put it in the skip. They can perhaps put it somewhere else, or sell it, live with it or pass it on. I think the longevity of things in our home is important. If we decided to change the kitchen, we could take out the dresser and it could be used in our bedroom, be something in the office or it could be some other piece of furniture that we store things in.*

For the good of our planet, we must collectively invest in materials that have longevity. In the same way that a betting-shop biro is far more likely to be thrown away than a fountain pen, so a plastic chair is more expendable than one crafted from natural materials.

A home should be able to expand and contract as our lives evolve. Early on in the growth journey of The Modern House, Albert and I realized that the main flaw in our model is the relative lack of repeat business – our clients don't move house very often, recognizing the rarity of their home and the value it adds to their lives.

Sometimes this means adapting the space and changing the materials. Sarah Wigglesworth and Jeremy Till are once again showing how it should be done, having made the decision to see out their days in their straw-bale shelter. Jeremy says:

> *All the research shows that people live much longer and happier lives when they're in their own home and they have autonomy and agency. We don't want to end up institutionalized in a care home.*

Sarah continues:

> *My advice to people in a home they love is to get on with adapting it early. Getting older is an inevitability, but it's best to face it and make your home work for you.*

For Jeremy and Sarah, that meant changes like switching to electric hobs ('so we don't have to worry about leaving the gas on'), repositioning the ovens so they won't have to bend down, creating a 'mini flat' in the ground-floor bedroom wing that could function independently from the main house if needed, and replacing some of the hardware that had come to the end of its natural lifespan with newer, better-performing technology. 'Annoyingly,' says Jeremy, 'the only thing people notice is that we got the furniture reupholstered!'

Playing with materials

When Faye and I got married back in 2008, we opted for a simple wedding attended by nine guests and a registrar in a flammable trouser suit, instead channelling our savings towards a honeymoon in Italy. Neither of us had been to Rome before, and the perched village of Ravello held a certain romantic allure, but, truth be told, the primary purpose of the trip was a pilgrimage to the Hotel Parco dei Principi in Sorrento, designed in the 1960s by Gio Ponti. We found it to be a slightly odd place. The food was pretty retro, and the guests were an unlikely combination of design tourists like us and perennial visitors who tapped their feet to plinkety-plonk piano music in the evenings.

The design of the building, however, felt as relevant today as when it was built. When we arrived in the lobby, Gio Ponti's artistry was immediately apparent, with every wall cloaked in a layer of blue-and-white pebbles, like the scales of a fantastical fish. Scattered across the tiled floor was a fleet of Ponti-designed chairs and sofas, all upholstered in blue, and boxy wall sconces shaped like abstract sculptures cast a gentle glow. Our bedroom didn't just have a sea view – it seemed to be a part of the ocean itself, with geometric floor tiles that danced their way out to the glinting waters beyond. At the Parco dei Principi, Gio Ponti used materials to conjure a sense of place but also to convey imagination and puckishness. Antoni Gaudí did a similar thing with mosaic, adopting the Moorish practice of using brilliantly coloured tile fragments to construct buildings with the wit and whimsy of fairy-tale palaces. Gaudí was a major influence on the French artist Niki de Saint Phalle, who had an equally smashing time working with ceramic fragments. In Tuscany, she conjured up an astonishing 14-acre sculpture garden based on the tarot, filled with huge mystical figures clad in kaleidoscopic mosaic and shards of mirror. It took her two decades to build, during which time she physically inhabited the sculpture of *The Empress*: her bedroom was inside one of its breasts, and the kitchen was in the other.

Follies, outbuildings, temporary dwellings and guest houses all give us a chance to experiment with different materials. A House for Essex, designed by FAT and Grayson Perry for Living Architecture, is a deliberately bonkers holiday house that looks like a Russian stave church parachuted into an English field. The design centres around a fictional character called Julie Cope, who appears as a saintly figure in the form of statues, tapestries, tiles and an aluminium weathervane. Dangling from the ceiling is the motorbike that Julie was riding when she suffered a fatal collision with a curry-delivery driver.

Not many of us could countenance living inside the mind of Grayson Perry, or indeed Niki de Saint Phalle's bosom, but we could certainly all learn to have a bit more fun. One man who knew how to enjoy himself was the architect Brian Muller. In the 1980s he acquired a conventional late-Victorian house in North-West London, and converted it into a fantastical nest with a tree growing through the middle of it. Muller removed large parts of the existing structure to create double-height spaces; the walls, ceilings and doors were stripped back to their structural fabric of brick, joists and lath; huge glazed up-and-over doors opened up to the garden; and metal service ducts referenced the High Tech structures of Norman Foster and Richard Rogers. Muller went on to become an experimental film-maker, which perhaps explains the house's theatrical quality. In later years it was owned by Stephen Fry, no stranger to showmanship himself, and, by the time we came to sell it in 2014, Muller's original vision still remained intact. It went for £300,000 over the asking price, and one man who was outbid never forgave himself: for years afterwards, he called us incessantly to ask if the owner would sell it to him.

Another place that went down well with the buying public is the Clock House in North London, a brilliantly imaginative reworking of a humdrum 1960s townhouse by the architecture practice Archmongers. The façade has been transformed with hand-made tiles from a Cotswolds pottery and a copper letterbox. At the rear is a dining extension with an exposed ceiling structure that combines steel, Douglas fir and the original concrete beams. Concentrated bursts of colour have been used throughout the house: the front elevation is marked with a bold green window, the rear with a small red vertical window, and nylon door handles give an individual palette to each floor.

A sense of playfulness doesn't have to be created from scratch – there are certain material products on the market that do the job for us. For example, 'Marmoreal', by the company Dzek, is a precast marble terrazzo with a flecked finish reminiscent of sweet nougat. Conceived by two friends of mine – curator Brent Dzekciorius and furniture designer Max Lamb – it has been steadily infiltrating the interiors of design-literate homeowners over the past few years, and has been specified by architects such as David Kohn and Nord Studio.

Brent says:

The domestic interior can be one of the most personal expressions of human creative spirit. Constructing one provides us with the rare opportunity to dance without fear of being watched. Marmoreal was kind of intended to be such a liberation for marble within the terrazzo tradition. As Max Lamb framed his intention, 'I wanted to emphasize the stoniness of stone.' This meant that the featured lumps of stone would need to be significantly larger than those found in standard terrazzos. The marble rocks needed to be of a scale that would allow one to fully experience the otherworldly qualities these metamorphic rocks contain.

Employing a single material in a grand gesture, even using it to cover every surface of a room, inevitably creates a sense of theatre. The Brick House by Caruso St John – which is squeezed into a densely occupied area of West London 'like a baroque chapel in Rome buried deep within the city's close pattern of narrow streets' – uses brick on both the floors and the ceilings, giving it a broodiness that is leavened by shafts of light from triangular rooflights. At Ochre Barn in Norfolk, a Victorian threshing barn transformed for modern living by Carl Turner, the architect has used great expanses of Oriented Strand Board (OSB) to visually reference the haystacks that originally would have filled the space.

Another trick is to manipulate a material in an unexpected way, to extend it beyond its existing state and alter its aesthetic impression. For his Chance Street project in East London, consisting of three small houses built on the site of a post-war print factory, Stephen Taylor used brass screens to provide a visual barrier against the street. Whereas the sombre engineering bricks of the façade deliberately reference the tones of the cobbled road and sooty neighbouring houses, the lustrous brass has been folded and perforated with thousands of holes, giving it the plasticity of a velvet stage curtain.

Such artisanship is worthy of the great French metal-worker and architect Jean Prouvé, whose output was so prolific and varied that he adopted the self-mocking moniker of 'the metal twister'. From his workshop in Nancy, Prouvé churned out everything from wrought-iron lamps to handrails, railings, lift cages and storefronts. In the 1950s he developed a prefabricated dwelling made from aluminium, called Maison Tropicale, which was designed to address the housing shortage in France's African colonies. For ease of transport, it could be packed down flat and bunged into the back of a cargo plane. In the end, only three prototypes were ever constructed, leading to the Maison Tropicale's eventual fetishization as a Modernist art object rather than an enabler of social change (the New York hotelier André Balazs reportedly paid almost $5 million for one at a Christie's auction in 2007).

Prouvé paved the way for the emergence of High Tech architecture in the 1970s, with its focus on structural transparency and factory aesthetics. The flats at No. 125 Park Road in London, designed by Nicholas Grimshaw, have a skin of ribbed aluminium with gently curved edges, a playful riff on the design of the Citroën van. Visiting the building is always a gratifying experience for me personally, as flats on the upper levels have views over the London Central Mosque in Regent's Park, which was designed by my Grandpa Whiskers (having also designed the Catholic cathedral in Liverpool, and a Benedictine monastery at Douai Abbey in Berkshire, he always joked that he had hedged his bets for the afterlife). The mosque is itself a melting pot of materials, including elevations clad in concrete panels with a Portland-stone aggregate, dark-brown aluminium window frames, and a precast concrete dome decorated with gold-coloured copper-alloy sheeting.

Concrete has a mixed reputation, but it is one of the most diverse materials we have, as Barnabas Calder points out in his book *Concrete: The Beauty of Brutalism*:

> *The uniform sobriety of concrete turns out, when you look at it more closely, to conceal a subtle gamut of textures and colours, beautiful in themselves and a permanent record of how the building was made . . . Whatever the excitement Modernist architects felt about its engineering possibilities and its aesthetics, concrete is seen by some as having the most generic-looking and uninteresting of finishes. Words which come up again and again are 'oppressive', 'grey', 'streaky', 'ugly' . . . but once you get your eye in you start to see a huge range of textures, tones and colours – a level of variety almost comparable to that of building stone.*

Indeed, concrete can be pigmented in all sorts of different colours (pink is a personal favourite). It can be as smooth as silk, or sludgy and coarse like a bowl of grits. One of its most intriguing characteristics is that it will faithfully adopt the texture of the formwork it is poured into. Le

Corbusier's Unité d'Habitation in Marseille, for example, has a beautiful grain imprinted in the *béton brut* concrete, derived from the shuttering of rough-sawn boards. Corb believed reinforced concrete to be 'a natural material of the same rank as stone, wood or terra cotta'.

Early in his career, Jamie Fobert experimented with the textural potential of concrete via a series of highly engaging residential projects. Anderson House in Central London is one of the most surprising private dwellings I've ever visited, a contemporary cave with the proportions of a chapel, parachuted into an invisible backyard site – here, the *in situ* concrete has been cast against plastic sheeting, giving it a satiny and wrinkled complexion like the weather-beaten brow of a rugged farmer. Fobert used a similar technique at a Victorian villa in Primrose Hill, where he completely opened up the lower floor and supported the upper storeys on what he describes as a 'concrete table'.

Architect Adam Richards has used concrete as the muscular core of his new house, Nithurst Farm, in West Sussex. Externally, it is wrapped in a layer of brick like a Roman ruin. Inside, meanwhile, the concrete has been left exposed; antique tapestries are hung in front of it, along with modern geometric artworks by Robert Mangold, bringing horizons of time into dialogue. Adam explains:

> *Concrete is quite a robust, aggressive material, some people might say, but I don't think that: it's got this beautiful silky quality. Obviously it tells this story about being a modern building, but it's essentially made of stone, which has associations with ancient buildings. Because of its structural qualities, it has allowed us to make a building that has certain spatial characteristics but also material characteristics that speak of 'ancient'.*

The Barbican Estate is made from concrete with a very different treatment. Here, the surface has been assiduously pick-hammered by hand to expose the aggregate underneath, giving it a coarse finish and a monumental presence. The Barbican is unquestionably a polarizing piece of architecture, but its popularity with creatives only continues to grow. One of its many illustrious residents is the artist Michael Craig-Martin, who, as Professor of Fine Art at Goldsmiths, oversaw the emergence of Damien Hirst and Sarah Lucas in the 1980s. When I interviewed him, he spoke effusively about the coherence of the design:

I was always fascinated by the Barbican and never understood why people didn't like it. I have to say, having the experience of living here, I think it's an architectural masterpiece. It is the true realization of the Modernist utopian idea of perfect urban living, where you have beautiful apartments filled with light, where everything is modern, simple and comfortable. Most of the buildings are lifted on pilotis, so the space flows underneath them. If they all went to the ground, the result would be heavy and bleak, but, because they are lifted up and penetrated everywhere by space and light, you can always see from one part of the estate to another. The mix of gardens, walkways, levels, terraces, vistas, 'lakes' and waterfalls combine to create a safe haven of public and private spaces. The materials used and the quality of the workmanship were exceptionally good – as in all truly important architecture, every detail has been thought through, and is coherent with the total vision. People who don't live here don't understand that, despite its immensity and Brutalist character, it is never oppressive: a fascinating and very comfortable place to live at the heart of the city.

As we have seen, there are more eco-friendly structural alternatives to concrete these days. However, when used at a domestic scale for a specific application like a kitchen floor or a worktop, it has a hardiness and handsomeness that's hard to match. Its naturally occurring blemishes and hairline cracks are all part of the fun.

Anyone who visited Tate Modern back in 2007 will remember the lightning-like fissure that ran all the way down the concrete ramp of the Turbine Hall. Created by the Colombian artist Doris Salcedo, this fault line was said to represent the socio-economic division between the Northern and Southern hemispheres, but it is also a playful comment on the transience and imperfection of materials. Once the exhibition had finished, Salcedo's crack was filled up again. However, the thing about concrete is that you can never match it exactly, and the jagged outlines remained visible, like a post-operative scar. It is a floor with flaws, and all the more beautiful for it.

Nature

'*Study nature, love nature, stay close
to nature. It will never fail you.*'
Frank Lloyd Wright

Putting nature first

Back when Faye and I lived in our basement flat in Camden, I spent the majority of our tenure painting over the patches of rising damp that bubbled up on the walls, and trying to catch the resident rat, a sinister fellow with a pronounced limp that miraculously healed itself whenever I got close (we named him Keyser Söze, after the fictional character from *The Usual Suspects*). Despite these inconveniences, it was the only place we could afford that had a garden. We cultivated great jungles of bamboo, in an attempt to block out some of the noise from the adjacent railway line, and woody fingers of rosemary that were thrown into hearty Sunday stews. We experimented with ferns in shadowy corners, and clematis up against sunlit stucco. Admittedly, we killed quite a few things through ineptitude and neglect, but overall our little sliver of urban greenery brought us a lot of joy.

From there, we graduated to our terraced townhouse in Islington, which we identified on the basis that it had a leafy outlook on both sides. At the front was a man-made waterway built in the seventeenth century to bring drinking water into London, and at the rear we looked down the gardens of the adjacent terrace. We figured that you can change almost anything about a house, but you can't alter the view. Waking up to nothing but trees in the morning, we couldn't help but feel uplifted, and we also discovered that there's something deeply liberating about being able to wander around *en déshabillé* without being overlooked.

Our next place in Highgate was essentially a garden with a house attached. Its size was relatively modest for a three-bedroom family dwelling, but the fully glazed south elevation opened on to a 40-metre-long lawn that bled into the sylvan setting of Hampstead Heath beyond. Indigo adored it, spending much of her day picking flowers, conducting archaeological digs and making dens inside the willow dome.

Our current house is in a National Park. Having always sought out nature in every home, we are now so thoroughly immersed in it that we cannot fathom how we ever survived in an urban environment. Ask any human being, and they will tell you that they feel good when they are surrounded by greenery. Despite this, we seem to be doing everything we can to deny our genetic programming. Thomas Gainsborough's wooded vales have given way to L. S. Lowry's sputtering factories and densely populated streets. In 1800 less than 10 per cent of the global population lived in urban areas, but by 2018 it was 55 per cent.

Of course, there are some significant benefits to all of this new-found comfort. We no longer need to hunter-gather our food; instead, it is decanted directly into our kitchens by cheerful delivery drivers. Buildings form a convenient barricade against predators, meaning that we no longer need to cower behind shrubbery to avoid them. Faye and I once stayed in a house without any walls on a Thai island, which was an enlightening experience – I awoke with a yelp to discover that a centipede had attached its pincers to my posterior.

However, having created this safety net for ourselves, we have become entangled in it like gormless bycatch. According to research by the World Health Organization and the US Environmental Protection Agency, Americans and Europeans spend approximately 90 per cent of their time indoors. As Martin Summer points out:

> *The lives of hunter-gatherers were the inverse of how we live today. We move from one shelter (our home) to another (our office) using a shelter on wheels (our car). We're rarely exposed to weather conditions. Often, we don't interact with a single sign of nature along the way.*

If you are on the lookout for a new home, a connection to nature should be the first thing on your wish list, regardless of budget. It always has been for me. In a densely built-up city, this might mean finding a flat that overlooks a communal garden, windows with ledges deep enough for plants or a location within walking distance of a park.

Take Fergus and Margot Henderson, for example. When they're not busy feeding brains-on-toast to London's creative community, these influential chefs are usually having an *offally* nice time in their South London garden, eating lunch at a table in the shade or pottering around to the buzzing of bees. They were previously living in a flat in the West End, but moved in order to get some outside space for themselves and their children. Margot says:

> *At first, I thought it was going to be terrible leaving Covent Garden: I'd miss being out late and walking home, watching the business of everyone going by and being close to all those restaurants. But I love being here. And I definitely don't miss Marks & Spencer, or all the tourists!*

'And it's better for our health here,' continues Fergus. 'The garden is like an urban lung.'

If you are moving to the countryside, remember that the landscape around you is just as important as the house itself. My family and I go for a local walk every day, exploring the network of river paths and blossom-lined bridleways. We see red kites circling over the fields, trout flipping out of the shallows and the occasional iridescent flash of a kingfisher.

During lockdown, these walks undoubtedly helped to keep us emotionally balanced. Indeed, if there is any upside to be found in the Covid-19 pandemic, it is that many of us have become more accepting of our place in the world. Rosa Park, the founder of *Cereal* magazine, is a seasoned traveller who was born in Seoul and now splits her time between Bath and Los Angeles, but 2020 was the first year of her life in which she was forced to stay put in a single country. She wrote:

> *Like many of us, I have become fixated on nature. Amidst Bath's parks, gardens, open fields and woodland, I've noticed how dramatically each season unfolds. The metamorphosis from bare, knotted branches to canopies of velvety cherry blossoms and wisteria felt performative, especially when the breeze sent flurries of petals descending like snowfall. Foraging for wild garlic in spring gave way to collecting elderflower in autumn, as I took an interest in cooking for the first time. At long last, I've learned how to make more than toast.*

People who place themselves in contact with nature tend to live happier lives. Indeed, gardeners and florists consistently top the charts in surveys about job satisfaction. This might be because nature teaches us about humility: anyone who has been out in a boat on a rough day knows about the swirling omnipotence of the sea, and a hike through the mountains generates a sense of rapture that puts everyday worries into perspective. As Peter Kahn, Professor of Psychology at the University of Washington, points out:

> *Interacting with nature teaches us to live in relation with the other, not in domination over the other: You don't control the birds flying overhead, or the moon rising, or the bear walking where it wouldn't like to walk . . . one of the overarching problems of the world today is that we see ourselves living in domination over rather than in relation with other people and with the natural world.*

Urban nature

Skulking among mature turkey oaks on a backland site in Sydenham is the aptly named Tree House, designed by Ian McChesney Architects, which is clad from head to foot in opaque black glass. Its façades reflect the surrounding foliage back on itself, enabling it to melt into the landscape like some kind of radar-defying vessel. When we sold it in 2015, it achieved a price premium of more than 50 per cent. Buyers will always pay more for a connection to nature. According to the Office for National Statistics, houses situated within 100 metres of a green space are typically £2,500 more expensive than those 500 metres away. I remember that we achieved a particularly eye-popping price for a flat in North London many years ago, purely because it had a big roof terrace – never mind the fact that it overlooked a square colonized by late-night ravers.

Just up the road from the Tree House is the Dulwich Estate, where more than 2,000 homes were built by Austin Vernon & Partners in the 1950s and 1960s. The architects took great care to respond to the natural contours of the site and the existing trees, separating roads from pedestrian areas and dedicating large swathes of land to communal spinneys. Corey Hemingway bought her apartment there specifically because of its connection to the landscape, and describes how she felt when she first viewed it:

> I bloody loved it! It was a really sunny day, with bright blue skies. I walked up the first set of stairs and into the original lift, which hadn't been changed since the block was first built in 1959 – it still had the original mustard-coloured rose-printed Formica and a mirror on the back wall. I remember looking at my reflection and grinning. It was autumn, and as soon as I walked into the apartment, I was drawn to the view out of the 5-metre-long living-room window – it felt as if I was in a treehouse. I immediately fell in love with the place. I'm surrounded by trees, and to watch them go through each season is very special.

In recent years, architects have sought increasingly innovative solutions to the problem of how to embed nature into an urban setting. Édouard François has managed to successfully elevate the traditional social-housing block with his Flower Tower in Paris – each of its ten storeys is defined by a concrete slab, the edges of which are lined with 380 suspended flowerpots planted with bamboo. From a distance it looks like a pistachio-filled baklava, and successfully imports an impressive amount of plant matter into its urban setting. Heatherwick Studio has applied a similar sensibility to its '1,000 Trees' project in Shanghai, where the structural columns double up as enormous planters with clusters of trees sprouting from them. It is less a building and more a piece of topography.

Much like green façades, sedum roofs bring a welcome carpet of nature to an otherwise neglected place. Flat roofs on house extensions and garages can be planted up in order to improve the view, create a habitat for wildlife and help to lower urban air temperatures. The simple act of establishing a window box, putting a pot on a doorstep or training a climber up a wall contributes to the collective greening of our streets. In general, the more leaves a plant has, the more useful it is in an urban environment. Living near a busy road has been linked with an increased incidence of Alzheimer's, but vigorous evergreens are among the greatest weapons in our armoury, filtering the air, trapping particulate matter and deflecting the sound of rumbling traffic.

I remember walking to work in North London many years ago, and coming across beautiful clusters of flowers emerging from the small patches of earth between paving slabs. The local residents had clubbed together to plant them, in an act of cooperative generosity towards their general wellbeing. Greening our cities is a collective social responsibility.

This responsibility extends to communal gardens. My mother-in-law, for example, has taken it upon herself to completely transform the patch of land outside her flat in Winchester, taming the tangles of shrubbery and planting up flowers and vegetables. Kaori Tatebayashi has performed similar miracles in Forest Hill. As she explains, her gardening exploits serve the common good but also help her own mental health:

> We have a communal front garden which I have been looking after ever since we
> moved into the building ten years ago, and I have felt extremely lucky to be able to
> experiment and grow things out there. There are endless jobs to do and it really helps
> keep me stay happy and sane! It's become known to locals as a rose garden, since I've

planted sixteen different roses over the years, with passers-by giving us constant compliments. I've started growing vegetables, too, but only a small amount at the side because I don't want to take over all the space.

For Tatebayashi, who is a ceramicist, putting herself in touch with nature transports her back to the rural village in Japan where she was born, firing her imagination and informing her work.

Communal outdoor spaces allow communities to come together, share ideas and show support for one another. For example, restaurateur Clare Lattin and her fellow residents congregate every Sunday at a shared table on the tarmac outside their converted factory in Hackney, where they break bread amid a family of eccentric pot plants. She sees it as part of a wider process of being accountable and finding a slower pace in the city:

It's about looking inwards, not out, being local, not global, and doing what I can in my tiny corner of the planet – be that composting my kitchen waste for the yard's pots or growing herbs and flowers to help wildlife where I can. We've become so disconnected from nature that now modern living has to be about reconnecting to it, touching it, living with it.

The grow-your-own movement has gripped the public consciousness in the wake of the Covid-19 pandemic, which has forced us to focus on our local neighbourhoods. Near where I live, there are little troughs of herbs and vegetables outside the railway station, which anyone is free to help themselves to. Many of my friends have a veg patch on the local allotment, which costs just £26 a year to rent. We should all do what we can to adopt a subsistence lifestyle, even if that simply amounts to a tuft of parsley on a windowsill. On The Modern House website, we publish a *Gardener's Diary* written by the organic-food grower Claire Ratinon, which explains what to plant and when.

For those of us with sufficiently large gardens, we owe it to the environment to cultivate some prize pumpkins and medal-winning marrows. When we bought our house, the bit that Faye was most excited about was the dishevelled kitchen garden, with its corrugated potting shed. Alison Lloyd, founder of bag company Ally Capellino, has a laudable level of respect for nature's abundant bounty. At her flat in Dalston, fingers of foliage are displayed on the walls like artworks, while, outside, the borders erupt with flowers, fruits and vegetables. She says:

> *I spend most of my time at home in the garden, although I find it impossible to just sit down. It's big, but I ended up buying half of next door's garden after a bit of negotiation. I tried to have a lawn, but it just didn't work and became a mud bath. The raised bed is for fruit and vegetables, and it's been particularly successful for blackberries, raspberries and rocket this year. I put in loads of artichokes to create some structure, and they're almost 12 feet high. It's been quite hard to keep up with the beans this summer. I can't help but keep adding things in – I'm very naughty and am always bringing plants back from holidays. I once brought an olive tree back from Greece because I felt sorry for it. I take great pleasure in the challenge of bringing things back to life again. I found an abandoned fiddle-leaf fig tree on the street the other day, and that ended up coming home with me, too.*

Cultivating your own produce encourages seasonality, which is better for your health and for the environment. And, much as a pint of Guinness tastes better in Dublin, so your own cockeyed courgettes will always bring about coos of approval for their depth of flavour. Gill Meller says:

> *So much of the fruit and veg we like to eat has become 'seasonless', and few illustrate this difficult truth more starkly than the tomato. Sadly, we've forgotten that tomatoes can be special; that a naturally grown, sun-ripened tomato, eaten when it's plump and warm and soft enough to split, can be a heartbreakingly wonderful experience.*

One of the most important things for a small urban garden is that it's low maintenance. Lawns require a lot more tending than people think, and there's nothing worse than a wisp of grass flailing in the wind like a geography teacher's combover. In my opinion, Astroturf looks naff anywhere outside of a hockey pitch, so hard landscaping is the logical choice, provided that it's augmented by enough easy-to-grow plant life. Slabs of York stone, flint, stone setts or

herringbones of brick – or indeed cheaper alternatives such as timber decking or compacted gravel – can be surrounded by borders of flowers, vegetables, shrubs and small trees. There is always some weeding to be done in the first year, but a certain amount of diligence and attention while the garden establishes itself will result in much less maintenance further down the line. If an outside space is easy to look after, then it invariably looks smarter, meaning that we are much more tempted to venture outside and use it.

Don't underestimate the value of a professional landscape designer. At our house in Islington, we worked with our friend Paul Gazerwitz, who set in place a series of loosely defined rooms that made the garden feel infinitely larger, more abundant and magical than we ever could have managed on our own. At our flat in Winchester, Harry and David Rich made sense of an awkward courtyard with beautifully wild planting and a bench made from flint. In my experience, people don't like to pay for garden design, but getting the structure right at the outset is imperative. If you can afford to instal it and plant it up all at once, you have an 'instant' garden that will give you an immense amount of pleasure from the outset.

Ceramicist and publisher Kate Griffin had help from designer Todd Longstaffe-Gowan when establishing her garden in North London many years ago. She explains:

> *I wrote him a letter and he happened to like it. I didn't really know who he was, I had just seen a garden of his I liked. He came along and turned out to be very famous and expensive. I thought I wouldn't be able to afford him and then he said, 'Just pay my wine bill.' I thought it would be really uncool to ask him how much that would be, but it turned out to not be too much.*

If you don't have the budget to work with a designer, the likes of Arne Maynard and Piet Oudolf have written books containing planting plans that you can take inspiration from.

Placing a chair on a balcony, a table on a terrace or a hammock between trees will encourage us to abandon the indoors and spend some extended time in nature. Eating a snack or reading a book can be a far more enlivening experience outside than in. Cultivate some herbs, keep some bees – anything that will tear you away from the sofa.

Taking into account the movement of the sun is crucial when planning any outside space. My friend Luke Chandresinghe, founder of Undercover Architecture, bought a Victorian terraced house with a shady north-facing garden. He populated it with a battalion of tree ferns, which thrive in sheltered conditions, and his young children were soon able to play games of hide-and-seek in a magical fairy-tale forest. If your home faces south, it can be a good idea to put deciduous trees close to the building. These will provide some solar screening during the hot summer months, and allow the winter sun to penetrate once the leaves fall off in the winter.

Planting up close to the house also creates drama. When Todd Longstaffe-Gowan designed a garden for Valentine and Régis Franc in West London, he installed a surreal screen of palms just outside the Crittall windows. Behind this, he planted what he calls 'rockets' of flowers and 'clouds' of box hedging. He explains:

> *The clients had never had a garden before. I decided that the only way they would venture to the back of it was to reverse the perspective. So we put all the trees in the foreground, which makes it seem more extensive, and from there the whole thing slopes upwards in a gentle ramp. The palms had to be pulled through the holes in the walls like missiles – it was part of the fun and the drama.*

When choosing a home to buy or rent, consider whether the outside space is truly useable. As discussed in the Light section, we are phototrophic creatures, and are naturally drawn to spots that are light and sunny. A survey of a residential block in Berkeley, California, confirmed this, as the authors of *A Pattern Language* explain:

> *Along Webster Street – an east–west street – 18 of 20 persons interviewed said they used only the sunny parts of their yards. Half of these were people living on the north side of the street – these people did not use their backyards at all, but would sit in the front yard, beside the sidewalk, to be in the south sun. The north-facing backyards were used primarily for storing junk. Not one of the persons interviewed indicated preference for a shady yard.*

Interestingly, the study also found that residents with a sunny yard wouldn't use it if they had to pass through a deep band of shade up against the house in order to reach the light. We need to differentiate between negative outdoor space, which is shapeless and occurs accidentally, like a void between buildings or a patch of asphalt between chimneys, and positive space, which is usually placed deliberately on the land and has the same definition as an indoor room.

Incorporating courtyards into housing design is a great way to embed nature into an urban milieu. The joy of a courtyard is that its walls filter out the majority of the wind, and, provided it's placed in a sunny spot, then it will be utilized regularly. A roof garden can be equally successful, dispensing clean air and distant views, promoting biodiversity and often improving the insulation of the building. We're not talking about a bench plonked beside a television aerial – to be truly useful, a terrace should be directly connected to the interior, like an extra room. An outside space perched right on top of a building and accessed by its own set of steps is usually forgotten about and seldom used; we enjoy the reassurance of feeling the building's presence behind us.

In the Space section, we saw how an entrance hall can create a satisfactory transition from outside to in, but we need to take things one step further back and consider the visitor's journey to the front door. If you are lucky enough to have a front garden, you might use a pergola or some trellis planted with climbers to create enclosure and build anticipation. Or you could twist the path to create an interesting voyage, with scented plants that provide an aromatic journey along the way. At my parents' old house in Devon, you were greeted by an explosion of lavender to either side of the path, which brushed against your legs and released its scent as you sidled through it. My dad had a knack of getting the best out of lavender, which involved slaying it every year like a berserk samurai warrior. He wasn't known for his subtlety, but gardens always came to life in his husky presence.

Bringing nature in

Before moving into The Modern House's HQ in London, we spent several months carrying out a much needed refurbishment. The previous occupants had colour-matched the walls to a Seville orange, and installed a complicated motorway network of plastic cable trunking, some of which inexplicably traversed the windows. One of the biggest design challenges was how to dampen the sound in the main space, formerly a church hall with double-height ceilings, where up to twenty-five members of our sales team would be on the phone simultaneously. I researched every form of acoustic panelling I could find, and discovered that they were either incredibly expensive, or incredibly ugly, or both. The solution was to instal a metal grid on the ceiling and suspend a miscellany of pot plants from it, which form dense clouds of sound-absorbent greenery. This canopy has become increasingly mature over the years, and now resembles Brian May's hair. Leaves cascade on to keyboards, and earlobes are tickled by errant fronds.

Increasingly, plants are being incorporated into domestic environments in a similar way, often in the form of 'living walls' with built-in irrigation systems. A standard interior wall can be transformed into a fast-growing vertical garden that absorbs microscopic pollutants, balances humidity and has a compelling visual impact. Indeed, house plants can be useful to us in many different ways, helping to demarcate space, regulate the temperature or add a flourish to an unremarkable room. At her rented flat near London Fields, East London, Rhonda Drakeford has used them as a screening device:

> The flat is right on the street, so privacy is an issue, but when I moved in the front window had frosted vinyl covering it. I took it off and put up these scaffolding planks, painted them and then put plants in. It's a natural screen, and if you're outside you really can't see in. People come right up to the window and take pictures, which at first was weird but they really can't see me! Using plants in an architectural way like this is something I've tried to bring into other projects, to see them not just as decoration but as performing a function, too. And I think especially for rented accommodation, plants are the easiest thing you can do to make the space feel alive.

Setting aside the aesthetic and functional benefits, incorporating plants into an interior can positively impact our wellbeing, lowering blood pressure and increasing attentiveness. This is an important point when we consider that the amount of vegetated land in our cities is steadily declining, and that more than one in five households in London has no access to a garden.

In our old house in Highgate, we cultivated a fiddle-leaf fig in a big concrete pot in the kitchen, which helped to edit out the view of the road. Its leathery leaves became increasingly humongous over the years, and I began to see it as a slightly eccentric member of the family, always there in the corner with a friendly outstretched palm. House plants manage to convey an element of unpredictability while at the same time reassuring us with their steady presence. The best examples add playfulness and movement, like the Swiss cheese plant, which has holes in its leaves like slices of Emmenthal.

The concept of keeping plants indoors has a fertile history, and the Egyptians, Greeks and Romans all used them to add colour to their grandiose estates. However, for today's urban-dwellers, it has become less about decorative garnish and more about finding a fundamental connection with the natural world.

Photographer Steph Wilson is part of this new generation. She shares her Brixton home with an extended family of pot plants, parrots and Pomeranians. This whimsical urban menagerie serves to remedy the anxieties of city life, as she explains:

> *Having a nice space is so integral to mental health. It makes me happy to sit in the living room with the sun moving across the plants, knowing it's keeping them alive; my blue parrotlet, Tomato, is doing his thing and I'm watching the birds. Then, in the summer, the plants come to life and start flowering. It's the most joyous thing. Any work of art is very secondary. It's always my main love to have a space that's nourishing me, and that I'm doing the same back. I feel at peace here.*

The botanical stylist Yasuyo Harvey, who grew up near Kyoto and now lives in a London suburb, uses plant matter as a form of sculpture. She makes seeds and dried foliage into the most exquisite mobiles, vessels and interior objects:

It's like meditation for me, a form of ritual. I am not good at drawing; combining textures is my skill. The raw materials always come first, and I get inspired by what's in front of me. I grow some of the seeds in my garden, and they come back every year. I also get things from markets and when I'm out walking in the fields. The best plants are usually in the alleyways between houses or in someone's front garden. I am always looking to discover new ways of using materials. I find it fascinating.

Much like Yasuyo does, we should try to keep things local and seasonal for the good of the environment. Grow some daffodils in a window box, or cut some hollyhocks and fragrant fronds of dill from your allotment. A bunch of flowers arranged in a vase on the kitchen table can do wonders for the spirit, bringing a blast of colour and texture to the dullest of days. Florence Nightingale wrote:

I shall never forget the rapture of fever patients over a bunch of bright-coloured flowers . . . People say the effect is only on the mind. It is no such thing. The effect is on the body, too.

Most fruits start their development as flowers, so our brains have been preconditioned by evolution to find them attractive, because they tell us that a food source is nearby. Try to choose flowers with a long lifespan, keep them in a cool place and change their water regularly to help them last longer.

In our house, we plant amaryllis bulbs in antique lustreware bowls, their delicate pink-and-white petals complementing the iridescent metallic glaze on the pottery. Our hallway is presided over by a family of geraniums in terracotta pots of assorted size. In spring, we cut stems from the magnolia tree, and wait patiently while the petals summon up the courage to burst from their buds; while in summer, sweet peas are dropped into expectant jugs. Often, we keep things in the house until they are long past their best. Sunflowers, for example, look much better when they rust and wither, and artichokes have a sculptural beauty post-mortem.

The natural matter we surround ourselves with doesn't have to be alive for it to be of value. As a child growing up in the countryside, Faye would spend hours in the woods collecting sticks and stones and broken bones, before endlessly rearranging them on the mantelpiece in her room. The creative director Lyndsay Milne had a similar compulsion:

> *I would take the brussels-sprout stems off the compost heap and hang them on string.*
> *I think my sister thought I was a witch.*

You only have to watch a toddler collecting shells on a beach to conclude that children have an urge to hunter-gather, to place themselves into physical contact with the natural world. Seemingly every time I reach into my coat pocket, I pull out a piece of flint or an acorn that one of my daughters has picked up on a windswept wander. I would proffer the view that most successful creatives have managed to retain this instinct into adulthood. In his book *Wabi Inspirations*, interior designer and antique dealer Axel Vervoordt writes:

> *Ever since I was a boy, I have been enthralled by the beauty found in nature's artistry.*
> *My room was always filled with little treasures I had lovingly collected* – objets
> trouvés *from the forests, fields, or seashore. To this day, I still prize pebbles, rocks, or*
> *old pieces of wood almost as much as I value art. For me, stones are living souls with*
> *a spirit that resonates for millions of years.*

Spatial designer Robert Storey, who has built his career working with brands like Nike, Prada and Hermès, keeps a collection of pebbles and pinecones above his bed, which he has picked up on his travels over the past ten years. He says:

> *They all have meaning, they're really stunning, and they don't cost anything. These*
> *tiny ones I found only a few months ago when I was in the New Forest with my*
> *godson, who lives in Hong Kong. It was such a sweet day, and now it's lodged into*
> *my mind through that object. And then these little ones over here were picked up from*
> *a tree at the top of a hill in Sri Lanka when I was travelling on my own. The memory*
> *is so strong when I look at them.*

One of my favourite places in the world is Kettle's Yard in Cambridge, a collection of workers' cottages that was transformed into a home and gallery by the art collector Jim Ede between 1957 and 1973. Here, nature's bounty is treated with as much reverence as a picture by Winifred Nicholson or William Scott, challenging traditional notions of artistic value. Seeds, shells, stones and bones are scattered among the sculptures and oil paintings. In Ede's bedroom, pebbles are arranged in a spiral on a tabletop, their edges perfectly rounded by the swirling seas. He spent hours scanning the beaches of north Norfolk, and the artists Henry Moore, Barbara Hepworth and William Congdon all donated stones to his collection. Elsewhere in the house, nature has been allowed to merge with the pieces themselves: Henri Gaudier-Brzeska's *Bird Swallowing a Fish*, for example, stands on a piece of driftwood found in the Scilly Isles. Ede once put his infatuation powerfully into words:

> *I have always been fascinated by pebbles without, I think, ever asking myself why –*
> *in flowers, too, and shells. Such things have been for me a sudden contact with*
> *the miraculous.*

Why, you might ask, did Jim Ede find humble hunks of rock quite so wondrous? Why does Faye always say that stones are more precious than silver? And why did I recently feel the urge to drag the moss-covered skull of a deer back to the house and plonk it on the kitchen dresser? In 1964 the German-born American psychoanalyst and philosopher Erich Fromm coined the term 'biophilia', which comes from the Greek and means 'love of life and living things', and it was popularized by Edward O. Wilson with his book of the same name twenty years later. Wilson's biophilia hypothesis asserts that human beings have an instinctive sense of affinity with nature, and that we require contact with it in the same way that we need air to breathe.

One of the principles of biophilia is that rounded forms make us feel calmer than jagged ones. An experiment by Moshe Bar and Maital Neta found that looking at images of sharp-angled objects stimulated the amygdala, which is the part of the brain associated with fear. We perceive such forms as desolate and inorganic, whereas gentler geometry is suggestive of life. 'I am of the opinion that anyone who wants to rest his rear end on a rectangle adheres in his heart of hearts to a totalitarian creed,' said Josef Frank provocatively. At home, Faye and I live with many of her curvaceous furniture prototypes. The 'Roly Poly' chair, which was

conceived during her first pregnancy, has the stout ankles and swollen belly of an expectant mother, and the 'Fudge' chair lives up to its name with a meltingly smooth silhouette. In my experience, living with soft edges rather than sharp corners is a lot less anxiety-inducing as the kids fly past like whirling dervishes.

As well as curves, nature contains an abundance of fractals: patterns that repeat themselves as they get smaller or larger. If you look closely at a fern, for example, you will see that its leaves are built up from the same shape used over and over again. My personal favourite is the Romanesco broccoli, a bonkers brassica that looks like a cauliflower in a nightclub.

In the unnatural world, these patterns have been replicated in everything from Gothic cathedrals to Leonardo da Vinci's drawing *A Deluge*. Jackson Pollock's paintings are fractal. The artist spent much of his time sitting on the back porch, assimilating the shapes in the landscape, before wandering inside to splat paint on to yachting canvas. Might the popularity of his artworks be explained by their natural geometry? Physicist Richard Taylor decided to put this to the test. He invented a device called the 'Pollockizer', a rather grandiose term for a container of paint hanging from a string. Using a nozzle to adjust the amount of drip, Taylor produced a series of patterns, some of which had fractal geometry and some of which did not. When he surveyed 120 people to find out which they preferred, 113 of them chose the fractals.

Man has always sought to integrate fractals and spirals into the design of buildings. The column capitals of Ancient Egypt were based on the form of lotus leaves, while the Greeks were inspired by acanthus leaves and rams' horns. Mimicking nature's patterns within the home can make it feel alive and uplifting. You might create a handrail with the 'golden spiral' of a snail shell, for example, or a tiled floor with a fractal motif. Luke Edward Hall and Duncan Campbell have shown the way at their flat in Camden, incorporating candleholders shaped like pieces of coral, shell wall sconces, Staffordshire dogs and a lamp that looks like a fish. Using botanical prints in your interior is an easy way to borrow from nature. The designs of Josef Frank, for example, combine daisies, tulips, roses, forget-me-nots and lilies of the valley with flowers from his own imagination.

Laura Hunter is a self-confessed pattern fanatic, who explores her passion for heritage and artisanal wallpaper in the blog *No Feature Walls*. In one of the bedrooms at her cottage in Oxfordshire, a still-life painting of a vase of flowers is hung on a 'Strawberry Thief' wallpaper by William Morris, with its depictions of thrushes in a kitchen garden. Another bedroom is swathed in Morris's 'Blackthorn', which she has deliberately hung upside down:

> *The flowers are supposed to be facing upwards, according to the sample, but I like them better the other way around. They look a bit melancholy – that probably says something about my personality!*

My heart's in the savannah (ooh na-na)

For months after we moved to our house in the countryside, I followed the same morning routine. I would get up, put my wellies on and march out into the garden to take a photograph of the valley. I have hundreds of versions of the same image, taken from the identical angle. On some days, mist is thrown over the fields like a quilt, while on others, the sunlight catches the tree canopy. Sometimes a horse wanders into view in the neighbouring paddock, or a buzzard swoops in for its breakfast. It's like having access to my own Gainsborough, one that gets repainted every day.

Of course, an environmental psychologist will tell you that the view makes me feel good because it is an archetypal savannah landscape. If Ocado went on strike and I had to depend on the land for survival, I could find my way down to the river easily enough, and there are plenty of copses in which to take refuge from passing tigers. Fashion designer Jasper Conran has his own savannah-like view at his house in Dorset, out through a pair of gates and into gently rolling fields dotted with trees; judging by his Instagram account, he photographs it with the same gusto that I do mine.

Professors Rachel and Stephen Kaplan, who have led the way in researching nature's impact on human health, have demonstrated that the most favoured natural surroundings have a balance between mystery and legibility. We like little collections of trees and hedgerows, bending pathways and interlocking hillocks, but we also like to be able to see into the distance. Lily Bernheimer calls it 'a mystery we can solve'.

This probably explains why, in common with many other people, I find sculpture parks so beguiling. In a place like Château La Coste, the Louisiana Museum of Modern Art or the Yorkshire Sculpture Park, the thrill comes not simply from the artworks themselves but from plotting a way through a legible landscape to certain tantalizing waypoints. For someone with a growth mindset, this has a highly narcotic effect. The great English landscape architect Capability Brown recognized this, which is why he designed gently contoured hillsides punctuated with Italianate bridges.

If we were to visualize the diametric opposite of the African savannah or a Capability Brown garden, it might look something like Manhattan. There is little mystery or visual intrigue in its grid layout, no curving vistas to tempt you down or secret gardens to discover.

When you throw in the sound of traffic rattling off its hard surfaces, and the fumes hanging in the air, it is as stressful an environment for a human being as you could possibly imagine. Thankfully for the residents of New York, they have Central Park in which to find some respite, which is a near-perfect spot for hunter-gatherers, with abundant water sources, trees and long views of incoming threats (especially those 600-pound grizzly bears in the zoo). It is little surprise that apartments on the Upper East and Upper West Side are so sought after.

My own experience suggests that people will pay more for the privilege of a home with a decent view. Crescent House forms part of the Golden Lane Estate in the City of London, which was designed in the 1950s by Chamberlin, Powell & Bon, as a precursor to the Barbican. Flats on one side of the block look across a busy road to some dreary buildings opposite, while those on the other side – which have the same layout – sell for a lot more because they have open views, suffer from reduced noise and are less exposed to pollutants.

When our clients talk about what's important to them in a home, the sense of feeling connected to the shifting seasons is something that comes up time and again. Creative director Jethro Marshall describes the joy of living in harmony with nature at his mid-century house in Lyme Regis:

> If I had to choose a favourite thing, it would probably be the three acer trees at the bottom of the garden. They have really delicate leaves which put on an amazing colour show for six months of the year. Seasonality is a big part of this house. It combines a well-considered modern living space with a beautiful natural environment. It's the combination of those two elements, for us, that brings happiness to raising a family, working, living in a space, and so on. It's difficult now to imagine living without those two things: they've become integral to our personalities, interests and lifestyles.

Modern architecture has always concerned itself with views of nature. Mies van der Rohe's Farnsworth House, which is steadfastly rectilinear and framed in steel, appears at first sight to completely reject the natural world; however, it is lifted from the earth on dainty *pilotis*, and huge swathes of glazing implore the occupants to immerse themselves in the beauty of the gardens. Unfortunately the client, Dr Farnsworth, didn't quite see it that way. She sued Mies for breach of contract after concluding that the house was far too open. Having lost her lawsuit, she gave an interview to *House Beautiful*, which described it as 'a glass cage on stilts'.

Despite Dr Farnsworth's misgivings, the architectural influence of her house is inestimable. In the early 1990s the architect Jonathan Ellis-Miller used it as the inspiration for an equally rigorous and transparent studio for the artist Mary Reyner Banham, incongruously sited on a nondescript road in the Cambridgeshire Fens. We sold it to Doug and Maureen Chadwick, who set about converting it into a full-time residence. They say:

> *We have yet to discover a downside to living here. The peacefulness suits us both ideally. The full-height glazing on the south and west elevations, and the elevated floor, are amazing features to live with. We have a long-distance, uninterrupted view towards Ely Cathedral from the front of the house. Living here has just got better and more enjoyable with time.*

Instinctively, we seem to know that a good view improves our wellbeing, but it was proven scientifically by Roger Ulrich, Professor of Architecture at the Centre for Healthcare Building Research at Chalmers University of Technology in Sweden. He published a seminal article in *Science* entitled 'View through a Window May Influence Recovery from Surgery'. Post-operative patients in a Pennsylvania hospital who were assigned to a room with leafy views received fewer negative comments in nurses' notes, took fewer potent painkillers and were released from hospital earlier than those who were placed in similar rooms with windows facing a brick wall.

Developing his findings further, Ulrich proved that simple views of nature could also alleviate anxiety. A group of 120 people were sat down in front of a stressful movie (*Santa Claus Conquers the Martians*, perhaps?), and afterwards were shown images of either a natural or an urban setting. The former group had an improved cardiac response and recovered their composure more quickly.

What can we learn from this that we can apply practically? It's certainly not feasible for everyone to up sticks and move to the countryside, but we all deserve a room with a view. Think about that when you're trawling through the property listings. A client of ours has built up a small portfolio of buy-to-let flats around London. He has invested in all sorts of different locations and buildings, but the one thing he won't compromise on is the view: every one of them overlooks surrounding trees or communal gardens.

If we are fortunate enough to live somewhere with a decent view, are we making the most of it? As I'm writing this, I have shifted my desk a few inches to the left to be able to peer through a gap in the trees. Can you position your bed to allow for an uplifting glimpse of nature first thing in the morning? Much like we discussed in the Light section, keeping windows clear of curtains and blinds allows the full extent of the view to be appreciated. We would never dream of cutting off the edges of a landscape painting using a clunky frame, so why do it with the real thing? Windowsills should be low enough to enable views from a seated position, and to give children a share in the spoils.

For those who don't have access to a view of nature, the next best thing is to replicate it using imagery. At The Modern House office in London, our marketing team work alongside a huge photograph of mountains in Ladakh by Tobias Harvey. In the space next door, the sales team have a painted canvas by Andreas Eriksson, an abstracted patchwork of rock formations and trees inspired by the Swedish landscape.

A civilized wilderness

If I conjure up an image of my Grandpa Whiskers in my mind's eye, I see a relaxed, affable fellow pottering around in his garden in Harlow on a sunny day. He always had a trowel in his hand and a pipe between his lips, and he lingered beneath a cumulus of Three Nuns tobacco smoke. It was not uncommon for him to absent-mindedly drop his pipe into his coat pocket and set fire to himself.

'Smoking jackets' aside, Grandpa had a talent for landscape design that more than equalled his architectural proficiency. His garden, which is open to the public, remains one of his greatest legacies. For me as a toddler, it was a source of constant adventure. My brother and I would scuttle around the Neoclassical columns that he had salvaged from Nash's Coutts Bank on the Strand (to which he contributed a spectacular modern atrium in 1978) and play war games on the moated 'castle' that he built for us using elm logs.

A journalist once visited his house for an interview and caught Grandpa backing out of a border in his civvies. Mistaking him for the gardener, he enquired after Sir Frederick's whereabouts. Grandpa duly doffed his cap and told the man to carry on up the path and ring the bell, before hurtling through the kitchen entrance and opening the front door with a flourish and a grin.

Speaking on Radio 4's *Desert Island Discs*, he declared that tinkering in his garden was the only way in which he could 'design without using a drawing board'. He worked on it tirelessly, to the extent that it always looked effortless. Having moved to the countryside myself, I can completely relate to the idea of seeing out one's days surrounded by nature, gently developing the contours of the landscape.

The Sri Lankan architect Geoffrey Bawa felt the same impulse. In 1949 he bought an undistinguished rubber plantation near Bentota, called Lunuganga, and spent the next fifty years steadily transforming it into an extraordinary pleasure garden, inspired by the landscapes of eighteenth-century England and Renaissance Italy. New pavilions and statues were erected, hills moved, trees planted and terraces created, and the old estate road was buried within a ha-ha.

Many years ago, Faye and I were assigned to review a new hotel in Sri Lanka by a travel company, which gave us the excuse we had always needed to visit Lunuganga. Walking through the garden in the afternoon, we encountered a bird of paradise flitting between the lake and the branch of a tree like a yo-yo, and then came face to face with an enormous monitor lizard, which flicked its forked tongue at us menacingly. Later, gin and tonics were served on the terrace, and we watched birds of prey picking off bats in the twilight.

In his expansive survey of the work of Geoffrey Bawa, David Robson describes Lunuganga as: 'A composition in monochrome, green on green, an ever changing play of light and shade, a succession of hidden surprises and sudden vistas, a landscape of memories and ideas.' In my view, it is this kind of civilized wilderness that we should be aiming for in a rural environment, not a Versailles of flowers and fountains. The benefits of allowing nature to take the driving seat were eloquently outlined in the book *Wilding* by the author and environmentalist Isabella Tree (now there's a case of nominative determinism if ever there was one). At their country estate in West Sussex, Tree and her husband, Charlie Burell, embarked on a process of 'rewilding', and, in doing so, were staggered by the number of birds and insects that descended on them. She writes:

> *The summer of 2002 was a revelation. Every morning we woke up cradled in undulating prairie. From our windows, industrial farming had vanished. No excavated soil, no machinery, no serried ranks of arable, no fences. Returning the park to permanent pasture was more than a lifeline for the oak trees: it was proving a tonic for us. The land, released from its cycle of drudgery, seemed to be breathing a sigh of relief. And as the land relaxed, so did we . . . Most conspicuous of all was the ambient noise: the low-level surround-sound thrumming of insects – something we hadn't even known we'd been missing.*

By 2009, eight years after they began the shift from intensive farming to rewilding, ravens appeared on the estate for the first time in over a hundred years, and there were visits by many birds on the UK's Red List, including redwings, fieldfares and lesser redpolls.

According to the RSPB, there were forty million more birds in the UK in 1966 than there are today. Insects and other invertebrates have more than halved since 1970, butterflies have declined by 76 per cent and moths by 88 per cent. As increasing amounts of our green and pleasant land have been built upon or repurposed for fast-growing agriculture, our wildlife

population has dwindled. Building on their own positive experiences, Tree and Burrell have established the Rewilding Britain charity. Its goals are commendably ambitious: to restore at least a million hectares, or 4.5 per cent of the British Isles, and 30 per cent of our territorial waters, to wild nature over the next hundred years.

Faye and I have decided to make our own, very small contribution. Our paddock, which was previously an area of pastureland surrounded by electric post-and-rail fencing, has been scarified and seeded with wildflowers. We sought advice from an expert in countryside restoration, a wonderful man called Charles Flower (there you go again). The plan is to mow some gentle paths through the meadow, with clearings for the children to play in. We will also plant some more trees. Yale School of Forestry and Environmental Studies states that the world's tree population has fallen by some 46 per cent since the start of human civilization. According to the German forester Peter Wohlleben, trees have families and social networks just like we do. Well-established 'parents' use their canopies to deliberately prevent the sunlight from reaching their offspring down below, ensuring that the little ones develop slowly and that their trunks grow thick and strong – this is crucial if they are to survive high winds and attacks from fungi when they get taller. If a member of their community has fallen over, they will keep its stump alive for centuries afterwards by feeding it nutrients and sugars.

Tolkien's talking Ents might be the stuff of fantasy, but trees do actually communicate with each other using their own chemical vocabulary, emitting volatile compounds called phytoncides to attract insects, kill pests and deter predators. Scientists found that acacia trees on the African savannah release these compounds into the air when giraffes come to feed, warning their friends of an incoming threat so that they can mobilize their immune systems.

Remarkably, the human body can also decode this plant language, and it responds in a similar way by strengthening its defences. Forest air triggers the formation of natural killer cells, which prevent the development of cancer and fight pre-existing tumours. A study carried out by Professor Qing Li from the Nippon Medical School has shown that a day spent walking in nature increases the number of natural killer cells in the blood by an average of 40 per cent.

Trees and plants also stimulate the human endocrine system, reducing our stress hormones. This is especially impactful after rainfall, when the earthy scent of mushrooms fills our nostrils. As usual, the Japanese have it all figured out. The term *shinrin-yoku* translates as 'forest bathing', and involves simply spending time in the wilderness, connecting with nature through all of our senses. It is promoted by the National Institute of Public Health for Japan as a legitimate form of physical and mental healing.

More than two-thirds of the land in Japan is forested, which perhaps explains why the country has a respect for trees that we in the UK have yet to muster. The majority of our countryside is given over to arable land, where nature struggles to impose itself. As Peter Wohlleben explains:

> When we step into farm fields, the vegetation becomes very quiet. Thanks to selective breeding, our cultivated plants have, for the most part, lost their ability to communicate above or below ground. Isolated by their silence, they are easy prey for insect pests. This is one reason why modern agriculture uses so many pesticides. Perhaps farmers can learn from the forests and breed a little more wildness back into their grain and potatoes so that they'll be more talkative in the future.

We can all do our bit to establish new trees and care for those that we have. I still feel regretful about cutting down a willow many years ago that was stealing lots of light and turning our lawn into a bog, despite the fact that we planted several new trees. Nowadays, I am more accepting of nature's natural frailties and inconveniences. I have become strangely attached to the disfigured old mulberry in our garden, which has one of its limbs propped up like a prostrate hospital patient. Trees don't subscribe to our visions of perfection, and over-pruning them can lead to their eventual demise. If a large percentage of the crown is removed and the level of photosynthesis reduces, then a similar percentage of the root system starves. Meanwhile, fungi penetrate the dead ends where branches have been removed, attacking a tree from the inside.

We need to be aware that our built environment has a detrimental effect on the health of trees. Increasing air temperatures and rising levels of carbon dioxide from the burning of fossil fuels have significantly reduced their global population. Just like humans, trees and plants use light as a source of energy and information, and their own day–night cycle is disrupted by exposure to light pollution. Wohlleben cites an article in the German journal *Das Gartenamt*, which reported that 4 per cent of oak deaths in an American city occurred because the trees were subjected to too much electric lighting at night-time. Drawing the curtains and dimming the lights in our homes will help the natural world outside to have its well-earned rest.

Trees have lives that far exceed our own, and in some cases they live for many thousands of years. If we must build new structures, we should do our best to preserve nature's noble elders. The Bass House, for example, which was part of the Case Study programme in California, was built around a giant Italian pine that acted like a parasol to provide shade. Tree House by 6a Architects, a timber extension to a family house for the architecture critic Rowan Moore, cinches itself in to circumnavigate a sumac tree and breathes out again beneath a eucalyptus.

Kind of blue

During a particularly potent heatwave last summer, I awoke to the sort of syrupy atmosphere in which you have a straight choice between lying very still or immersing yourself in as much cold water as possible. Remaining motionless isn't an option when you have young children, so, dressed like a washed-up 1980s tennis player in absorbent terry towelling, I cajoled them into the car and drove to the most easily accessible body of moving water that I know: a tributary of the River Test. We arrived to find that several hundred other people had had the same idea. This most bucolic of locations, where it's usually just us and a herd of apathetic cattle, had been transformed into some kind of Spanish seaside resort. The banks were a sea of towels and picnic blankets, couples cavorted on inflatable flamingos, and naked children stabbed their fishing nets into the reeds. Even the cows were paddling steamily in the shallows, surveying their human companions beneath weary eyelids.

While some of this stretched the definition of respect as far as the environment is concerned, the sentiment was sound and the collective urge was clear. We have a magnetic attraction to water, hence why most of our communities are built close to it. When I lived in Highgate, I often went swimming in the bathing pond on Hampstead Heath, even on a chilly winter day, its murky depths proving a welcome distraction for my overloaded mind.

Empirical research into so-called 'blue health' lags behind other forms of environmental psychology, but it's clear that spending time in nature's rivers, lakes and oceans makes us feel better and reduces our stress levels. Roger Ulrich's experiment with green views in the 1980s was replicated by a team from the European Centre for Environment and Human Health at the University of Exeter, who showed photographs of a variety of landscapes to a group of participants, but this time introducing aquatic elements. Scenes containing water were associated with higher preferences, greater positive effect and higher perceived restorative qualities than those without. Interestingly, images of urban areas containing water were rated just as positively as natural 'green' space.

Expanding on these findings, the team used data from Natural England to establish that the closer you live to the coast, the healthier you tend to be. This goes some way to explaining why houses by the sea tend to command a premium. We sold my parents' house, for example, which has views across an estuary to the English Channel, for 25 per cent more than the asking price. The same is true in urban areas, where homes beside a canal or river are always more sought-after.

When Patrick Michell of Platform 5 Architects decided to build himself a holiday home, he was driven by the desire to find a site with a waterside setting rather than one by a fixed area. He settled on a secluded lagoon in the Norfolk Broads, raising the house above the waterline and allowing floodwater to flow beneath its timber deck. He explains the positive influence that weekend visits have on his family's collective wellbeing:

We come up on a Friday evening after rush hour and put the kids to bed – they fall asleep in the car! We'll wake up, have breakfast, and then fill our day with things like canoeing, going to the beach, watching seals in winter, swimming, venturing down the coast, pub lunches and hiring boats. Sometimes we go for a paddle as the sun sets over the Broads. For me, that's what this house is all about. Coming in here, it's almost like a meditative experience. You're surrounded by nature and feel cleansed by the time you have to leave. You almost have to remember to start thinking again!

It is this sense of getting away from it all, of being at the outer reaches of a land-mass with nothing much to do except potter around, that enables the human brain to truly decompress. Architect Paul Scrivener describes the state of mindfulness he is able to reach when he visits his coastal home in Anderby, Lincolnshire:

A friend of mine once said, 'How do you get to Anderby Creek? You go to the end of the world and keep going for half an hour!' Other than reading, painting, cooking and generally just chilling out, there isn't a whole lot more to do here. I put a studio in the garden, so I go out there to paint, but it would be a great place to write or just relax. It's all about communing with nature, and having my dogs is great because I take them for walks on the beach and in the Lincolnshire Wolds. If I get here on a Friday afternoon, I feel like I've had a week-long holiday in the space of a weekend.

There are things we can all do to incorporate water into our everyday lives. The majority of off-the-shelf water features are unutterably ghastly (urinating Classical cupids, anyone?),

but a body of water that is carefully integrated into the structure of a terrace can be a very fine thing, generating reflections and attracting glittering dragonflies.

We had a pond in our garden when I was a child – my dad decided to build it on a sloping patch of ground, so that one end was always exposed. We had a lot of fun filling it with tadpoles and watching the frogs leaping about. You can make a simple pond from an old plant pot, disused sink or a washing-up bowl, and it's amazing how even the most modest body of water will start to attract wildlife: newts and freshwater shrimp will take up residence, birds will use it as a lido, and water boatmen will conduct furious rowing races on its surface. Simon Barnes writes:

> An Englishman's home is his castle; but a castle is nothing without a moat. A little water defines the place, makes sense of it, adds a richness to everything all around. A pond is the centre of the stage; the garden's focal point, drawing the eye, bringing in many other living things. More than that: it's a statement of what a garden is for. Once you have a pond, it's a sign that you have abnegated some of your sovereignty. The garden is not there to show off your gardening skills: it's there to gratify a far deeper level of human pleasure. The garden is not for humans first and foremost and always and only; it's for every living thing that might find the place of use.

In his modest town garden in Queen's Park, Jonathan Tuckey has created a plunge pool in which to cool off on a hot day. The water is fed from a tap in the kitchen and channelled along a gulley to the outside, and his children enjoy floating model boats down it. He explains:

> London has got to be one of the best places on earth – its diversity, its richness is so energizing. But sometimes, in urban architecture, you can be somewhat alienated from your core senses. We were very keen to make sure that those elemental aspects of life, of our planet, were brought right into the house.

One of those senses, of course, is hearing. Aside from stimulating our bladders, which can be somewhat inconvenient, the sound of moving water tends to put us into a relaxed state. This is probably because, for our ancestors, it would have been an auditory signal that sustenance was nearby. Moving water can also be a very helpful tool in filtering out the noise of a busy road or aircraft overhead. Using galvanized metal gutters and downpipes instead of plastic, or even simple rain chains, amplifies the orchestral thrum of raindrops during a deluge.

When I was growing up, we spent many holidays at a converted sailing school on stilts in Norfolk, which had the upturned hull of a boat as its front door. The walls were adorned with old sailing ropes, buoys, fishing reels and a twenty-pound pike in a box – you were never in any doubt about your connection to the water. Children's bathrooms are an obvious place in which to have fun, and a wallpaper with fish motifs or some tiles hand-painted with newts or ducks can conjure up the spirit of an aquatic environment. Painting the walls of a house in natural colours is also an easy win: try a splash of ultramarine to help ward off the blues.

At a base level, we can all resolve to have more showers. I recently had a genetic test, which revealed a predisposition towards dementia. My prescription? A cold shower every day and three wild swims a week. Cold water wakes up our immune systems and provides a boost for our white blood cells. It also burns calories, activates endorphins and is thought to improve levels of the sex hormones testosterone and oestrogen. Standing in the shower is the closest thing we have to immersing ourselves in the ocean waves, the steady stream of 'blue noise' removing us from the visual overstimulation of the day.

For a shower to be truly effective, it needs to thud against the skin with an element of force – imagine a Scandinavian woman standing beneath a waterfall in an advert for conditioner. It requires an effective thermostatic mixer tap and decent water pressure, which means installing a pump if necessary. There are few things bleaker than a dribbly shower head. If you have enough room, it is preferable to incorporate the design of the shower into the bathroom in a coherent way, surrounding it with bespoke glass panels, perhaps leaving one side of it open, and making sure that the drain is seamless with the floor. Stepping into an off-the-peg plastic cubicle doesn't hold quite the same appeal.

If a cold shower in the morning is nature's equivalent of an iced coffee, then an evening bath is its mug of steaming Bovril. A friend of mine spends several hours in his tub every weekend, daydreaming, reading books and allowing the heat to penetrate his brain cells, before finally emerging with the wrinkled complexion of a Shar-Pei dog. Bathing is a ritual that's taken very seriously throughout the world: in Bali they submerge themselves in water strewn with flowers; the Japanese congregate in geothermally heated *onsens*; and the Ayurvedic Indians marinate themselves in milk (is this how cottage cheese was invented?).

Placing the bathtub in the middle of the room is an act of generosity that resolutely defines its purpose. You might even decide to raise it up symbolically on a plinth, like a royal throne or ancient sarcophagus. As discussed in the Light section, the bathroom should always be dimly lit to allow the mind to unwind. If you are brave enough, you might even consider following Jonathan Tuckey's lead by omitting artificial lighting altogether. He explains:

> *We had visited Japan in the early stages of designing our house. The importance they place on bathing was really inspiring – it's something that we all do every day, but it has somehow been overlooked and buried away into slightly sterile spaces. So we didn't put any lighting in the family bathroom, to try and make bathing a more celebrated and heightened experience, forcing us to light candles in there. For the last twenty years, it has always been candle-lit.*

The Ritalin of nature

One of the main reasons Faye and I decided to move out of London is that, despite the good fortune of having a big garden, our house was situated just off an arterial road, with buses and lorries thundering past. Indigo developed 'viral-induced wheeze', a respiratory condition similar to asthma, and we were regular visitors to Accident & Emergency. On each visit, she shared a hospital ward with many other pre-school children, all puffing away on ventilators and high as kites on salbutamol.

If we're honest, her behaviour wasn't great either. Might this have been, at least to some extent, environmental? The nursery she attended was unquestionably brilliant in terms of teaching and care, but it didn't have any outside space to speak of. Not even a tuft of grass between two paving slabs. Equipment such as slides and bikes had to be set up inside, and a few times a week the kids would be loaded on to a bus and driven to a small garden square for half an hour of outside play (on condition that the teachers had eaten their biscuits, the wind was blowing gently from the south, and the mustachioed man in a trench coat wasn't shouting at the pigeons).

Patrik Grahn, Professor of Environmental Psychology at the Swedish University of Agricultural Sciences, has shown that kids need contact with nature for their physical and mental development. He carried out a study that compared children in two contrasting kindergartens, one with a paved playground surrounded by high-rise buildings, and the other located amid woods and meadows. Those who were able to play in nature exhibited better physical coordination and significantly improved levels of concentration.

American author and journalist Richard Louv refers to the 'Ritalin of nature', because of its abilities to regulate behaviour. In his book *Last Child in the Woods: Saving Our Children From Nature-Deficit Disorder*, he argues that a childhood deprived of physical contact with the natural world contributes to depression and attention disorders. As Isabella Tree points out:

> *Measurements of blood pressure, pulse rates and cortisol levels of young adults demonstrate a decrease in anger and an increase in positive mood when walking in a nature reserve, while the reverse is true walking in an urban environment. Low*

levels of self-discipline, impulsive behaviour, aggression, hyperactivity and inattention in young people all improve through contact with nature. Studies on children who were being bullied, punished, relocated or suffering from family strife all showed that they benefitted from closeness to nature, both in levels of stress and self-worth.

Spending time outside sparks a child's imagination and helps to heal any mental wounds they may be carrying around. It also encourages them to assess risks, solve problems and develop creativity. Watching Wren and Etta creating a fairy garden or tottering around collecting twigs, it is clear to me that they are operating on instinct. They have an impulse to take their shoes off and go barefoot, connecting them to the earth and allowing them to feel its natural textures. Admittedly, they spend quite a lot of their time beheading our favourite flowers, but at least they're breathing in some clean air while they do it. Rachel and Steven Kaplan talk about the 'effortless fascination' provided by nature, the way in which it engages us without the need for conscious thought.

Depressingly, a survey in the UK found that 74 per cent of children spend less time outdoors than prison inmates. Therefore, we must give them as many excuses as we can to get out into nature. In my experience, making sure that you have the right kit is half of the battle. Our kids are generally happy to venture into the garden on a rainy day because they have wellies, proper waterproof coats and fleece-lined dungarees with stirrup straps that stop the legs from riding up. When we go on local walks, we carry our sandwiches in metal mess tins, inside a fully waterproof backpack. We have gloves for snowball fights, pull-on water shoes for paddling in the river and dry robes for warming up afterwards.

If you have toddlers, a magnifying glass in the Christmas stocking can buy you at least ten minutes of peace as they go on the hunt for ants, woodlice, worms and beetles. They will enjoy working with you to build a bug hotel, gathering up logs, dry leaves and velvety carpets of moss (sure, it will end up looking more like the Bates Motel than the Four Seasons, but the chances are they won't notice). For older children, a pair of binoculars and a book about birds or butterflies encourages them to really observe the natural world around them. Even a cheap football can be a very fine investment: when I was a boy, we spent virtually every waking hour of every weekend playing 'Wembley' in the garden.

Cobbling together a treehouse or erecting a tepee gives kids their own defensible space, and our daughters can spend hours in a sandpit or a paddling pool with a colander and a wooden spoon. We've also given them their own patch of earth, some seeds and a little gardening set, including some child-sized trowels and a watering can. Much like looking after a beloved family pet, growing plants teaches children about responsibility and how to care for living things. By exposing them to the magic of nature from an early age, we can create a new generation of human beings who have nothing but respect for the environment. After all, they are its future custodians.

The architect Sally Mackereth deliberately sought out a *Swallows & Amazons* existence when she converted a lighthouse in Norfolk into a weekend retreat for her family. She explains:

> *What I really noticed was that raising children in London, I was nostalgic for a childhood that I had, which wasn't about being ferried around to play dates, sports centres and activities. People with young children fill their weekends with doing things, and I think it's very important to just be, rather than do. The interesting thing about being here is that everyone finds a place to just be. And, while city life doesn't get completely forgotten, it's relaxing to throw on a sweatshirt with holes in it, stick your wellies on and wander on the beach to look at the seals. We do things here that we just don't do in London, like picking fruit and making jam, which has now become a tradition.*

Indeed, families tend to work together when they are in the garden. Some of my own vivid childhood memories involve shelling peas with my mum and making bonfires with my dad.

Babies, with their endless cycles of feeds and naps, often don't spend as much time in the open air as they should. Being outside helps to develop their motor skills, stimulates their learning, helps ward off illnesses and establishes their circadian rhythm. Many parents I know have adopted a Scandinavian mindset, and park their pram in a safe place outside for the afternoon nap.

Shortly after Indigo was born, we took an ill-advised holiday to Andalusia. As anxious first-time parents, we packed everything except the Smeg, and I had a meltdown at the

Ryanair check-in desk after being charged £300 for a suitcase full of wet wipes and formula milk. When we finally reached our rental house, we discovered that it was just like being at home, except a lot hotter and a lot harder. Our days were spent blearily careening around the supermarket, preparing meals, washing up, changing nappies and, mostly, trying to stop our baby from wailing. And then, a few days in, we noticed a beautiful mature olive tree in a corner of the garden. I picked Indigo up and parked her on a sheepskin in the dappled shade cast by its branches. She stopped crying, her pupils widened, and she gazed up into its complex canopy, cooing contentedly and kicking her legs. Faye and I lay down beside her, and, to the soundtrack of birdsong and the gentle rustling of leaves, dropped into a life-giving afternoon nap. Not for the first time, nature had saved us.

Decoration

'A decorator has to have a feel for a house's personality and try not to fight against it. I like to get the juice out of a house and not spoil it.'
Nancy Lancaster

I was ten years old when I realized that our house might not be like other people's. One morning, I went downstairs as usual to remove my palate with a searingly hot Pop Tart, and there on the table was a picture of our family bathroom, gaudily arranged across the pages of a book about interior design. The floor was covered in red rubber tiles – those ones with raised anti-slip discs on them – which continued up the sides of the free-standing bath. The taps, blind and door furniture were all picked out in matching crimson. On the wall beside the sash window was a cardboard cut-out of Superwoman, her legs arranged in a position of supreme compromise.

Inspired by Jocasta Innes and the eighties spirit of DIY decoration, my mum spent several days with a sponge and a brush faux-marbling the entrance hall, so that it resembled Stilton cheese. In the dining room, floor-to-ceiling shelves flexed under the weight of hundreds of toast racks: a mixture of sterling-silver, Spode creamware and Art Deco ceramic examples with gold edges. When he came to visit in our teenage years, Albert referred to the house as 'the toast-rack museum'. It wasn't like anybody else's place, and we loved it for that. And then, one day in the mid-1990s, my parents sold it to Clive Anderson, the dry-witted man from the telly.

We moved to another nineteenth-century terraced house nearby, and by this stage I was obsessed with interior decoration. I helped my dad to create a teenagers' lair in the basement. At the foot of the staircase, we exposed the original barrel vaults and left the walls as bare render, with an orange-and-shocking-pink curtain at the end to draw the eye through. A Habitat sofa was drafted in alongside some family heirlooms, including a 'Wassily' chair and a vintage fruit machine. We wedged a little shower room into a corner of the bedroom, with a curved wall like a pocket on a snooker table. The only thing on my Christmas list that year was a Philippe Starck mixer tap.

When my first job selling makeovers over the telephone didn't really work out, I realized that I should try to combine my passions for design and writing. Albert had managed to bag himself a job as Editorial Assistant at the architecture magazine *Blueprint*, which seemed to me the very summit of cool. Armed with a betting-shop biro and a notebook, I went to the newsagent and scribbled down the name of the Editor-in-Chief of every glossy magazine with a room on the cover. I then wrote a begging letter to each: 'Dear Mr Brûlé', 'Dear Ms Crewe', and so on. At the top of the masthead in *The World of Interiors* was the puzzling name

Min Hogg. 'Is that a man or a woman?' I asked Albert. 'Just write "Dear Min Hogg",' he advised.

In the event, it was Rupert Thomas who invited me for an interview. Impeccably attired in a tweed jacket and Vivienne Westwood bondage trousers, he explained that he was just taking over as Editor and could use all the help he could get. For the first few months I spent a lot of time fetching provisions from Vogue House's diminutive canteen, 'The Hatch', where a mustachioed Portuguese called Tony slathered margarine on to toast with practised bonhomie. But once Rupert gave me my first writing assignment, I never looked back, thanks largely to his generosity and mentorship. My understanding of good taste was challenged constantly, especially the day that my new business cards arrived: urine-yellow lettering on a poo-brown background.

Writing for a magazine is strange, because you rarely get any feedback from readers unless you've made a blunder. I once received a handwritten letter of complaint from the art historian Sister Wendy Beckett after a misjudged comment, and Rei Kawakubo was understandably miffed when I got the address of her new Comme des Garçons store wrong. However, when an antique rooster came up for sale one month, no one seemed to notice when I wrote, 'Get your hands on a gleaming gold cock' in the auction listings. Even when using 'fowl language', one rarely had the sense of being able to shift public opinion.

And yet the best interiors magazines have always managed to influence the way we live. In the 1950s *House & Garden* developed its own colour range, which was updated annually and persuaded people that a fresh lick of paint 'not only delights the eye, but raises the spirit and challenges the imagination'. In the 1980s *The World of Interiors* burst on to the scene like feathers from an overstuffed cushion, extolling the virtues of peeling paint and shabby-chic furniture. The following decade Tyler Brûlé's *Wallpaper* magazine showed us how to live the Scandinavian urban dream. More recently we've gorged ourselves on the louche and flash-lit interiors of *Apartamento*, then buttoned up our shirt collars in the carefully curated world of *Kinfolk*.

Certain product designs have also helped to define an era. I will always remember the 1990s, for example, as the age of Philippe Starck's rocket-like lemon squeezer and the brightly coloured Apple iMac. A visit to the fabulous Museum of the Home (formerly the Geffrye Museum), which displays life-sized mock-ups of interiors from different points throughout history, shows how aesthetics change and certain ways of living come and go. Nowadays we are presented with a bewildering bundle of styles and products to choose from, and it feels like we have experienced every conceivable movement and anti-movement. In the end, good design is timeless. It is also deeply personal. Whether we choose to live minimally or maximally, we should think about the emotional resonance of our decisions, and educate ourselves about the past so that we may create something that is distinctly our own.

Adding colour

From a decoration perspective, the first step towards personalizing the home is to add some colour. Like so many issues that we face these days, the dilemma of what to choose is complicated by the overwhelming array of choices on offer. Early man did not suffer from this problem, as the Danish urban planner Steen Eiler Rasmussen explained in his book *Experiencing Architecture*:

> *Man used the materials which Nature supplied and which experience taught him were strong and serviceable. The walls of his dwelling might be of hard-packed mud dug up on the building site or of stones gathered nearby. To these he added twigs, withes and straw. The result was a structure in nature's own colours, a human dwelling which, like a bird's nest, was an integral part of the landscape. Primitive man decorated his neutral-coloured wooden cot or adobe hut by festooning it with garlands of flowers or by covering the grey walls with coloured fabrics. Thus he sought to improve on the rawness of nature, just as he might hang colourful ornaments on his sun-tanned body.*

Clay ochre was the first pigment used by humans, and is still visible in the dramatic depictions of animals in prehistoric cave paintings. Earthy tones were the order of the day for many thousands of years, until the Egyptians invented blue. They believed it to be the hue of the heavens, and it is still the most popular colour used in interior decoration. All of the colours we live with now have a long-standing meaning. Tyrian purple was affordable only for the elite during Antiquity, and its regal significance has endured – Queen Elizabeth I forbade anyone from wearing it except close members of the royal family. Red has been synonymous with courage ever since Roman soldiers wore crimson tunics, and yellow is associated with the divine power of the sun.

Given the choices we have and the array of connotations to consider, it is best to use the attributes of the building as a starting point. Correctly used, colour can unlock its natural character and spirit. If you have decorative features like panelling, cornices, fire surrounds or old doors, use tonal changes to emphasize them. At our Georgian house in Islington, Faye and I decorated the joinery in inky-blue and aubergine gloss paint from Emery & Cie, to bring out the richness and integrity of the original architecture. When we got to our Modernist house in Highgate, we realized that only a neutral palette would work with the simple lines and humble materials of the building. Every surface of our Victorian flat in Winchester was painted in Farrow & Ball's 'Cornforth White' – including the ceilings, skirtings, cupboards and kitchen cabinets – because the height of the rooms and absence of decorative mouldings or cornicing seemed to warrant a single treatment.

The next thing to think about is the movement of the sun, because natural light has a significant impact on the way a colour feels. Rasmussen points out that Johannes Vermeer's studio had a northern exposure, giving his paintings a cool, blue light, whereas the warmth of Pieter de Hooch's pictures was dictated by the afternoon glow in his west-facing room. Using a neutral tint in a south-facing room will reflect the light and create an uplifting environment, whereas warm tones can rescue the insipid atmosphere of a north-facing room. A dining room can be dark and sultry, and is one of the few rooms in the house that works well in red, the colour of romance. Try a gloss ceiling, which will dance in the candlelight.

The kitchen is a daytime room, and should feel bright and buoyant. The colours of nature work well in bedrooms because of their calmness. Light levels vary significantly even within the various parts of an individual room, so I recommend ordering some sample pots of your preferred paints and trying them out in different areas – beside the window, above the mantelpiece, and so on. Assess them at various times of the day, as they will look very different depending on the cloud cover and intensity of light.

In general, light colours tend to bring big rooms to life, and dark colours enhance the intimacy of small ones. Our dining room at home is painted in gloss ochre, giving it a primordial and cosy atmosphere, especially when the wood-burner is ablaze. You can afford to be a bit more daring in the spaces that are used less, like spare bedrooms and cloakrooms. We have covered the walls of our entrance hall in a wallpaper designed by Faye, which depicts a panoramic landscape scene that she painted herself in sooty blacks and deep browns. The gnarly oak floor and the smell of chopped logs leaves you in no doubt that you are in a country house. As you come off the dark hallway, the kitchen and sitting room seem much bigger and brighter than they otherwise would. We have used red-based neutrals rather than blue-based

ones so that they don't feel jarring. Indeed, using the same family of colours throughout the home leads to a much more cohesive result. In my view, floors can afford to be dark, as it helps to anchor the room, but ceilings should always be painted in a light colour – a dark ceiling makes it feel like the sky is falling in.

Not long ago, I paid a visit to Rosa Park, editor of *Cereal* magazine, and her husband, Rich Stapleton, whose wonderfully pared-back photographs of architecture and landscape have helped to define the magazine's refined aesthetic. Their gallery and office space in Bath is a serene sequence of rooms that hangs together beautifully because of the careful gradation of warm neutrals (or what Rosa self-deprecatingly calls 'shades of beige'). When I asked Rich which colour he used in a particular area, he started digging out endless pots of paint from different manufacturers, each specially chosen to account for the aspect, light and materiality of the room.

The Italian artist Alessandra Taccia paints still-lifes of bottles, jugs and mugs in creams and greys and washed-out greens, and she prefers to live with a similarly restrained palette at home. She says:

> *I believe that colours have a voice. Strong colours have a really loud voice, so for me it's a lot of distraction. The colours in this house are very gentle – they don't seek attention at all. When people come round, they relax and feel really at ease. They feel like they can be themselves.*

We all have our own personal preferences around colour, defined by the homes we grew up in and the clothes we wear to suit our natural complexions. I tend to gravitate towards cooler colours – our walls at home were usually painted in standard-issue architect's white, and my skin is fair and freckled, so I quickly learnt that certain warm colours make me look like a gingerbread man. Raising identical twins is like conducting some kind of extended social experiment, and even at the age of three Wren and Etta have developed their own preferred palettes. Wren has a cool complexion, and her favourite colour is blue; Etta has a warmer skin tone, and is obsessed with pink. Is this nature or nurture? Since the day they were born, we have dressed them differently so that friends and family can tell them apart.

Richard Rogers has always dressed like his buildings, and it is interesting to note that his son, Ab Rogers, has adopted the same primary palette. Albert has a fondness for these bold hues, as well as a weakness for browns and oranges. Perhaps this is why we have been judicious in our use of colour when it comes to The Modern House: on our website; in our marketing material; in our offices – because we recognize that everyone has their own viewpoint. If there is a colour that we are both drawn to, which sits in the middle of our Venn diagram, it is a dusty, dirty pink, the colour of dried plaster.

The artist John Booth inhabits a space that is as boldly variegated as his work, a happy arrangement of graphic textiles, yellow walls, and pieces by Vernon Panton and Ettore Sottsass, held together by a colour scheme derived from childhood nostalgia and Italian Postmodernism. He explains:

> It's a rented house, which means there are some limits on what I can do, but my landlords are pretty chilled and like what I've done . . . I love colour, and I think I always have. In my head, colour is linked to childhood memories, a lot of which are based on logos and motifs of clothes I liked. I've got a twin sister, so we shared clothes quite a bit – we had lots of yellow and green things.

Designer Yinka Ilori is equally comfortable around brilliant colour, which he uses in both his work and his spaces as a form of memory:

> As a kid, I saw my parents wear colourful garments to weddings, churches and celebrations, so using colour makes me think of happy times. It's an extension of my identity because Nigerians love colour, and I want to express and celebrate that in my work.

This predilection for primaries betrays a fun-loving spirit that harks back to childhood colour preferences. Young children are drawn to bold colours in their early years, because their eyes are still developing, and they stand out more in their field of vision. However, this quickly changes, and it has been interesting to watch how Indigo's tastes have shifted over the years: by the age of six, she disclosed a preference for black and, perhaps inevitably, indigo. In fact, our reactions to colour continue to develop throughout our lives. My dad did a lot of painting in his spare time, and his canvases became noticeable brighter and more vivid in his later years. In her book *Biophilia*, author Sally Coulthard explains:

> *Adults tend to have a strong liking for colours in short wavelengths – such as blues and greens – and have much less preference for the longer wavelength, warm colours such as reds, oranges and yellows. In our sixties and beyond, our preference then seems to revert back to our childhood favourites – the bright, primary colours, possibly a function of physical changes in our eyes and how we perceive colour in later life.*

Our impression of a particular colour is affected by its 'chroma', or vividness. A heavily saturated version with a high chroma will make us feel stimulated, whereas a washed-out version has a more calming influence. Regardless of where your preferences sit within the colour wheel, consider using less intense versions that are representative of those found in the landscape and build upon our biophilic preferences: the green of the sea on an overcast day; the grey of a craggy rockface; the quiet yellow of sand.

We often think of Modernism as a monochromatic movement, but that's partly because we are so used to looking at black-and-white photographs. You only have to consider the balconies at Le Corbusier's Unité d'Habitation to appreciate how its leading exponents embraced the use of colour. Corb felt it was 'a means as powerful as the ground plan and section', and went so far as to develop his own tool for architectural colour design, the *Polychromie*, in which sixty-three different hues are arranged in rows like keyboards in wonderfully unexpected combinations. Luis Barragán famously used planes of cobalt-blue, sunshine-yellow and flamingo-pink to create pictorial depth and dramatically enhance the contrast of light and shade.

I have a book by Duncan Miller entitled *More Colour Schemes for the Modern Home*, which is old enough that the colour plates have been glued in rather than printed. One of the homes featured is a London flat designed by Serge Chermayeff, in which the neutral palette of ivory walls, natural wool rugs and a walnut partition are in service to the colourful canvas by Christopher Wood above the fireplace. In this case, the painting provides a concentrated burst of colour that doesn't overwhelm.

In other cases, a favourite artwork might be used as the sounding-off point for a room's palette. Personally, I use fine art as the visual inspiration for almost everything. When thinking about how the branding for The Modern House might look, for example, I was inspired by the paper collages of Eduardo Chillida and the paintings of Richard Serra; for Inigo, it was the landscapes of Paul Nash and George Stubbs's muscular horses.

Painting the inside of a cupboard in a deliberately jarring hue always provides a licentious thrill. The upside of using concentrated pops of colour is that we can easily redecorate the furniture or swap out the object, if our tastes change and we get bored by them. Using them in a more wholesale way is a difficult thing to get right, as Duncan Miller amusingly describes:

> *I once heard of somebody in charge of a regimental mess during the war who produced, as a tour de force, a meal in which everything looked like a poached egg. One course was indeed a poached egg, another half a tomato upside down on mashed potatoes, and the sweet was half an apricot on rice. Presumably they all tasted different, but one can imagine the feeling of nausea by the end of the meal. That is the kind of mistake that can be made in a colour scheme by somebody who is not sure of what he is doing.*

This reminds me of a 'Henry Ford' dinner we held at Albert's house in our early twenties, where the guests could eat anything they liked so long as it was black. Russian rye bread, squid-ink risotto and black-velvet cupcakes were among the macabre morsels on offer. We didn't have the décor to go with it, sadly, but black paint can sometimes be a very fine thing, especially if it is used to accentuate the diminutive proportions of a larder or loo.

The importance of pattern and texture

Most of us can visualize the patterns from our childhood homes. For me, it's a checked oil cloth on the dining table, the bergère sofa with its meticulous marquetry, and curtains with daisies on them that hovered just above the floor. Patterns can make a small room seem bigger, or a bland room come to life. They can generate mind-boggling optical illusions like Bridget Riley paintings. See what happens, for example, if you lay square black-and-white floor tiles in a staggered formation rather than in straight lines – the eye starts to bend them out of shape. In an interiors project she did in Notting Hill, Faye laid the ceramic floor tiles in a chevron pattern but used a contrasting colour in the high-impact areas of the house – in front of the bathroom basins; around the kitchen island – in a witty riff on the ageing process. Anyone who has paraded across the marble courtyard at Versailles or admired their reflection in the golden mirrors of the City Palace in Udaipur is aware of the emotional power of a heavily patterned surface. Terence Conran, who advocated a contemporary way of life with a respect for the past, considered pattern to be a fundamental contributor to the success of any interior. He wrote:

> As subtle as the self-coloured design of a damask cloth or as bold as a sofa layered in Oriental textiles, pattern transforms our appreciation of colour and texture, adding rhythm and movement, intrinsically suggestive of order and repose. A well-balanced print is a good way of living with the intensity of strong colour and an excellent mediating influence between strong shapes and plain surfaces.

At Conran's country house in Berkshire, patterned floor tiles ushered you through the entrance hall; a decidedly stripped-back bedroom was enlivened by a red-and-white-striped bedspread; and in the living room, a faded Oriental rug with a pile of cushions on top of it implored you to lie down by the fire. To live without texture is to risk denying our natural instincts, as Lily Bernheimer explains:

> Environments devoid of neurologically nourishing information mimic signs of human pathology. For example, colourless, drab, minimalist surfaces and spaces

reproduce clinical symptoms of macular degeneration, stroke, cerebral achromatopsia,
and visual agnosia.

Textile designer Eleanor Pritchard creates blankets, cushions and upholstery fabrics that render twentieth-century references, such as early television technology, radio waves and Art Deco design, into geometric shapes and textural flourishes. All of her designs first take shape on her peg-and-lag dobby loom in her Deptford studio, before going into production at mills in west Wales, Lancashire or the west coast of Scotland. She says:

> *You might think, why are blankets relevant to modern living? Why does anybody need one if we have thick duvets and central heating? But there's something very primeval about getting out a blanket and wrapping yourself with it, or putting it on your bed – there are nurturing, homely connotations associated with blankets. They also feel both timeless and yet very ancient to me – they seem to hold a lot of cultural and emotional symbolism. I recently inherited a blanket which has been handed down in my family from a forebear's wedding trousseau from 1842 – a beautiful double-cloth pattern in indigo blue and white. It is 178 years old now and still feels completely relevant.*

In her own home, Pritchard uses textiles sparingly. She likes the contrast that they provide with hard materials: a napkin on a wooden table, for example, or curtains against concrete. She prefers to see the structure of a chair rather than the whole thing being upholstered, so that there is a juxtaposition of materials. You can replicate this approach by placing a simple rug on a hard floor.

Personally, I prefer rugs to fitted carpets, which are liable to make a room look like an executive suite just off the North Circular. Natural floor coverings such as sisal and jute often look better if they are loose-laid, with a 50-centimetre gap between the edging and the wall. In our sitting room at home, we have used an expanse of woven water reed, placing it on top of the dark-stained floorboards to provide texture, warmth and a colour that references the landscape outside. In the master bathroom, a rug made of natural rush happily imbibes the drips from an overfilled tub, while on the stairs, a runner absorbs the sound of heavy footsteps and provides a visual link between the two storeys.

Using floor coverings in this way doesn't prevent you from adding a more graphic rug on top. Indeed, many people take a much more Maximalist approach to textiles, layering them like a pastry chef making millefeuille. The legendary English decorator David Hicks pioneered the use of pattern on pattern, declaring that it gave a room 'guts and distinction'. Lucinda Chambers, founder of Collagerie and erstwhile fashion director of British *Vogue*, is another who is able to combine chevrons, checks and stripes with great dexterity. At her holiday house in the south of France, the seating is scattered with jumbles of cushions in contrasting motifs, and colourful straw hats are hung on the walls like a form of decoration. She told me that her use of textiles is about generating comfort rather than an outward demonstration of taste – she always provides a blanket on a sofa, for example, so that a guest can pull it over themselves if they get cold. The hats have been accumulated from gatherings of family and friends that have taken place over many years; each time someone revisits, they take their chosen headpiece off the wall and wear it for the duration of their stay.

We can all take inspiration from Lucinda by employing textiles as a form of collage: placing rugs in differing sizes to fill the redundant spaces around a bed, for example, or a perfectly proportioned Asafo flag above a fireplace. Using textiles for wall decoration instead of paintings or photographs often gives a more nuanced effect, and is usually a lot cheaper, too. We live with some of Faye's tapestries, which are digitally printed on wool and cotton, and up to 3 metres wide. I love looking at the intricacies of their abstract shapes, but they also provide a texture and warmth that you don't get from a flat canvas. Albert has some pieces by the American artist Alice Adams, who learnt traditional Aubusson techniques and then subverted them by adding surface articulation and found objects to her 'woven forms'.

Chintz has enjoyed something of a renaissance in recent years. The aforementioned Min Hogg, founding editor of *The World of Interiors*, had a self-confessed weakness for the stuff:

> *From their origins in sixteenth-century India to the present day, examples of repeat floral patterns on furnishing materials have me in their thrall, but selecting just the one for curtains, covers and cushions is not my thing at all. Open the drawers or cupboards in my establishment and you will find heaps of neatly folded chintzes. Anything from a snippet to a 25-metre roll, pristine or in shreds – the pleasure in these designs is limitless.*

A new generation of designers, like Matilda Goad, Flora Soames and Beata Heuman, have figured out how to incorporate chintz into a contemporary setting without its becoming overwhelming. An upholstered chair, a pair of curtains or simply a solitary cushion in a pretty floral can conjure up the unpretentious elegance of a Colefax & Fowler decorative scheme.

Textiles need not be bright, brash or heavily patterned for them to contribute texture. Kirsten Hecktermann's linens and velvets, which she makes by hand in her garden, are the sort of thing that even battle-hardened architects can get on board with, with their vegetable dyes and subtle detailing. Even a simple grasscloth wallpaper generates a much more characterful finish than conventional matt emulsion. In our flat in Winchester, we made window blinds using off-white artist canvas, which showed its veins and ripples as the sun shone through it, like an eyelid in the glare of an optician's torch.

The new Minimalism

Early in my career, *The World of Interiors* commissioned me to write about an apartment in the Belgian seaside town of Knokke, designed by the Minimalist architect John Pawson. The charming couple who owned it put me up in a separate flat on the seafront, and I was taxied over to their place in an Aston Martin for dinner and a bottle of Barolo. It was the sort of thing that very rarely happens to a wide-eyed young design journalist. On the short car journey, the driver told me that the locals have an old saying: 'Every Belgian is born with a stone in his stomach.' Surveying the town through the window, I started to see what he meant. Drunk on dormers and pissed on pilasters, its inhabitants seemed to have indulged in a ritual regurgitation, throwing up a mishmash of buildings in every conceivable architectural style. Of course, witnessing this prelude meant that by the time I reached the Pawson apartment, its sublime focus felt all the more pronounced. The pared-back interior was as quietly beautiful as the washed-out landscape beyond, and I was struck by the quality of the craftsmanship and the expertly judged junctions. The walls, which were painted in characteristic Pawson white, evolved from grey to yellow as the sun descended towards the sea.

The travel writer Bruce Chatwin recalls visiting John Pawson's first-ever project, an apartment in Elvaston Place, South Kensington:

> *I was taken to a flat in an ornate but slightly down-at-heel Victorian terrace and shown into a room in which, it seemed to me, the notes were almost perfect . . . I walked around the walls, watching its planes, shadows and proportions in a state of near elation.*

Pawson's clients, and those of his fellow Minimalists such as Claudio Silvestrin and Alberto Campo Baeza, talk about being able to leave their emotional baggage at the door and exist in a space of aesthetic silence. Such rarefied rigour is incredibly difficult to achieve, and has spawned a surfeit of substandard imitations by property developers. Take a room with basic geometry, add some laminate flooring, a wash of white emulsion and – hey presto! – you have your very own lunatic asylum.

The success of a Minimalist style of decoration depends on the quality of the materials.

You also need to be prepared to do some maintenance every once in a while: I have visited other John Pawson projects where the doors dangle drunkenly from their hinges, and the heavily fingered paintwork looks like a crime scene that's been dusted for evidence.

Funnily enough, the current masters of the realm – Vincent van Duysen and Axel Vervoordt – are both Belgian. Their interiors tend towards a neutral palette, with comparatively little furniture or art to distract the eye, but they are utterly alive with texture and patina. Vervoordt is heavily inspired by the cultivated simplicity of Japanese *wabi-sabi*, which we discussed in the Materials section. He believes it gives his houses a timelessness that transcends any decorative fads:

> Wabi *is not a style, a fashion or a design trend . . . It avoids showy objects and conspicuous displays of wealth. The defining factor that sets* wabi *apart is its purity and simplicity. It is free from eclectic clutter and distractions that prevent us from finding inner peace. As such it is tranquil, calm, and reassuring – completely centered.*

The present-day version of Minimalism is about making sure that there is enough comfort and warmth despite the lack of ornamentation. Designer Rose Uniacke creates interiors that somehow manage to combine the serenity of a monastery with the reassurance of an old smoking jacket, using relaxed upholstered furniture alongside muted colours and natural materials.

The architect Jamie Fobert lives in a flat on the top floors of a Victorian warehouse, in an environment that is calm and ordered but never precious. He explains:

> *There's a wonderful text by Dom Hans van der Laan, a Belgian monk who built beautiful buildings. He wrote that architecture should be like a sandal to a foot: just hard enough to withstand the rough ground and just soft enough to be comfortable. I think it sums up how I approach domestic spaces.*

Paring down an interior takes skill and sound judgement – much like an egg, if you don't boil it enough it becomes a watery mess, but overdo it and you end up with rubber. It's all about being an effective curator, choosing furniture and objects with personality embedded

into their form and materiality. Get it right, and the effect can be truly liberating. Jim Ede was one of the most accomplished curators of them all, and the success of Kettle's Yard owes much to his talent for reducing things to just the right extent. Despite his weakness for paintings and pebbles, he always maintained that space is the most important element in any interior:

> *How often indeed have we found our room too small for us – it gets so crowded with things, we don't know where to move and the eye has no whither to rest. We all want space – we are spatial beings – we move in space – we ask primarily for space in our daily lives . . . The space which we so much want, we can create in our home, in our room. And how? By clearing away all that is in it, coming back to its bare walls, its full spaciousness, and then putting into it only those things which we absolutely need and endeavouring to put them in such a way that they do not seem to make the room look any smaller.*

This is a methodology that I would encourage everyone to adopt. A room will always seem small when it's empty, but as soon as you add some pieces of furniture, the spaces between them start to assume importance and give it a sense of scale. However, if you go too far and add too many things, it begins to look constricted again, so the trick is to stop right at the top of the parabola.

For many creatives and entrepreneurs, being in a space that's devoid of visual distractions allows a busy mind to find its focus. Ross Bailey, CEO and founder of Appear Here, told me that he takes his management team to the Cotswolds for a few days every year, to give them a break from the everyday noise of the business in order to concentrate on higher-level strategic planning. Their chosen venue is the Minimalist home of the architect Richard Found, which has a 23-metre-long space with a continuous band of floor-to-ceiling glazing overlooking the valley. Bailey says:

> *There really is nothing in it: concrete, glass and white walls, with one beautiful sofa. There is zero distraction, and nothing changes. It really gives me an opportunity to just think, without any clutter. The moment I walk through the door, I remember the conversations we had the year before, and the year before that.*

Another of my early writing assignments at *The World of Interiors* involved a visit to an extraordinary studio flat in Notting Hill, belonging to a theatrical man called Peter Hone. He answered the door with a fruity giggle, wearing a pair of wellingtons, and I was immediately struck by the intense whiff of cheese-and-pickle sandwiches. 'I'm making chutney,' he offered casually, as if it were an everyday occurrence. After his Jack Russell performed a canine breakdance around my ankles in the dimly lit entrance hall, I was ushered into the sitting-room-cum-bedroom, which looked like a miniature version of Sir John Soane's Museum. Every inch of wall space was covered with architectural fragments, marble busts stood regally on plinths, and Roman and Greek statuettes skulked in corners. At one end of the room was a four-poster bed and a replica of the Pope's throne, while, at the other, a round table was draped with a stripy tablecloth in white and bubble-gum-pink. For every Minimalist one meets, there is always a committed Maximalist like Peter, who can feel truly at home only when surrounded by their worldly possessions.

Albert has always been a collector. In a moment of weakness in our early twenties, he showed me into his dad's garage in Lyme Regis, where he stored his outstanding collection of furniture by the Postmodern designer Ettore Sottsass. There were teetering bookcases, sofas and lamps, their peculiar limbs adorned with all manner of spots, stripes and zigzags. It looked like the sort of thing that might happen if Roy Lichtenstein was locked in with a pile of wood and a spray gun.

Sottsass and the Memphis Group produced objects that recalled the spirit of everything from Eastern decorative traditions to Arts and Crafts and suburban Pop. Their fantastical forms and preposterous patterns reached a level of deliberate absurdity that held a mirror up to the decadence of early-eighties consumer culture. They may not be to everyone's taste, but they have an exuberance that is hard to deny, with an enduring appeal in their ability to pervert the seriousness of a room. Sometimes you need to send things up a bit. For Raphaël Zerbib, who works in finance, his PoMo pieces lend humour and movement to his otherwise-demure flat in Stoke Newington. He explains:

I love the Memphis style, because I think their work is still culturally and artistically relevant. They decided to take a completely different direction, in contradiction with architectural and design movements at the time, to offer a new vision of what furniture could be, and presented a new way of living, too.

One of Postmodernism's most esteemed exponents is the architect Sir Terry Farrell. A few years ago we sold his London apartment, which was sprawled across the top floor of an Art Deco Spitfire factory. Pot plants were offered up on metal plinths emerging from the staircase, model aeroplanes dangled from the corrugated-steel roof, and everywhere you looked there was colour, pattern and a layering of materials. In his book *Interiors and the Legacy of Postmodernism*, Farrell explains his Maximalist mindset:

> *The home has to have the element of chance and time and ordered chaos. It has to have a spatial discontinuity, and the complexity of decorative and personal expression. The minimalist idea of creating order in chaos is a kind of aristocratic elitist order wherein a house or apartment is walled off from the disorder of the uncontrollable, real-life chaos outside its boundaries. But one day the walls will be breached – one day the order, the appearance of order, will inevitably go, history has always shown us that.*

A different brand of ordered chaos was brought to bear upon the stately home by the decorator John Fowler. What we now think of as the 'English country-house style' is actually a construct of the mid-twentieth century, when Fowler borrowed the best bits from Georgian-era houses and mashed them together with outside influences to create something much less stiff. His style reached full maturity once he teamed up with the American Nancy Lancaster, who described decorating as 'a bit like mixing a salad'.

Inspired by this laid-back legacy, a new generation of interior decorators are busy mixing salads of their own using an abundance of produce from throughout history (just don't give them an iceberg lettuce). Martin Brudnizki is the man behind the wonderfully flamboyant Annabel's private members' club in London, where hand-painted murals of flamingos cavorting through country gardens coexist with Murano-glass chandeliers shaped like tulips. He describes how he takes inspiration from the past to create something new and unexpected:

You need to look at everything from Baroque to Rococo in order to understand how we got here, and how Modernism happened, for example. The trick is to never do a pastiche of the past. You need to be inspired by it, but then reinterpret it for a contemporary context. I believe my job is to look back to be able to look forward, and create something that is actually going to work emotionally for people today.

If that sounds potentially lawless, then a look at Brudnizki's diminutive flat in a Victorian mansion block makes you realize that everything has its place. Each room has a distinct purpose, the pictures are arranged with the merest sliver of circulation between them, and the furniture is the perfect proportion for the space.

The Swedish-born designer Beata Heuman shares a similar outlook. She learnt her craft under Nicky Haslam, the society decorator whose weakness for fabulous fakery was revealed at an early age, when he garnished his room at Eton with ostrich-plume pelmets and a carpet of artificial grass. Heuman's own eclectic interiors are formed of ebullient colour palettes, recherché antiques and a catholic approach to materials. She explains:

I think mixing things from different eras, and from all over the world, makes things more interesting and livelier. That's what human nature is: a great big mix.

Personally, I have always liked the approach of amalgamating old and new. For some people, that might mean combining a vintage Hans Wegner chair with a contemporary one by Martino Gamper. For others with a more adventurous outlook, it will have a much broader meaning. David Hicks would place Louis XVI chairs alongside Lucite tables, for example. In my house, the Georgian kitchen table is surrounded by some Gio Ponti 'Superlegerra' chairs and a couple of high-back Windsors, while elsewhere, a polystyrene bench by Max Lamb is an anarchic presence alongside a pair of Regency library chairs.

Surround yourself with meaningful things

Whether you believe that 'less is more' like Mies van der Rohe, or 'less is a bore' like Robert Venturi and Denise Scott Brown, the things you choose to live with must have a personal meaning. Any interior should represent the personalities of the people who occupy it rather than being some sort of ersatz appropriation. These days, we are bombarded by seductive images of houses on Instagram feeds and Pinterest boards, and it is tempting to copy them. We can all get hung up on the idea of buying the latest thing that everyone else seems to have.

Shortly after we got married, Faye and I acquired a vintage rocking chair by Charles and Ray Eames; we kept it for a year or so, until it became apparent that every Mid-Mod enthusiast in the Western world had one, too, at which point it was shipped off to its next victim. Nowadays we use the 'Golden Arches test'. When assessing a piece of furniture, we ask ourselves: 'Might this turn up in a branch of McDonald's one day?' Arne Jacobsen's wonderful 'Egg' chair, for example, has sadly become as ubiquitous as the morning McMuffin.

When I used to show people around houses that were for sale, it always surprised me how animated they became when they encountered a piece of furniture that they recognized. 'Look, Dennis, they've got the same sofa as us!' Time and again, it was apparent that people were more likely to buy a place if they felt safe among familiar objects. I always found this a bit depressing. There was a formula that seemed to work, and therefore the same things began to appear in seemingly every home I visited: a mid-century Danish sideboard; a Castiglioni floor lamp; and so on.

The issue with this decoration-by-numbers approach is that, aside from being disingenuous, it feels like something that is intended to appeal to the visitor rather than the person who lives there. The authors of *A Pattern Language* write:

> *The things around you should be the things which mean most to you, which have the power to play a part in the continuous process of self-transformation, which is your life. That much is clear. But this function has been eroded, gradually, in modern times because people have begun to look outward, to others, and over their shoulders, at the people who are coming to visit them, and have replaced their natural instinctive decorations with the things which they believe will please and impress their*

visitors . . . But the irony is, the visitors who come into a room don't want this nonsense any more than the people who live there. It is far more fascinating to come into a room which is the living expression of a person, or a group of people, so that you can see their lives, their histories, their inclinations, displayed in manifest form around the walls, in the furniture, on the shelves.

As we found with our Eames rocker, fashions change and so do our tastes. By investing in pieces that feel right for today, we are unquestionably creating a headache for tomorrow. As Alain de Botton points out:

Our impressions of beauty continually swing between stylistic polarities: between the restrained and the exuberant; the rustic and the urban; the feminine and the masculine – leading us ruthlessly to abandon objects to expire in junk shops at every swerve.

It is best to stick with objects that have a sense of timelessness and mean the most to you emotionally. When my father died, the things that my brother and I chose to inherit were those with the most personal memories: the pictures he painted; his box of fishing flies; our grandfather's 1940s cigarette case from the Architectural Association. The choices we made bore no relation to size, function or monetary value. Most of the bigger pieces of furniture were sold in a garage sale or given away to family and friends.

This emotional connection is the reason why Faye and I have so much of her own work in the house: furniture prototypes, sculptures, tapestries, wallpapers and door furniture. Artists and makers are not always comfortable with the idea of living with their own stuff, but for us it seems completely logical. The artworks on our walls are a mixture of family heirlooms, photographs and abstracts by our friends, and pieces we have bought for each other across many Christmases, anniversaries and birthdays. Each one represents a particular memory or moment in time, and has its own reason for being there.

Glenn Adamson counsels us to see the objects we live with as points of contact between people rather than as meaningless props to put on the mantelpiece. He writes:

By better understanding the tangible things in our lives, we better understand our fellow humans . . . the real test of an object's worth lies not in its efficiency, novelty, or even beauty (which, in any case, is in the eye of the beholder), but in whether it gives us a sense of our shared humanity . . . Just as a skilled maker will anticipate a user's needs, a really attentive user will be able to imagine the way something was made. The material object serves as a bridge between these two perspectives.

This sense of social connection is the reason why Faye decided to give away fifty of her cast-aluminium 'Spade' chairs (so-named because they are shaped like a shovel, with a narrow back topped by a handle) to some of her favourite artists, architects, photographers and product designers. Each maker was encouraged to donate a piece of their own work in return, and these formed the basis for an exhibition at the London Design Festival in 2017, entitled *The Trade Show*. The idea of artists supporting each other through mutually beneficial barter goes back centuries. However, it doesn't have to be a museum-quality oil painting in order to have meaning. Children seem to intuitively understand the emotional significance in handing over something they have made themselves – I have drawers full of sketches, paper snowflakes and clay animals that my daughters have enthusiastically thrust into my possession over the years.

In her book *On Longing*, Susan Stewart analyses why we develop a fascination for certain objects in our lives. Sometimes, she says, it relates to scale: a doll's house, for example, is so out of kilter with the real world that we can only enter it through our imagination. At other times we become gripped by the idea of amassing a collection – like my mum and her toast racks, or Albert and his Memphis furniture. An assemblage like this can never be truly completed, which drives us on to greater heights of obsession. Or it might be a souvenir, which allows us to reinhabit the past: a tribal nose flute from a particularly momentous holiday, perhaps.

Putting your collection of books on display is an easy way to surround yourself with memories and instil some personality. Whether you arrange them on a Dieter Rams shelving system or a mahogany chiffonier, a row of well-thumbed tomes conveys warmth and agelessness, and helps to dampen the acoustics of a room. Every kitchen feels somehow more welcoming with an assortment of cookbooks on the shelf.

It is challenging to arrange a group of hardbacks on the coffee table in an unselfconscious manner, but, rather than thinking about the intellectual rigour they project, I tend to consider

them more as decorative objects in their own right. An obscure book about aircraft often finds its way to the top of the pile in our sitting room, simply because the hardback cover, with its faded blue and functional graphics, seems to work best with everything else. I remember that my parents once used a similarly beaten-up book about Alvar Aalto as the basis for an interior scheme.

In an increasingly fluid world, where many of us live in several different countries during a lifetime, personal possessions can provide an anchor and remind us of the singular journey we have been on. The home of musically monikered designer Oscar Piccolo is a symphony of treasures that tell the story of his life, as he explains:

> *All my friends make fun of me because I have wooden fruit in my fruit bowl. Why?! To me, they're beautiful objects I happened upon in a charity shop, and they remind me of the places I grew up in. I was born in Sicily, but we lived in Ghana, Turkey, Egypt and Libya throughout my childhood. I think the fruit reminds me of Ghana the most because everything there was made of wood; it was like being in the wooden version of* The Flintstones – *I loved it. When we went to Ghana, we moved into a big, beautiful house with nothing in it but mattresses. My mum, being the creative one, started to source and draw furniture, which she would then have made. I grew up with the idea that you could make things from scratch rather than just buy them. Then, when we moved to Istanbul and later Egypt, all the things we had accumulated came with us, so that the idea of home became less about a physical place but more about the objects that carried meaning.*

Building things with your own hands undeniably gives them greater significance. At the Tin House in West London, architect Henning Stummel has made a walnut dining table with a stainless-steel ribbon running across the surface, a coffee table from a slab of fossilized stone brought back from a holiday, and an ingenious modular sofa cut from a single sheet of ply (which he has since put into production). Malgorzata Bany and her partner Tycjan Knut have hand-made almost everything in their flat, including the kitchen units. Their friend gave them an IKEA sofa, and they deconstructed it and repurposed it into a base for a Donald Judd-inspired daybed.

It doesn't have to be a piece of furniture – a lopsided pinch-pot or a spoon that you have whittled yourself will always bear the marks of your own fair hands, regardless of how clumsy the result. Donna Wilson talks about creating 'installation areas' on shelves and in cupboards, where she arranges the things that she and her kids have made together.

Having children should not put you off keeping precious objects. Ours have grown up in a house where ceramics by Paul Philp and Akiko Hirai, with their naive forms and tempting textures, are within easy reach of destructive hands. Etta or Wren will occasionally take a sharpie to the sofa during a moment of rebellion, but in general they understand which things can be bashed with a pretend hammer and which need to be skirted around. My artist friend Sarah Kaye Rodden describes a similar experience:

> *Because I have always loved to collect objects to draw, the house is full of quite dangerous things! But the children have never broken or touched any of it. There are brass poles, cannonballs, shark teeth, meteor fragments, dinosaur eggshell pieces, but they've never gone near them.*

Nathalie Assi knows a thing or two about this, having transformed her family home in Kensington into a retail gallery, where cereal packets jostle with ceramics and the kids are free to bounce around on the merchandise. She says:

> *The children understand that it's important not to destroy things around them, that they should appreciate them. We tell them about the designers, and they have met a few of them, so they wouldn't knock or damage the pieces. When you are not too careful with things and are natural around objects, children also become more relaxed and don't think they should transgress things that are forbidden. It becomes natural for them to touch and use objects without feeling too stressed out by them, or, on the other hand, too relaxed.*

Wearing it well

There's a wonderful photograph from 1939 that shows Le Corbusier standing outside Villa E-1027, a Modernist house on the Côte d'Azur built by the Irish furniture designer Eileen Gray. Completely starkers apart from his trademark spectacles, he is captured gleefully defacing the house with colourful murals like an impish graffiti artist. A hefty scar is visible on his right leg, a bit like a shark bite, caused when he was struck head-on by a motorized yacht, sucked beneath its keel and spat out by the propeller blades.

Gray considered Le Corbusier's murals to be an act of supreme vandalism. Was he a little jealous of the place? How could a woman have created such a magnificent monument to Modernism, he might have wondered, especially in this otherworldly location on the French Riviera. She wasn't even a trained architect, for heaven's sake. E-1027 has all the ingredients of the Corbusian canon: a flat roof, structural columns, floor-to-ceiling glazing, open floor plates and acres of painted render. However, it represents something far more than that, because inside its rectilinear shell is one of the most thoughtful and multisensory interiors ever made, enlivened by the presence of Gray's remarkable custom-made furnishings.

Her ingenious 'Satellite' mirror, for example, has a secondary magnifier on an adjustable arm that allows the user to shave the back of their neck (or lament their bald patch, as the case may be). At the rear of the dining alcove is a folding table which, when opened, transforms the corridor into a bar. There's the debonair 'Transat' chair, with its heavily reclined profile influenced by transatlantic steamship travel, and the 'Bibendum' chair, with voluptuous folds inspired by the inflated torso of the Michelin man. Peter Adam, who has written extensively about Eileen Gray's life and work, says:

> *Every detail had to be considered with the human body in mind. Things turned, bent, tilted, opened up. With a simple gesture one could rotate a cake tray . . . With another, a writing desk could be transformed into a low coffee table. The movements of elements created a mechanical ballet that became a hallmark of her design.*

We took The Modern House team on a trip to Villa E-1027 a few years ago, and I came away feeling like I had got to know Eileen Gray, her sensibility and supreme sense of wit. Indeed,

the most interesting interiors are those which are unmistakably imbued with the character of their creator. A home should be eclectic, singular, and potentially even a bit odd. My advice is to try not to conform to some prescribed vision. The great curse of modern decorating is the ubiquitous 'hotel style', a bogus and buttoned-up attempt at glamour using lamps with mirrored bases and clocks pretending to be from a French *brocante*. Sometimes I daydream about rounding up all of the Union Jack cushions in the world and lobbing them on a bonfire when no one is looking.

The success of an interior is in no way commensurate with the money that has been spent on it, and indeed many of the most memorable homes we have featured on The Modern House website were created on a budget. The wonderfully weird Margate home of musician and stylist Whinnie Williams, for example, is a testament to her original taste, DIY spirit and eye for a bargain. It is a riotous mash-up of vintage furniture, patterned wallpaper and red-and-white painted floors, with individually themed rooms that encompass gold swan taps and shell-covered fireplaces. Many pieces in the house have either been home-made, like the graphic black-and-white artwork in the living room (which was painted with an old mop) or found trawling auction houses and eBay ('old chair' being one of Whinnie's favourite searches). Even the society decorator David Hicks, who moved in rarefied circles, had a certain thriftiness to his approach, preferring to let gloss paint or vivid upholstery do the hard work of providing impact. He said:

> *Good design is in no way dependent upon money. I like to spend the minimum of money and yet gain the maximum effect. Style is not what you do but how you do it.*

There is nothing wrong with spending money on beautiful things if you can afford it, but it's all to do with wearing it well. Nancy Lancaster had what Cecil Beaton called a talent for 'making a grand house appear less grand', a trick that only the most accomplished aesthetes can pull off. Rarely have I seen it achieved with such effortless aplomb than at the 1960s home of Jane Wenner, which was built by Ward Bennett in the sand dunes of Amagansett. Jane is the ex-wife of *Rolling Stone* founder Jann Wenner and one-time muse of Annie Liebowitz, and a rock-and-roll spirit infuses every gently faded corner. Nineteenth-century

English furniture is mixed with Modernist classics, loose-covered Italian sofas and contemporary pieces by Rick Owens.

We can all channel this comfortable bohemianism using, say, slouchy sofas and stout armchairs with quilts thrown over them. Modern furniture doesn't have to be slick. My favourite Marcel Breuer armchair is tarnished and scuffed, and one of its arms has come unstitched, but guests feel comfortable about throwing themselves into it as a result.

By their very nature, occasional tables have a relaxed air about them, and are one of the most useful pieces of furniture you can own. They allow a guest to put their drink down, they can be used as a makeshift stool when a room reaches capacity, and they can be moved from one space to another with the minimum of fuss. In my opinion, one of the greatest pieces of product design ever made is the '60' stool by Alvar Aalto: it is lightweight, stackable and beautiful, and works equally well as a bedside table or a seat for a meeting. Conscious that it will adapt to any interior of any style, we gave one to every member of our team as a thank-you for their hard work during the Covid-19 pandemic.

Somewhere along the line, wall-mounted televisions started to become the focal point for our living spaces, but we need to get back to something more elemental. Although we no longer formally withdraw to our drawing rooms, there is still a logic to using the hearth as the centrepiece of an interior arrangement. According to Terence Conran, making fires accounted for an estimated ten hours a week of housework in the mid-1930s. Nowadays we have central heating, but a fireplace still has a timeless appeal. A pair of wing chairs either side of a flickering fire is always a welcome sight after a winter walk – add a damp spaniel and a bag of pork scratchings, and you have your very own wayfarer's inn.

How to arrange

When I was a subeditor at *The World of Interiors*, the highlight of every month was when the fax machine would spurt out the latest piece of copy from Alistair McAlpine, who wrote a column in the back of the magazine. Editing it was like trying to crack the Enigma Code. McAlpine wrote in one continuous sentence, scrawling his thoughts in black felt-tip pen without any thought for a comma, full stop or hoarse intake of breath. I became increasingly proficient at deciphering both his handwriting and his thought processes, and learnt a lot about collecting art in the process. McAlpine was one of the first to discover Mark Rothko, and later in life he became infatuated with the nuanced naivety of Aboriginal art. He invested in everything from police truncheons to dinosaur penises.

In his latter years, McAlpine restored an old convent in Puglia, southern Italy, which he ran as a rarefied B&B with his wife, Athena. Visiting the place, I realized that this inveterate magpie was just as accomplished at arranging as he was at collecting. Tribal masks were hung on the walls like fighter planes in formation; a humongous pile of quinces from the garden formed the centrepiece of the breakfast table, suggesting generosity and a connection to the soil; the rooftop terrace contained many hundreds of cacti and succulents in pots, standing proud like spiky soldiers. I remember him telling me that he could never make do with one of anything – he had to have the whole set.

This fondness for abundance should not be confused with artless clutter. A collection of objects from the same family, arranged in a contained way, will always have a greater aesthetic and emotional impact than something on its own. David Hicks was another master of the genre. He said:

> *My passion for arranging masses of things together is part of the way that I see objects and use them. It not only looks mean, but is visually meaningless, to have one bottle of gin, one of whisky, a couple of tonic water and a soda syphon on a table in the living room . . . If you are going to have a table with photographs, you must have enough of them – the more you have, the more interesting the table will become.*

In his book *Arranging Things*, Leonard Koren talks about displaying objects as a form of 'rhetoric': the power of persuasion through communication. Illustrating his arguments using still-lifes that he has come across in shop windows and people's houses, he carefully analyses the various elements that contribute to their success, such as their proximity to each other, their hierarchy and their sensual appeal. However, in the end, a successful composition really arises from what feels right, as Koren acknowledges:

> *Most arrangers of things work intuitively. They have 'feelings' about what objects go where, with what. They 'sense' when arrangements 'work', or don't. They create in a non-analytical state of mind.*

When my mum, who is an accomplished artist, taught me to draw as a child, she would always talk about the magic that is created when two lines don't quite meet. 'The bit you leave out is the most important,' she said. The interval between things creates a dynamic tension that heightens our appreciation of the overall composition. Lucio Fontana exploited this idea when he first slashed a canvas with a utility knife, transforming the traditional painting from a two-dimensional object into a three-dimensional one with thrilling mystery in its gaping abyss. Within our homes, we should think carefully about both solid and void when making small arrangements of objects on a table, or indeed when positioning large pieces of furniture in a room. Alex Eagle, who lives in a light-filled loft in London's Soho, describes how she was influenced by Donald Judd in this regard:

> *He had a really good use of the empty space, which I feel is what I'm constantly having to balance here: to try not to overfill and remember that empty space is as beautiful as filled space, that there's a luxury to the space you could fill but don't.*

When arranging furniture, considering the contours of the room is a useful starting point. Will the bed nestle in that natural niche? Is it best to have a sofa in this space, or will a pair of chairs work better? Think about the proportions of the building and find furniture with a corresponding scale; many interiors are let down by an oafish reclining chair lurking in the room like a lost elephant. When we bought our little nineteenth-century house in Islington, we had to downscale to some narrow upright seating because it was the only thing that seemed to work.

One of my favourite pictures is a lithograph of *Three Reclining Figures* by Henry Moore, which Faye gave me one Christmas. Somehow the trio of forms looks exactly right on the paper. From a visual perspective, odd numbers of things always seem to work better than even numbers. Next time you go to your favourite restaurant, have a look at the plate: the chances are, there will be three main elements grouped together in a harmonious way. If things are arranged asymmetrically, the eye is forced to move around them to fully absorb what it sees. In the home, this rule applies on every scale, so you might place a sofa and two chairs together, three pendant lights over a dining table, or a trio of ceramics on a tabletop.

Even the most ordinary household objects benefit from being displayed in a thoughtful way. If you have an old Japanese chef's knife, mount it on the wall so that you can appreciate the mottled beauty of its hand-forged blade. Arrange your collection of slipware on the open dresser. Put spices in little jars and let the deep red of smoked paprika and the burnt-orange of turmeric make a visual contribution. On the wall in our house is an assortment of old shaving mirrors that we brought back from India – you can't see your face in them, but there is a painterly beauty in their heavily foxed glass. Create your own cabinet of curiosities. Carlo Viscione has done this with an antique display case from a shop, filling it with things that remind him of his travels, including a collection of shells from Cuba, Vietnam and China.

When hanging pictures, think about how they occupy the space, and their relationship to the floor and the ceiling. The most common mistake is to place them too high. When I was a teenager, a friend came round to my house and remarked on the positioning of the paintings. 'Are your parents really short?' he asked. If you're standing there with a hammer and a picture hook, wondering whereabouts on the wall you should whack it in, the answer is this: use your eye to find what feels like the right place instinctively, then take it down by six inches. A picture that's hung too high looks bereft; it ceases to relate to the furniture or the other objects in the room.

The absolute exemplar of satisfactory picture-hanging is Kettle's Yard. In some cases, they are placed so low as to touch the floor. Invariably they are off-centre, creating a pleasing tension between the piece and the space around it. The placement of ship paintings by Alfred Wallis is as naive as the wibbly-wobbly works themselves, with the wooden frames slightly

askew and not quite lining up. On one wall, three monochrome collages by Italo Valenti have been butted up against each other, frame to frame, above an altar-like table. The arrangement suggests they were created as a triptych, but, in fact, they were part of a much larger group and never intended to be exhibited together. By treating them as a single artwork, Ede somehow elevated each picture and gave it greater purpose (Valenti himself grew to like this idea so much that the works appeared together as a trio in later monographs about the artist).

Mathieu Paris, senior director at the contemporary-art gallery White Cube, took inspiration from Kettle's Yard when decorating his flat in Pimlico. He says:

> *The process of hanging paintings feels instinctive to me – it's what I do every day, whether in the gallery or in the homes of collectors. There is no one recipe to showcase art, but the way you place art in your own house says a lot about your personality. I guess I match artworks to the architecture of the space. Kettle's Yard has taught me a lot about how to live with art and design. When I first went there four years ago, it was one of the great moments I've had in the UK, and we've collaborated with them a few times at The White Cube now. Like at Kettle's Yard, many of the artists I've worked with don't believe in the hierarchy of presentation. There's beauty in everything.*

Think about placing one big canvas on a wall, or a series of mismatched pictures scattered around. Put them above light switches, around corners, beside the loo – anywhere that they might cause surprise. You don't always have to hang them: put up a shelf and arrange them along its length, or lean them up on a cabinet. Use a variety of pictures at different scales, in assorted frames. Add a postcard into the mix. Writing in *The World of Interiors*, Alan Bennett recalls his early life as an artful arranger:

> *I didn't see paintings as art objects so much as objects in a setting, and had the unashamedly English notion of pictures as furniture. I preferred them above tables, behind flowers, say, dimly lit by lamps or even half hidden by books. I would never want a room in which a painting was spotlit; it smacks too much of a museum, or a certain sort of gallery.*

How to collect

When choosing what to buy for your home, try to follow your instincts rather than any preconceived notions about what constitutes good taste. Assemble a magpie's collection of pieces of different sizes, from different eras, that reflect your own personal view of the world. Use your eyes, look closely at the shape of something and how it has been made – the curve of a handle on a jug, for example, or the way that a set of cutlery feels in the palm. Only by freeing ourselves from prevailing aesthetic trends can we start to really see objects for what they are.

Many of the best things you can buy have not been designed by well-known creators, cannot be found in textbooks and do not cost a great deal. Often they have a kind of accidental beauty that is the result of fulfilling utilitarian needs. Yanagi Sōetsu was the founder of the *mingei*, or folk art, movement in Japan in the late 1920s. His book *The Beauty of Everyday Things* urges us to adopt an accepting attitude. He writes:

> *To be highly intelligent does not necessarily mean that one has an eye for beauty. Detailed knowledge does not in itself qualify one to be called a lover of art . . . intuition is far more important than intellect, far closer to the essence of beauty.*

One of the most memorable art exhibitions I have visited was called the *Museum of Everything*, which took place in a rambling former recording studio in Primrose Hill back in 2009. It was dedicated to work by untrained, undiscovered and unintentional artists. Wonderfully intricate mobiles made from baling wire and aluminium foil by the hirsute Nebraskan Emery Blagdon hung in a cupboard, which he intended as a 'healing machine' to harness the power of the earth to alleviate pain and illness (Blagdon started work on them after the death of both of his parents). There were paintings created by Josef Karl Rädler in a psychiatric hospital, and textile pieces by Judith Scott, who had Down's syndrome. I found it to be both exhilarating and unsettling, like being granted access to something you were never supposed to see, but it shone a light on the presumptuousness of the contemporary-art world.

Alfred Wallis is one of Britain's most celebrated painters, but he would have been baffled by the adulation and auction prices attached to his innocent renderings of the Cornish coast.

With no artistic training and little understanding of perspective, he daubed marine paint on to everything from advertisement cards to Quaker Oats packets. He came to public attention when he was 'discovered' by the prodigious young artists Ben Nicholson and Christopher Wood, who happened to be strolling past his cottage in St Ives in 1928 when they glimpsed his work through the open door. Struck by the purity of Wallis's paintings, they purchased some of them and brought them to the attention of the London avant-garde.

I encourage you to use your own judgement about what you think is beautiful. The other day Faye came home with a fibreglass sheep salvaged from a butcher's shop, its head far too small for its bulbous body. 'It reminds me of those naive nineteenth-century trophy paintings,' she explained, as Wren and Etta eyed it suspiciously. The antique dealer Robert Young has the most perfectly honed eye when it comes to primitive art, and specializes in strangely proportioned paintings of horses and livestock by unnamed artists. Maria Speake and Adam Hills from the architectural salvage company Retrouvius are also expert editors, sourcing everything from foxed mirrors to second-hand artists' palettes.

A visit to the Peanut Vendor website, which is run by Becky Nolan and Barny Read, might reveal an original Olivier Mourgue chair or Mario Bellini sofa, but it's usually the little abstract sculpture by an unknown artist or uncomplicated timber cabinet that really catches the eye. When I was looking for some decorative pieces for our office, I used it as a one-stop shop to buy some beautifully aged marble platters, ceramic vases and wooden bowls. Becky describes the joy of living with a piece that has value because of its honesty rather than its rarity:

> It's not important to us to have collectable items. Our dining-room table, for example, didn't make it to the shop because we love it so much, but we don't know who made it. There's one in the kitchen which is such a nothing table, but it collapses and folds out in a great way. And somebody has painted it black, so it's not in its original state, but it just looks so good. I don't know why, but every time I use it I enjoy it.

The more integrity an object has, the more likely it is to survive and be passed down the generations. Shaker furniture, for example, was designed to be long-lasting and allow the greatest efficiency – even the tacks, rivets and nails were made by hand. 'Brown furniture', which is a disparaging term used to describe wooden antiques from the seventeenth, eighteenth and nineteenth centuries, is the kind of thing that has been unfashionable for years, but is again making its presence felt in the interiors of knowing millennials because of its enduring quality. A Windsor chair is a marvellous thing, and looks just as good in a modern interior as it does in a period setting. Even better if it bears the war wounds of a thousand fireside chats: gouges and scratches and curves in the spindles. Georgian furniture is particularly beautiful, and tends to be finer and more elegant than later Victorian examples. Don't be precious about it. Personally I love an armchair with the upholstery exploding out of it and the hessian on show like a salacious undergarment.

Antiques fairs, *brocantes*, local auctions and markets can be a great starting point, and part of the fun is in sifting through all of the substandard trinkets to unearth a hidden gem. We all love a bargain, too. When I visited the chef Anna Barnett, she showed me her haul of wares from the Princess May car-boot sale, including a Portuguese lamp that she bought for £20 but is worth closer to £300.

Hairstylist Cyndia Harvey, who moved to the UK from Jamaica at the age of eleven, lived in hostels and temporary accommodation before finally putting down roots at a mews house in Brockley. Her fabulously personal interior is the result of following her instincts, as she explains:

> *I didn't set out to decorate in a specific way. I'd just go to markets – pretty much everything is from Kempton – and pick out what I liked. I wasn't in a rush to buy anything, and I wasn't like, 'Oh, this goes with that.' It was a bit of 'I like that thing. That's what I'm going to get.' And somehow it all came together pretty nicely. I figured out my aesthetic just through looking, and if a piece jumped out at me, I'd go for it . . . Everything in here puts a smile on my face and – it sounds pretentious to say – I feel really connected to everything because it all has a story behind it. When you buy vintage, you're buying all the stories from the person who sold it to you, even though some of them seem so outrageous I'm not even sure if they're true!*

The layering that Terry Farrell has achieved in his flat is largely the result of dragging things back from the local market stalls and antiques shops over several decades. As a passionate place-maker who has helped regenerate areas like the Greenwich Peninsula, Newcastle Quayside and Brindleyplace in Birmingham, he revels in the notion that buying locally connects him to his neighbourhood and the people around him.

Indeed, much of the joy is in the human interaction and the characters you come across. When model Emma Champtaloup and her husband, Jack, a music manager for the likes of Sam Smith and Disclosure, moved to their family home in North London, they opted to start with a blank slate, leaving everything behind except their clothes and a single beloved light fixture. On a trip to Portobello Market, Emma met the interior designer Hollie Bowden, who ended up consulting with her on the decoration of the house:

> *I was sitting on a chair, feeling sick and pregnant, and Hollie was easy to notice running around scanning the stalls, and we just got talking. Not being from London, I didn't know where to go to fill the house with eclectic pieces. It's such a hard one: where do you find amazing, one-off furniture? And then Hollie suddenly entered my life and she just knew! I got to do the whole thing with her, and now we're really close friends! I love that side of doing the house: the markets, the antique stores, and the people you meet. It's a total treasure hunt. I remember finding the tree that's now above my bed – it's so precious to me. We bought it off this amazing man in an antique shop near Pimlico. I walked in, saw it, and knew it was a piece I had to have. Every person you meet in these antique shops, they're such enthusiasts. They've all got so much sparkle.*

Buying art should be approached in the same way as buying furniture and objects: follow your gut. Second-guessing the vagaries of the market is a difficult trick to pull off, so rather than 'investing' for monetary gain, instead think about how a piece makes you feel. It is easy to forget that a painting can look very dominant once you hang it on the wall, so consider the colours and forms you would like to live with. Art can have a significant bearing on the atmosphere of a room, which perhaps explains why the painter Michael Craig-Martin is an arch-Minimalist. In both his home on the Barbican Estate and his holiday apartment on the *piano nobile* of a Venice palazzo, Michael has used his own canvases – dazzling depictions of everyday household objects – as the primary decorative device. I was fascinated to discover

that this man, whose whole career has been defined by his use of intense colour, chooses to live in a decidedly ascetic manner, with neutrally coloured walls, minimal architraves and an absence of objects.

Setting some parameters around what you buy can be a way to ensure that an art collection feels coherent. You might decide to focus on landscapes, for example, or a particular historical movement. Curator Oscar Humphries, who is a specialist on the artist Sean Scully and was responsible for the first selling shows of Pierre Jeanneret and Jean Prouvé furniture in London, encourages his friends and clients to be disciplined in their buying habits:

> I used to collect lots of different things: one Roman object, one tribal mask, one ancient Greek ceramic, one modern piece . . . I've come to realize it's really important to focus, so now I collect with purpose because, otherwise, you just end up with lots of stuff; it becomes shopping. I don't even want to look at the remnants of my old collections any more for that reason. Forming a focused collection looks much better in the end – to have consistency in something – it's intellectually more stimulating because you actually learn about the subject and, finally, if you ever need to sell, it's much easier if you have a collection of X, rather than saying, 'I've got one of this, one of that.'

Grandpa Whiskers, who was an avid collector, imposed three rules upon himself: each picture must be a watercolour, drawing or print; the artist must be British; and the artist must be alive. The last of these was important because it enabled him to show support for young and emerging talents. A large part of his collection, including works by John Nash, Elizabeth Blackadder, John Piper and Edward Bawden, now resides in the Gibberd Gallery in Harlow. Many of these artists were personal friends of his. Henry Moore, for example, would often come over for lunch. My aunt Sophie recalls that, during one particular visit, Moore began absent-mindedly playing with the children's Plasticine, fashioning it into the shape of farmyard animals. The room fell silent as everyone looked at these 'sculptures' on the table, conducting internal estimations of their financial value, before the artist dramatically crushed them flat with his palm.

My grandpa gave me a Henry Moore picture in his will – a little lithograph of a sheep. It is one of my favourite things, not because of its value but because of what it represents emotionally. Pictures, objects, books and collectables remind us of family members, friends and special experiences. Very early in our relationship, some twenty years ago, Faye and I visited St Ives for the first time. Having been exhilarated by the colours of Patrick Heron and Roger Hilton at the Tate, and by the forms of Barbara Hepworth at her home and studio, we spent our *World of Interiors* wages on a pair of small seascapes from a gallery in the town's cobbled backstreets. These paintings will always have a scintilla of reflected glory, and forever remind me of that weekend. Whenever I look at them, I remember the feeling of the sun on my neck, the chattering of seagulls and the apprehensive tangle of young love in my stomach.

These pictures have shared our journey of moving from home to home, being shrouded in bubble wrap and loaded on to lorries, before settling on to a hook in their new environment. In our current house, they hang next to a swirling painting of Constantine Bay by my late father. It was his favourite beach, and we spent every summer there when I was a boy, building teetering sandcastles and chasing gobies in the rockpools. Beneath it is a wooden table that my mum gave me, its wobbly drawer filled with faded family photographs. In the end, decorating a home is a deeply personal and heartfelt process. It is about building memories of the ones we love the most.

Epilogue

It is the brightest of winter days. Through the window of my study, I can see a pheasant pottering around in the borders, pecking at seeds that have fallen from the bird-feeder and ruffling its frumpy plumage. Wren and Etta have loaded their favourite dollies into prams, and are busy steering them into the wooden Wendy house in the kitchen garden.

The door creaks open, and Indigo scuttles in brandishing a pair of felt-tip drawings that she has just completed. The first one has 'My Dream Home' scrawled across the top of it. It looks like an unlikely marriage between our house and a Moorish palace, with Victorian windows, battlements, a set of gold domes and a flag adorned with the face of a tiger. Grapevines adorn its sun-baked façade. The second drawing depicts the interior of the house, where three staircases snake their way through its six sizeable storeys. On the ground floor is a dining room with red walls, an eight-seater table and a 'chandelier' made from palm fronds. The adjacent sitting room, in baby-blue, has soft furnishings, lamps on occasional tables and a thriving pot plant in the corner. Further up the building, there is a yellow-painted wet room with the most tremendous of rainfall showers, and Indigo's own bedroom, which is decorated in pink. The other members of our family, she tells me, sleep inside the domes at the top (she seems to have grasped the notion of refuge already).

For as long as I can remember, Indigo has drawn pictures of imaginary houses. Each one is more elaborate than the last, and incorporates her latest thoughts on colour, interior layout and architectural detail. Looking at her latest decadent domicile, I am reminded of something that Albert once told me. Back in the early days of The Modern House, when he and I were tearing around the country visiting prospective clients, he began to keep a little notebook of 'self-build dreams'. Every time a particular detail caught his eye, he would write it down – a thigh-level window seat; an unusually broad hallway; a study space squirrelled away in a teetering turret. The idea was that, one day, these elements would all come together in a triumphant Casa Albert.

Looking at this notebook with fresh eyes, Albert confesses that the resulting house would be a Frankenstein's monster that is better off remaining on the page. However, perhaps it is the act of dreaming about a future dwelling rather than its physical manifestation that holds significance. The philosopher Gaston Bachelard wrote:

Sometimes the house of the future is better built, lighter and larger than all the houses of the past . . . Late in life, with indomitable courage, we continue to say that we are going to do what we have not yet done: we are going to build a house . . . Maybe it is a good thing for us to keep a few dreams of a house that we shall live in later, always later, so much later, in fact, that we shall not have time to achieve it. For a house that was final, one that stood in symmetrical relation to the house we were born in, would lead to thoughts – serious, sad thoughts – and not to dreams. It is better to live in a state of impermanence than in one of finality.

My mum, who is in her mid-seventies, is just coming to the end of a major renovation at her house in a Devon seaside village. Having been married for half a century, she is adjusting to life on her own. She has lived on a building site for more than a year, and is dreading the day that the builders finally pack up their tools and leave her alone with her thoughts. Already she is talking about moving on, about a new home that might better support her needs and allow her to be closer to family.

Much like Albert, I have found the experience of visiting hundreds of extraordinary private homes both inspiring and slightly perilous. As a design and architecture obsessive, as someone who appreciates beautiful things, I have continually had my head turned by the allure of another building – a Georgian rectory winking at me with its perfectly symmetrical face, or a neglected coastal cottage raising an ear like a puppy in a rescue centre. Since Faye and I have been together, we have moved house every three years or so, largely on my insistence. She sometimes describes herself as a hen waddling around trying to make its nest, only to have it whipped away before she can lay any eggs.

This constant quest for the next thing is innate. The neuroscientist Jaak Panksepp identified seven networks of emotion in the brain: anger, fear, panic/grief, maternal care, pleasure/lust, play and seeking. It is the last of these that is potentially the most potent. For me, an afternoon at an antiques fair is just as fun if I come away empty-handed, in the same way that I can spend hours on travel websites looking at holidays I will never go on. In the end, it is the seeking rather than the achieving that administers a syringe of dopamine.

Much like my mum, I don't think I will ever accept a particular home as my final resting place. However, with practice and careful thought, I am learning to be more accepting of what

I have. Writing this book has definitely helped. Looking around my house now, I am acutely aware of its flaws and foibles – the way the wind whistles down the chimney; the slate roof tiles that don't quite match; the poplar in the garden that's leaning perilously – but, overall, it manages to embody the timeless principles set out in these pages. The trade-off for a cold winter is that its sturdy concrete frame stands up resolutely in the face of a howling gale. The windows in Faye's studio have clunky aluminium frames, but they emit the most wonderful westerly light. The reproduction marble fireplace in the drawing room that was added by our predecessors looks troublingly gaudy and lacking in patina, but the proportions are rather lovely; instead of getting rid of it, we will have a go at dulling it down with a damp teabag. Even in a child's imagination, a home is not a perfect place. Indigo has drawn a pair of towers on hers, which are rendered in grey and occupied by men with miserable faces. 'These are all the people on the island who have done bad things,' she explains.

Buildings are fluid; they change with the seasons. Roof tiles fall off and need replacing, lawns need mowing, and hedges with shaggy hairdos demand to be clipped. In the end, modern living should be about investing yourself in the home you have. Only when you devote yourself to it will it devote itself to you. It may not be the perfect home, but it is yours.

Acknowledgements

This book owes its existence to a friendship that dates back thirty years. I first met Albert Hill in an English lesson at school; he had an explosion of dark hair and – for reasons known only to himself – the name 'Keith' sewn on to the back pocket of his pleated trousers. His early days as an innovator were revealed when he turned up to the football pitch wearing a pair of gleaming white boots, while the rest of us were still in black Umbros; unfortunately, they were two sizes too small, which meant that he stalked across the pitch like an egret in stilettos. Albert has always been a creative thinker, and I will be forever grateful that he came up with the idea for The Modern House and asked me to be his partner. Like any successful relationship, ours is founded on trust and mutual respect.

I want to say a heartfelt thank you to our wonderful team at The Modern House and Inigo; there are too many to name here, but I am proud of them all. Particular mention is due to Emma Mansell for her overall contribution, to Charlie Monaghan for writing many of the original interviews featured in these pages, and to Emily Stevens for helping with the permissions. Thank you to the generous people who have allowed us into their homes over the years, especially those who are quoted or pictured in the book, and to the photographers who have captured them so beautifully, not least Elliot Sheppard.

Thank you to the brilliant Tom Killingbeck for his insightful feedback and unerring positivity, and to the rest of the team at Penguin Life, especially Richard Bravery, Saffron Stocker, Julia Murday and Donna Poppy. I am grateful to Emma Paterson at Aitken Alexander Associates for her expert guidance; to Cecilia Stein, Morgwn Rimel and Nicola Loughton for their encouragement and support during the gestation of the project; to Alistair O'Neill and Brent Dezkciorius for nobly wading through the first draft of the copy; and to Guy Marshall for his skilful stewardship of The Modern House brand.

Bookshelf

At The Modern House, we have a reference library containing several thousand books, encompassing everything from design dictionaries to gardening manuals, dusty psychology books and architectural classics in suitably rectilinear jackets. I won't claim to have read them all, but putting together *A Modern Way to Live* has provided a welcome excuse to spend many hours in a Scandinavian lounge chair in the name of research.

Rather than reference each and every one in a bibliography, instead I have consulted with Albert to compile a boil-in-the-bag list of the books we value the most. These are the timeless tomes that usually end up at the top of the teetering pile. If I could pick just one, it would be *The Modern House* by F. R. S. Yorke, a 1934 classic that unleashed the startling forms of Modernist architecture on a buttoned-up British audience, and, some seventy years later, gave our company its name.

Adamson, Glenn, *Fewer, Better Things: The Hidden Wisdom of Objects* (2018)

Alexander, Christopher, et al., *A Pattern Language: Towns, Buildings, Construction* (1977)

Bachelard, Gaston, *The Poetics of Space* (1994)

Barthes, Roland, *How to Live Together: Novelistic Simulations of Some Everyday Spaces. Notes for a Lecture Course and Seminar at the Collège de France, 1976–7* (2013)

Bernheimer, Lily, *The Shaping of Us* (2017)

Cantacuzino, Sherban, *New Uses for Old Buildings* (1975)

Conran, Terence, *The Essential House Book* (2000)

de Botton, Alain, *The Architecture of Happiness* (2007)

Ede, Jim, *A Way of Life: Kettle's Yard* (1984)

Einzig, Richard, *Classic Modern Houses in Europe* (1981)

Harwood, Elain, *Space, Hope, and Brutalism: English Architecture, 1945–1975* (2015)

Koren, Leonard, *Arranging Things: A Rhetoric of Object Placement* (2003)

Le Corbusier, *Polychromie architecturale: les claviers de couleurs de Le Corbusier de 1931 et de 1959*, Arthur Rüegg (ed.) (1997)

—, *Toward an Architecture* (1924)

McGrath, Raymond, *Twentieth-Century Houses* (1934)

Nairn, Ian, *Nairn's London* (1966)

Newton, Miranda H., *Architects' London Houses: The Homes of Thirty Architects since the 1930s* (1992)

Pallasmaa, Juhani, *The Eyes of the Skin: Architecture and the Senses* (1996)

Pevsner, Nikolaus, *Pevsner Architectural Guides: Buildings of England* (1951–74; 46 vols.)

Pidgeon, Monica, and Theo Crosby, *An Anthology of Houses* (1960)

Powers, Alan, *The Twentieth-Century House in Britain: From the Archives of 'Country Life'* (2004)

—, *Modern: The Modern Movement in Britain* (2005)

Rasmussen, Steen Eiler, *Experiencing Architecture* (1960)

Reed, Christopher, *Bloomsbury Rooms* (2004)

Ruskin, John, *The Seven Lamps of Architecture* (1849)

Tanizaki, Jun'ichirō, *In Praise of Shadows* (1991)

Tree, Isabella, *Wilding: The Return of Nature to an English Farm* (2018)

Tuan, Yi-Fu, *Space and Place: The Perspective of Experience* (1977)

Venturi, Robert, *Complexity and Contradiction in Architecture* (1966)

Williamson, Leslie, *Interior Portraits: At Home with Cultural Pioneers and Creative Mavericks* (2018)

Wohlleben, Peter, *The Hidden Life of Trees: What They Feel, How They Communicate – Discoveries from a Secret World* (2016)

Picture credits

pp. vi–1: Ferrum House, by John S. Bonnington. Thanks to Louise Bonnington. Photography by Dan Glasser.

pp. 4–5: Housden House, by Brian Housden. Thanks to Beth and Tess Housden. Photography by Taran Wilkhu.

p. 6: Albert Hill (*left*) and Matt Gibberd. Thanks to Hole & Corner. Photography by Carol Sachs.

pp. 10–11 (*from left*): Clerkenwell Cooperage, by Chris Dyson Architects. Thanks to Shane McKenna. Photography by Dan Glasser. Copenhagen house, by Niels Strøyer Christophersen of Frama. Thanks to Niels Strøyer Christophersen. Photography by Maja Karen. Hackney flat, by Rhonda Drakeford. Thanks to Rhonda Drakeford. Photography by Mariell Lind Hansen. Thanks to Dominic

Weil. Photography by Elliot Sheppard.

pp. 16–17: Cheshire house, by Annabelle Tugby. Thanks to Annabelle Tugby. Photography by Elliot Sheppard.

p. 22: Suffolk house, by Birkin Haward. Thanks to Chris and Susannah Burke. Photography by Elliot Sheppard.

p. 25: Gin Distillery, by Open Practice Architecture. Thanks

to Rupert Scott and Leo Wood. Photography by French & Tye.

pp. 30–31: High Sunderland, by Peter Womersley. Thanks to Paul Stirton. Photography by Taran Wilkhu.

p. 34: Severels, by Walter Greaves. Thanks to Hannah Greaves. Photography by Taran Wilkhu.

pp. 38–9: Collage House,

by Jonathan Tuckey Design. Thanks to Jonathan Tuckey. Photography by Elliot Sheppard.

p. 41: Heron Cottage, by Sue Skeen. Thanks to Sue Skeen. Photography by Jonathan Gooch.

p. 42: Converted Methodist church, by West Architecture. Thanks to Morgwn Rimel. Photography by Taran Wilkhu.

pp. 46–7: Severels, by Walter Greaves. Thanks to Hannah Greaves. Photography by Taran Wilkhu.

p. 50: Coach House, by Matheson Whiteley. Thanks to Stuart Shave. Photography by Taran Wilkhu.

pp. 52–3: Coward House, by David Shelley. Thanks to Monica and Simon Siegel. Photography by Elliot Sheppard.

pp. 56–7: Heron Cottage, by Sue Skeen. Thanks to Sue Skeen. Photography by Jonathan Gooch.

p. 61: Canonbury house, by Faye Toogood and Matt Gibberd. Photography by French & Tye.

p. 66: Clerkenwell Cooperage, by Chris Dyson Architects. Thanks to Shane McKenna. Photography by Dan Glasser.

p. 71: Thanks to Maya Njie. Photography by Mariell Lind Hansen.

pp. 74–5: Nithurst Farm, by Adam Richards Architects. Thanks to Adam Richards. Photography by Elliot Sheppard.

p. 76: Gin Distillery, by Open Practice Architecture. Thanks to Rupert Scott and Leo Wood. Photography by French & Tye.

p. 81: Cotswolds house, by Found Associates. Thanks to Richard Found. Photography by Elliot Sheppard.

pp. 82–3: Mancett House, by Michael Manser and Guard Tillman Pollock Architects. Thanks to David Liddiment and Michael Denardo. Photography by Elliot Sheppard.

p. 86: Islington house, by Niall McLaughlin Architects. Thanks to Penny Mason. Photography by Dan Glasser.

pp. 90–91: Heron Cottage, by Sue Skeen. Thanks to Sue Skeen. Photography by Jonathan Gooch.

p. 95: London house, by Thomas Downes and Erica Toogood. Thanks to Thomas Downes and Erica Toogood. Photography by Elliot Sheppard.

p. 98: Peckham house, by Jonathan Nicholls and Alex Randall. Thanks to Jonathan Nicholls and Alex Randall. Photography by French & Tye.

pp.102–103: Ghost House, by BPN Architects. Thanks to Steve Smith. Photography by Dan Glasser.

p. 105: London house, by 6a Architects. Thanks to Louise Clarke. Photography by French & Tye.

pp. 108–109 (from left): Gin Distillery, by Open Practice Architecture. Thanks to Rupert Scott and Leo Wood. Photography by French & Tye. Thanks to Laura Jackson. Photography by Mariell Lind Hansen. Thanks to Jamie Smith. Photography by Elliot Sheppard.

p. 111: Thanks to Amy Yalland. Photography by Mariell Lind Hansen.

p. 115: Lost House, by Adjaye Associates. Thanks to Brian and Jessica Robinson. Photography by Taran Wilkhu.

p. 117: Lost House, by Adjaye Associates. Thanks to Brian and Jessica Robinson. Photography by Taran Wilkhu.

pp. 122–3: Nithurst Farm, by Adam Richards Architects. Thanks to Adam Richards. Photography by Elliot Sheppard.

p. 124: Copenhagen house, by Niels Strøyer Christophersen of Frama. Thanks to Niels Strøyer Christophersen. Photography by Maja Karen.

pp. 128–9: Winchester flat, by Faye Toogood and Matt Gibberd. Photography by Taran Wilkhu.

p. 133: Walter Segal house in Highgate, by Faye Toogood and Matt Gibberd. Photography by Taran Wilkhu.

pp. 136–7 (from left): Parliament Hill house, by Woollacott Gilmartin. Thanks to Katy Woollacott and Patrick Gilmartin. Photography by Dan Glasser. Ferrum House, by John S. Bonnington. Thanks to Louise Bonnington. Photography by Dan Glasser. Isokon Building penthouse, by Wells Coates. Thanks to Tom Broughton. Photography by Elliot Sheppard.

pp. 140–41: Copenhagen house, by Niels Strøyer Christophersen of Frama. Thanks to Niels Strøyer Christophersen. Photography by Maja Karen.

pp. 144–5: The Beldi, by Chan & Eayrs. Thanks to Zoe Chan and Merlin Eayrs. Photography by Taran Wilkhu.

p. 148: Padbury Court. Thanks to Kate Christie. Photography by Stephen Bishop.

pp. 152–3: Hampshire house. Thanks to Sheridan Coakley. Photography by Taran Wilkhu.

p. 156: Strange House, by Hugh Strange Architects. Thanks to Hugh Strange. Photography by Dan Glasser.

p. 161: Clay House, by Szczepaniak Astridge. Thanks to Simon Astridge. Photography by Taran Wilkhu.

pp. 164–5: Sussex house, by England Architecture. Thanks to Gina Portman. Photography by Elliot Sheppard.

p. 168: Nithurst Farm, by Adam Richards Architects. Thanks to Adam Richards. Photography by Elliot Sheppard.

pp. 172–3: Gingerbread House, by Laura Dewe Mathews. Thanks to Laura Dewe Mathews. Photography by Mariell Lind Hansen.

p. 176: Mountain View, by CAN. Thanks to Mat Barnes and Laura Dubeck. Photography by Elliot Sheppard.

p. 180: Kander House, by Jamie Fobert. Thanks to the Kanders. Photography by Dan Glasser.

p. 187: Outhouse, by Loyn & Co. Thanks to Jean and Michael Dunwell. Photography by French & Tye.

pp. 190–91: Thanks to Fergus and Margot Henderson. Photography by Elliot Sheppard.

p. 194: Stoke Newington house, by Kate Griffin. Thanks to Kate Griffin. Photography by French & Tye.

pp. 200–201: Brixton house, by Steph Wilson. Thanks to Steph Wilson. Photography by Veerle Evens.

p. 205: Worcester Park house, by Yasuyo Harvey. Thanks to Yasuyo Harvey. Photography by Taran Wilkhu.

pp. 208–209 (from left): Thanks to Louisa Grey. Photography by Veerle Evens. Thanks to Gill Meller. Photography by Kim Lightbody. Noble Barn, by McLaren.Excell. Thanks to John Bateman. Photography by Elliot Sheppard.

p. 214: Sartfell Retreat, by Foster Lomas Architects. Thanks to Dr Peter Lillywhite & Carole Lillywhite. Photography by Elliot Sheppard.

p. 218: Wimbledon house, by Foggo & Thomas. Thanks to Adam Sykes. Photography by Elliot Sheppard.

pp. 222–3: Los Angeles studio, by Raina Lee. Thanks to Raina Lee. Photography by Kate Berry.

p. 226: Cotswolds house, by Found Associates. Thanks to Richard Found. Photography by Elliot Sheppard.

pp. 230–31: Kent beach house, by Marcia Mihotich. Thanks to Marcia Mihotich. Photography by Elyse Kennedy.

pp. 236–7: Thanks to Alison Lloyd. Photography by Genevieve Lutkin.

p. 238: Strange House, by Hugh Strange Architects. Thanks to Hugh Strange. Photography by Dan Glasser.

p. 243: Whitechapel house, by Pedro da Costa Felgueiras of Lacquer Studios. Thanks to Pedro da Costa Felgueiras. Photography by Taran Wilkhu.

pp. 246–7: Hoxton house, by Morag Myerscough. Thanks to Morag Myerscough. Photography by Dan Glasser.

pp. 252–3: High Sunderland, by Peter Womersley. Thanks to Paul Stirton. Photography by Taran Wilkhu.

pp. 256–7: London house, by Lucinda Chambers. Thanks to Lucinda Chambers. Photography by Kensington Leverne.

pp. 262–3: London house, by 6a Architects. Thanks to Louise Clarke. Photography by French & Tye.

p. 265: Cotswolds house, by Found Associates. Thanks to Richard Found. Photography by Elliot Sheppard.

p. 269: London flat, by Martin Brudnizki. Thanks to Martin Brudnizki. Photography by Mariell Lind Hansen.

p. 273: Mile End house, by Charles and Romilly Saumarez Smith. Thanks to Charles and Romilly Saumarez Smith. Photography by Elliot Sheppard.

p. 277: Los Angeles house, by Merchant Modern. Thanks to Denise Portmans. Photography by Kate Berry.

pp. 280-81: London flat, by Keith Coventry. Thanks to Keith Coventry. Photography by Elliot Sheppard.

p. 283: Walter Segal house in Highgate, by Faye Toogood and Matt Gibberd. Photography by Taran Wilkhu.

p. 286: Camberwell house, by Corinna Dean. Thanks to Corinna Dean. Photography by Elliot Sheppard.

pp. 288–9: Camden flat, by Duncan Campbell and Luke Edward Hall. Thanks to Duncan Campbell and Luke Edward Hall. Photography by Mariell Lind Hansen.

pp. 294–5: Brockley flat, by Cyndia Harvey. Thanks to Cyndia Harvey. Photography by Elliot Sheppard.

pp. 298–9: St Ann's Court, by Raymond McGrath. Thanks to Osman Kent. Photography by French & Tye.

p. 303: Gingerbread House, by Laura Dewe Mathews. Thanks to Laura Dewe Mathews. Photography by Mariell Lind Hansen.

Every effort has been made to trace copyright holders and to obtain their permission for the use of copyright material. The publisher apologizes for any errors or omissions and would be grateful to be notified of any corrections that should be incorporated in future editions of this book.

Index

Aalto, Alvar 24, 154, 169, 274, 279
Accoya 167
Adam, Peter 276
Adams, Alice 258
Adamson, Glenn 131, 158, 271–2
Adjaye, David 106, 113, 147
Airlite 159
air quality 155, 158–9, 207
Akari light 120
Alexandra & Ainsworth Estate 150
Alexander, Christopher: *Community and Privacy* 97
allotments 29, 192, 202
Anastassiades, Michael 107
Anderson House 179
Ando, Tadao 23, 106
Annabel's 267

Ansty Plum 60
Appleton, Jay 24
Appleton-Sas, Agatha and Robert 170–71
arakabe 160
Archmongers 175
Art Nouveau 146
Arts and Crafts Movement 134, 266
Asplund, Erik Gunnar 126
Assi, Nathalie 275
Astridge, Simon 53, 160
Astroturf 54, 193
'Atollo' lamp 121
Aubusson techniques 258
Austin Vernon & Partners 188

Bachelard, Gaston: *The Poetics of Space* 26, 73, 300–301
Bailey, Ross 264
Banham, Mary Reyner 212
Bany, Malgorzata 274
Barbican Estate, City of London 49, 179, 181, 211, 293
Bar, Moshe 192
Barnes, Mat 142
Barnes, Simon 227
Barnett, Anna 292
Baroque 12, 60, 62, 177, 268
Barragán, Luis 250
Bass House, The 221
Bath 87, 92, 186, 248
Bawa, Geoffrey 216, 217

BBC Television Centre, West London 163
Beaton, Cecil 276
Beckett, Sister Wendy 229
Bennett, Alan 142, 287, 290
Bennett, Ward 278
Benson & Forsyth 150
Bentley Hagen Hall 49
Bentley Wood 132
Bernheimer, Lily 210, 254–5
'Bibendum' chair 276
biophilia 18, 204, 250
Blagdon, Emery 290
blue (colour) 244, 248
blue health 224
Bofill, Ricardo 147, 149
Bonham Carter, Helena 44
Booth, John 249
Botsford, Gianni 101
Bowden, Hollie 119, 293
Breuer, Marcel 7, 147, 279
Brick House, The 177
broken plan 48, 97
Broughton, Tom 146–7
Brown, Capability 210
'Brown furniture' 291–2
Brown, Neave 150
Brudnizki, Martin 267–8
Brûlé, Tyler 240, 241
Brutalism 3, 8, 28, 130, 178, 181
Bulmer, Edward 159
Bunten, Claire 62
Burke, Chris and Susannah 151
Burne-Jones, Edward 93–4
Burnside, Della 106
Burell, Charlie 217, 219
Burton, Tim 44
buy-to-let landlords 130, 212
Byrne, Neil 35–6

Calatrava, Santiago 100
Calder, Barnabas: Concrete: The Beauty of Brutalism 178
Californian Modernism 135
Campbell, Duncan 206
Campo Baeza, Alberto 260

CAN 142
Case Study House No. 8, Pacific Palisades, Los Angeles 37
Case Study programme, California 221
Chadwick, Doug and Maureen 212
Chamberlin, Powell & Bon 49, 211
Chambers, Lucinda 258
Champtaloup, Emma 293
Chance Street project, East London 177
Chandresinghe, Luke 195
Chapel of Notre-Dame du Haut, Ronchamp 78
Château La Coste 210
Chatsworth House, Derbyshire 80
Chatwin, Bruce 260
Chaudhuri, Mallika 110
Chermayeff, Serge 97, 132, 134, 250; Community and Privacy 97
Cheval, Ferdinand 169–70
Chillida, Eduardo 251
chintz 258, 259
Chipperfield, David 138
Choi, Eudon 35–6
Church of the Light, Japan 106
circadian rhythm 94, 119, 234
City Palace, Udaipur 254
Clark, Sam and Sam 31
Classical architecture 8, 12, 96, 225
Clayworks 148
climate change 163
Clock House, North London 175
Cockaigne Houses 97
Colefax & Fowler 259
Collagerie 258
Congdon, William 204
Conran, Jasper 13, 210
Conran, Terence 58, 254, 279
cooking 29, 32, 186, 225
Cook, Sydney 150
Coppin, Sandra 60
Cornforth White 245
Cotswolds pottery 175
Coulthard, Sally: Biophilia 250
Coutts Bank, Strand 216
Covid-19 pandemic 20, 154, 186, 192, 279
Craig-Martin, Michael 179, 181, 293, 296

Crawford, Ilse 127
Crescent House 211
Croft, Thomas 97, 99
Cross Laminated Timber (CLT) 62, 167
Cruickshank, Dan 167, 169
Crystal Palace 80
Culley, Peter 112

Dapple House 112
Davison, Katy 33
da Vinci, Leonardo: A Deluge 206
de Botton, Alain 87, 271
De Stijl art movement 48
de Waal, Edmund 135, 138
DIY decoration 240
Drakeford, Rhonda 198
DSDHA 169
Dubeck, Laura 142
Dulwich Estate 188
Dzek 175
Dzekciorius, Brent 175, 177

Eagle, Alex 284
Eames, Charles and Ray 2, 37, 270, 271
eco-friendly 151, 162, 163, 181
Ede, Jim 204, 264
'Egg' chair 270
Egypt, Ancient 104, 155, 199, 206, 244, 274
Ellington Court, Southgate 48–9
Ellis-Miller, Jonathan 212
Elvaston Place, South Kensington 260
Emery & Cie 245
E-1027 (Modernist house, Côte d'Azur) 276, 278
European Centre for Environment and Human Health, University of Exeter 224
European Modernism 3, 48
Experimental House, Muuratsalo 169

Farnsworth House, Illinois 80, 211–12
Farrell, Sir Terry 267, 292;
    Interiors and the Legacy of
    Postmodernism 267
Farrow & Ball 159, 245
FAT 174
Ferrock 166
First World War (1914–18) 28
Fisher, Geoffrey 169
'flat architect' 49
flexible living 48–51
Flower, Charles 219
Flower Tower, Paris 188–9
Fobert, Jamie 179, 261
Fog House, Clerkenwell 106
Fontana, Lucio 284
formaldehyde 158
Foster, Norman 175
Found, Richard 264
Fowler, John 267
Franc, Valentine and Régis 196
François, Édouard 188–9
Frank, Josef 204, 206
Freud, Bella 163
Fromm, Erich 204
Fry, Stephen 175
'Fudge' chair 206

Gainsborough, Thomas 184, 210
Gamper, Martino 268
Gaudí, Antoni 174
Gaudier-Brzeska, Henri: *Bird*
    Swallowing a Fish 204
Gazerwitz, Paul 195
Georgian architecture 49, 64, 87, 96,
    132, 142, 245, 267, 268, 292, 301
Gervasoni 'Ghost' sofas 155
Gibberd, Sir Frederick (Grandpa
    Whiskers) 18, 48–9, 178, 216, 296;
    The Modern Flat 49
Gibberd Gallery, Harlow 296
Gibbons, Steve 88
Gingerbread House, Hackney, East
    London 62
Glass House, Connecticut 80
Golden Arches test 270

Golden Lane Estate, City of London
    211
Goldfinger, Ernő 28, 100
Gothic architecture 104, 206
Gothic Revival architecture 134
Gough, Piers 79
Grade I listing 147
Grade II listing 3, 7, 84, 88, 151
Grahn, Patrik 232
Grand Designs 162
Gray, Eileen 276, 278
Great Hanshin earthquake, Kobe 170
Greaves, Hannah 84
Greaves, Walter 84
Greeks, Ancient 155, 199, 206, 266, 296
Grey, Louisa 121
Griffin, Kate 195
Grimshaw, Nicholas 178
guest permissions 62–3
guest quarters 72–3
Guhl, Willy 138

Hackney, London 49, 62, 147, 192
Hadrian, Emperor 100
half levels 35, 114
Hall, Luke Edward 206
Hall, William: *Brick* 167
hammock 45, 195
Harris-Taylor, Sophie 101
Harvey, Cyndia 202
Harvey, Yasuyo 199, 202
Haslam, Nicky 268
Haward, Birkin 151
Hayden, Anna and Russel 85
Heatherwick Studio 189
Hecktermann, Kirsten 259
Hemingway, Corey 188
Henderson, Fergus and Margot 185–6
Hepworth, Barbara 79, 204, 297
Heron, Brian 55
Heron, Patrick 79, 297
Heuman, Beata 259, 268
Hicks, David 258, 268, 278, 282
High Tech structures 175
Hill, Albert 3, 7, 9, 19–20, 171, 240, 249,
    251, 258, 266, 272, 300

Hills, Adam 291
Hilton, Roger 297
Hirai, Akiko 275
Historic England 146
Hix, Mark 55, 58
Hogg, Min 240–41, 258–9
Holland, Mina 139
Hone, Peter 266
Hooch, Pieter de 245
Hotel Parco dei Principi, Sorrento 174
'hotel style' 278
Housden House 3, 35
House & Garden 241
House for Essex, A 174–5
Hoxton Square, London 26–7
Hugo, Victor: *Hunchback of Notre-Dame*
    26
Humphries, Oscar 120, 296
Hunter, Laura 206–7

Ian McChesney Architects 188
Ilori, Yinka 249
immune systems 118, 219, 228
Innes, Jocasta 240
intern, or 'CAD monkey' 138
International Journal of Environmental
    Research and Public Health 166–7
International Style 59
Irons, Felicity 166
island unit 55, 116
Isokon Building, Hampstead 146–7
Italian Postmodernism 249

Jackson, Duncan 94
Jacobsen, Arne 136, 270
Japan 49, 59, 99, 106, 113, 120, 138, 143,
    160, 170, 192, 219–20, 229, 261,
    285, 290
Jeanneret, Pierre 296
Johnson, Philip 80
Journal of Clinical Sleep Medicine 94
Journal of Environmental Psychology 36
Judd, Donald 274, 284
Jun'ichirō Tanizaki: *In Praise of Shadows*
    113, 116, 118, 143

Kahn, Louis 77, 169
Kahn, Peter 186
Kaplan, Professors Rachel and Stephen 210, 233
Kawakubo, Rei 241
Keeling House 55
Keller, Helen: *The World I Live In* 126–7
Kettle's Yard, Cambridge 203–4
killer cells 219
Kintsugi 143
Knut, Tycjan 274
Koenig, Pierre 116
Kohn, David 175
Koren, Leonard: *Arranging Things* 284

Lab Architects 62
Lamb, Max 175, 177
laminate flooring 142, 260
'Lampada Cappello' lamp 114
Lancaster, Nancy 239, 267, 278
Langhorne, Alistair 62
Lasdun, Denys 55
Lattin, Clare 192
Laurent, Marie 79
Leach, Bernard 138
Le Corbusier 8, 28, 36, 78, 106, 250, 276
L'Espérance, Sara 51
Levitt, David 60
Lichtenstein, Roy 266
Lightfoot, Heidi 88
Light House 101
Little House, Highgate 59
Living Architecture 174
living walls 198
Lloyd, Alison 192–3
Lloyd Wright, Frank 104, 183
locally sourced materials 170
Locher, Heidi 44, 104
London Central Mosque, Regent's Park 178
London Design Festival (2017) 272
Longstaffe-Gowan, Todd 195, 196
Loos, Adolf 36
Lost House 113
Louisiana Museum of Modern Art 210

Louv, Richard: *Last Child in the Woods: Saving Our Children from Nature-Deficit Disorder* 232
Lowry, L. S. 184
L-shaped room 49, 51
Lunuganga, Sri Lanka 216–17
Lyons, Eric 87

Mackereth, Sally 67, 234
Magistretti, Vico 121
Maison Dom-Ino 28
Maison Tropicale 177–8
Mangold, Robert 179
Marmoreal 175, 177
Marshall, Jethro 211
Martello tower 94–5
material intelligence 131
Mathews, Laura Dewe 62
maximalism 258, 266, 267
Maynard, Arne 195
McAlpine, Alistair 282
McAtamney, Gerard 28
McLeod, Duncan 54
medieval-guild model 134
Meller, Gill 32, 193
Memphis Group 266–7
Meyers-Levy, Joan 22
Michaelis, Alex 69
Michell, Patrick 225
Mid-Mod 270
Miller, Duncan: *More Colour Schemes for the Modern Home* 250, 251
Milne McLeod, Lyndsay 54, 203
mindfulness 225
mingei, or folk art, movement, Japan 290
minimalism 254–5, 260–61, 264, 266, 267
Miyako Hotel, Kyoto 116, 118
Modern House, The 7, 8, 9, 82, 84, 171, 192, 198, 213, 249, 251, 276, 278, 300
Modernism 3, 8, 10–11, 28, 30, 43, 48, 49, 59, 68, 78, 79, 80, 135, 150, 151, 154; 178, 181, 245, 250, 268, 276, 279, 305
Modern Movement 36, 48, 59

Mondrian, Piet 48
Moore, Henry Moore 132, 134, 204, 296–7; *Recumbent Figure* 132; *Three Reclining Figures* 285
Moore, Rowan 221
Moro, Peter 84
Morris, William 18, 59, 93–4, 134, 207
Muller, Brian 175
Munch, Edvard 80, 143
Murphy, Sheena 159
Museum of Everything art exhibition 290
Museum of the Home 241–2

NASA 158
National Institute of Public Health for Japan 220
National Trust 88
Natural England 212
Navone, Paola 155
Neoclassicism 12, 106, 216
Neofunctionalism 138
Neta, Maital 204
Neues Museum, Berlin 138
Nicholson, Ben 147, 291
Nightingale, Florence 202
nimbyism 132
Nithurst Farm, West Sussex 64, 179
No Feature Walls blog 206
Noguchi, Isamu 114
Nolan, Becky 130, 291
Nord Studio 175
Nune 159

Ochre Barn, Norfolk 177
oculus 100
Oculus Transportation Hub 100
Oliver, Jamie 29
'1,000 Trees' project, Shanghai 189
open-plan 2, 26, 28, 35, 99, 154
Oriented Strand Board (OSB) 177
Oudolf, Piet 195
Owens, Rick 279

Pacific Gas & Electric Company, California 94
'Paimio' armchair 144
Paimio tuberculosis sanitorium 154
Pajon-Leite, Andres 28
Palace of Westminster 134
Palais Idéal, Hauterives 169–70
Palladian architecture 96
Pallasmaa, Juhani: *The Eyes of the Skin* 14, 126
Panksepp, Jaak 301
Pantheon, Rome 100
Panton, Vernon 249
Paper Log House 170
Park Road, No. 125, London 178
Paris, Mathieu 287
Park Court, Sydenham 48
Park, Rosa 186
Parsons, David 112–13
Passivhaus 85
Pattern Language, A 62–3, 65, 96–7, 196, 270–71
Pawson, John 58–9, 260, 261
Paxton, Joseph 80
Paxton, Richard 44, 104
Peanut Vendor website 291
Perry, Grayson 174, 175
Peru 62–3
pets 69, 70, 72
Philp, Paul 275
Phippen, Randall & Parkes 97
piano nobile 96, 293
Piccolo, Oscar 120, 274
Piercy, Stuart 94, 96
Plain English 55
Platform 5 Architects 225
playfulness, sense of 175, 177, 199
Pollock, Jackson 32, 206
pollution 92, 155, 158–9, 198, 211, 220
Polychromie 250
Pomyers, Édouard de 79
Ponti, Gio 174, 268
Postmodernism 79, 96, 249, 266, 267
Pre-Raphaelite Brotherhood 93, 134
Pritchard, Eleanor 255
Pritchard, Jack 147
prospect (ability to observe) 24, 26–7, 43

Proust, Marcel 154, 166
Prouvé, Jean 177–8, 296
Pugin, Augustus 134
Pullman Court, Streatham 48–9
Putman, Michael 51

Qing Li, Professor 219

Rädler, Josef Karl 290
Rainbow House 69
Rasmussen, Steen Eiler: *Experiencing Architecture* 244, 245
Ratinon, Claire 192
Raumplan 36
Read, Barny 130, 291
Red House 93–4, 134–5
Retrouvius 291
rewilding 217, 219
Richards, Adam 64, 179
Rich, Harry and David 195
Rietveld, Gerrit 48
Rietveld Schrsöder House, Utrecht 48
Riley, Bridget 254
Rimel, Morgwn 43–4
Robinson, Jessica 114
Robinson, Vishaka 92
Robson, David 217
Rodden, Sarah Kaye 93, 275
Rogers, Ab 67
Rogers, Richard 7, 69, 175, 248–9
Rogers, Ruth 69
'Roly Poly' chair 204, 206
Roman Empire 12, 24, 100, 155, 179, 199, 244, 266, 296
Ronnie Hill, Sean 110
Rothko, Mark 282
Royal Festival Hall, London 84
RSPB 217
Ruskin, John 110; *Seven Lamps of Architecture* 134

Saint Phalle, Niki de 174, 175; *The Empress* 174
Salcedo, Doris 181
'Satellite' mirror 276
Savannah, African 24, 210, 219
Scheerbart, Paul 80; *Glasarchitektur* 80
Schindler, Rudolf 135
School of Life 43
Schräder-Schröder, Mrs Truus 48
Scott Brown, Denise 270
Scott, Judith 290
Scrivener, Paul 225
Scully, Sean 296
Segal Method 59–60
Segal, Walter 59–60
Serra, Richard 132, 251
Shaker furniture 291
Shigeru Ban 170
shinrin-yoku ('forest bathing') 219–20
Shulman, Julius 116
Silvestrin, Claudio 260
6a Architects 51, 221
'60' stool 279
'sky façade' roof 101
skyspaces 100
Smith Papyrus, The 155
Smithsons 84
Soane, Sir John 106–7, 266
Solidspace 35
Somerford Estate, Hackney 49
Sottsass, Ettore 249, 266
South Downs National Park 19, 170
'Spade' chairs 272
'Span' house 87
Speake, Maria 291
Spode creamware 240
Stahl House 116
Stapleton, Rich 248
Starck, Philippe 240
Stewart, Susan: *On Longing* 272
Stirling, James 84
St Ives 79, 291, 297
St John, Caruso 177
Storey, Robert 203
Straw Bale House 162–3
Street Porter, Janet 106
Strindberg, August 80
Stummel, Henning 27, 274

Sudjic, Deyan 138–9
Summer, Martin 185
Summerson, John 40, 134
sunken sitting 68
Suprblk 51
sustainable materials 151, 162–3,
    166, 170
Swift, Tim and Emily 32
Syrett, Jason 92–3

Tabori, Peter 150
Taccia, Alessandra 248
tadelakt 160
Tate Gallery 132
Tate Modern 181
Tatebayashi, Kaori 189, 192
Taylor, Richard 206
Taylor, Stephen 177
tea ceremony 138
The Trade Show exhibition 272
Thomas, Carol and Philip 132
Thomas, Rupert 142, 241
Till, Jeremy 162, 171
Tin House, West London 274
Townsend, Geoffrey 87
'Transat' chair 276
Tree House 188, 221
Tree, Isabella 217; *Wilding* 217, 232–3
Trellick Tower 28
Tuckey, Jonathan 68, 227, 229
Turner, Carl 177
Turner, Sam and Nelli 150–51
Turrell, James 100
Twain, Mark 44
'Type 20' 49

Ulrich, Roger: 'View through a
    Window May Influence Recovery
    from Surgery' 212, 224
Undercover Architecture 195
Uniacke, Rose 261
Unité d'Habitation, Marseille 178–9
U-value (rate at which heat escapes
    through glass) 85

Valenti, Italo 287
van der Laan, Dom Hans 261
van der Rohe, Mies 80, 211, 270
van Duysen, Vincent 261
Van Gogh, Vincent 40
Vartanian, Dr Oshin 36
Venetian blinds 88
Venturi, Robert 270
Vermeer, Johannes 245
Versailles, Palace of 217, 254
Vervoordt, Axel 261; *Wabi Inspirations*
    203
Villa Müller, Prague 36
Villa Savoye 36
Viscione, Carlo 149–50, 285
volume 35–7, 49, 64, 104, 154

wabi-sabi 138, 143, 146, 261
Wallis, Alfred 79, 285–6, 290–91
Wallpaper 7, 8, 241
'Wassily' chair 240
Webb, Philip 89, 124
Webster, Sue 147, 149
Wegner, Hans 268
Wenner, Jane 278
West Architecture 43
Whittington Estate 112–13
Wigglesworth, Sarah 162, 171
Williams, Whinnie 278
Willow Road, No. 2, Hampstead 100
Wilson, Donna 64–5, 275
Wilson, Edward O. 204
Wilson, Steph 199
Windsor chair 268, 292
Wohlleben, Peter 219, 220–21
Wood, Christopher 250, 291
World Health Organization 158, 185
World of Interiors, The 7, 8–9, 107, 142,
    240–41, 258–9, 260, 266, 287, 297
Wright of Derby, Joseph 110; *An
    Experiment on a Bird in the Air
    Pump* 110

Yale School of Forestry and
    Environmental Studies 219
Yalland, Amy 149
Yanagi Sōetsu: *The Beauty of Everyday
    Things* 290
Yi-Fu Tuan 70
Yorke, F. R. S.: *The Modern Flat* 49
Yorkshire Sculpture Park 210
Young, Robert 291

Zellige tiles 107, 143
Zennor 79
Zerbib, Raphaël 266–7
Zhu, Rui 36
Zogolovitch, Roger 35
Zumthor, Peter 125

PENGUIN LIFE

UK | USA | Canada | Ireland | Australia
India | New Zealand | South Africa

Penguin Life is part of the Penguin Random House group of companies
whose addresses can be found at global.penguinrandomhouse.com.

First published 2021
002

Colour reproduction by Altaimage Ltd
Printed and bound in Italy by L.E.G.O. S.p.A.

The authorized representative in the EEA is Penguin Random House Ireland,
Morrison Chambers, 32 Nassau Street, Dublin D02 YH68

A CIP catalogue record for this book is available from the British Library

ISBN: 978–0–241–48049–6

www.greenpenguin.co.uk